Democracy

by

Decree

_____

Democracy
by Decree

What Happens When
Courts Run Government

Ross Sandler and David Schoenbrod

Yale University Press   *New Haven & London*

To Alice Mintzer Sandler and Jan Selby,
our partners in all things

Production of this book was supported by the Mary Cady Tew Memorial Fund, an
internal publication fund of Yale University Press.

Set in Minion type by Keystone Typesetting, Inc.
Printed in the United States of America.

Library of Congress Cataloging-in-Publication Data
Sandler, Ross.
Democracy by decree : what happens when courts run government / Ross Sandler &
David Schoenbrod.
        p.   cm.
Includes bibliographical references and index.
ISBN 0-300-09272-5 (cloth : alk. paper)
1. Judge-made law—United States. 2. Judicial power—United States. 3. Courts—United
States. 4. Democracy—United States. I. Schoenbrod, David. II. Title.
KF4575 .S26 2003
347.73′1—dc21
2002009650

A catalogue record for this book is available from the British Library.

The paper in this book meets the guidelines for permanence and durability
of the Committee on Production Guidelines for Book Longevity of the
Council on Library Resources.

10 9 8 7 6 5 4 3 2 1

Contents

Preface

When we began work on this book on federal court orders that manage state and local government, we intended to call it *Government by Decree*. The title had been used almost a century ago in books on decrees designed to kill unions. Those books chastised judges for unilaterally making the kind of judgments that in a democracy ought be left to legislatures. By borrowing the old title, we meant to suggest that the concerns of democracy that counted against the antiunion decrees should also count against the supposedly progressive decrees of today.

It took us some time to see that the parallel was not as neat as we had wished. The judges in the old union cases had acted unilaterally, but most of the modern decrees have come with the explicit approval of elected officials. In most cases, Congress had enacted a law that told federal judges to enter decrees against state and local governments, or the state and local officials had consented to the entry of the decree against themselves, or both.

The modern decrees are nonetheless antidemocratic. Elected officials invite judges to take charge of policy making in order to evade responsibility for politically controversial choices. This is a core argument of this book. Because the decrees that concern us have their origins in democratically elected institutions yet work to thwart democratic accountability, we have given the book the ironic but more exact title _Democracy by Decree._

Introduction
The Legal Hook

Carol Sherman, a young legal aid attorney practicing before New York City's family court in 1972, could do nothing to help her twelve-year-old client Shirley Wilder.[1] Shirley urgently needed to escape her abusive relatives. Her mother had died when she was four, and her grandmother, who took her in, died when she was eleven. Shirley had most recently been living with her father, whose common-law wife beat and brutalized her. Eleven times Sherman had asked the family court to place Shirley with one of the private foster care homes under contract with New York City. These private homes were managed largely by Jewish and Catholic agencies that were allowed by state law to give preference to children of their own religion. None of these homes would take Shirley, who, besides being troubled, was black and Protestant.

Sherman made a twelfth application before Family Court Judge Justine Wise Polier, a well-connected reformer and crusader against the inadequacies of the city's foster care system. The only facility that would take the child was the poorly managed state Training School for Girls in Hudson, New York, 130 miles north of New York City. The state had built the training school in the nineteenth century as a reformatory for female criminals and now operated it as a foster home. Its small, inept staff tolerated rampant gang activity while enforcing dozens of trivial rules with brutal discipline, including solitary confinement in bare, dark, padded cells. It was a horrible place to send Shirley, but she had to go somewhere. Judge Polier, after an angry attack on the city's foster care system, assigned her to the training school.

While Sherman worked on Shirley's case, Marcia Lowry, another public interest lawyer, was working on similar child welfare cases from her office with Mobilization for Youth, a public interest law firm located on Manhattan's Lower East Side. Private agencies were similarly giving Lowry's clients of the wrong religion or race the cold shoulder unless they were very young and trouble free. Lowry's work came to the attention of the New York Civil Liberties Union, which had, like Lowry, come to believe that getting rid of religious preferences was key to providing adequate care for children like Shirley. The Civil Liberties Union asked Lowry to head its newly created Children's Rights Project, whose first step would be to file a lawsuit charging that the religious preference violated the First Amendment's separation of church and state and discriminated against black, Protestant children.

Lowry needed a plaintiff to bring the lawsuit, and Sherman suggested that Shirley would be ideal. In the spring of 1973 Lowry drove up to Hudson, New York, met Shirley for the first time, and obtained her agreement to be lead plaintiff. On June 14, 1973, Lowry, in *Wilder v. Sugarman,* asked the federal court in Manhattan to declare unconstitutional New York's law that allowed religious preferences in foster care assignments and to require that all children be placed on a first-come, first-served basis. The federal court ruled, however, that the statute's religious preference was not unconstitutional as written.[2] For Lowry now to win, she would have to prove at a trial the more difficult charge that the state law as it was actually applied discriminated against black and Puerto Rican children. Pretrial discovery and procedural maneuvering began and dragged on for almost a decade.

In 1983, as the trial date approached, New York City's chief lawyer, Frederick A. O. Schwarz, Jr., initiated settlement negotiations. He was embarrassed by the failures of the city's child welfare system, feared Lowry might win, and resolved that it was in the city's interest to work out a solution rather than litigate. In 1986, after three years of intensive and sometimes acrimonious negotiations, the group of lawyers presented to Judge Robert J. Ward a detailed forty-page order that moderated the effect of the state law, substituted an amalgam of negotiated compromises, and added a number of rigid specifics designed to improve the city's foster care program generally. The appellate court later called the negotiated order "a blueprint to implement a broad change in municipal policy."[3]

New York City's child welfare system did not, however, improve, and Lowry in 1990 and again in 1993 moved to hold New York City and its officials in contempt. She told Judge Ward at the time of the 1993 motion, "To tell you the truth, your Honor, I don't know what we really accomplished."[4] The article in *Newsday* reporting Lowry's 1993 comment summed up the situation with this headline: "Despite 20-Year Effort, City Can't Fix System."[5]

In 1995, the city's child welfare system erupted into a major scandal when five-year-old Elisa Izquierdo was murdered by her mother. The mother's earlier abuse of the child had come to the attention of the city's child welfare authorities, but they had failed to act. The murder and reports of similar outrages were for Lowry the last straw. She filed a new federal lawsuit, this time asking the court to take over the New York City Child Welfare Administration as if it were a bankrupt company run by incompetents.

The *Wilder* litigation typifies thousands of cases brought over the past forty years to reform institutions of state and local government. Reform-minded attorneys identify a program that needs change, construct a legal theory that some constitutional or statutory requirement has been violated, and file a lawsuit. The alleged violation becomes, in the parlance of lawyers, a "legal hook" for seeking broader reform. In *Wilder*, for example, Lowry converted the complexity and failures of the New York City foster care system into a single legal question: Did it discriminate unconstitutionally? When such a legal claim is accepted as appropriate for the court to entertain, lawyers for plaintiffs and defendants are encouraged to negotiate a detailed plan to fix the entire system. The plan is then reduced to a court order, known variously as a *decree*, a *consent decree*, or an *injunction*. Mayors, governors, or commissioners who agree to such decrees, and their successors, must then obey the orders by implementing all of their provisions. Defiance would be contempt of court, a crime potentially punishable by imprisonment or other severe sanctions. Compliance is monitored by the lawyers and, often, court-appointed experts.

This template for reform has been applied to the full range of governmental programs, including, to name just a few examples, special education, mental hospitals, environmental protection, and prisons. The decrees cover not only an enormous range of programs but also an enormous range of states and cities. Decrees have ruled prisons in forty-one states and local jails in fifty states.[6] A recent study counted more than six hundred school districts subject to desegregation decrees and found that the "vast majority" continue "with no hint of impending termination."[7] The template has acquired a name: *institutional reform litigation*.

Institutional reform litigation promises to protect the powerless by making politicians cede some of their power to apolitical judges and public interest lawyers who will be guided by experts concerned with doing the right thing rather than the politically opportune thing. Congress has warmly encouraged institutional reform litigation in many statutes. Mayors and governors, when cornered, bless institutional reform litigation by consenting to decrees against themselves rather than fighting. University faculties and the national press generally applaud institutional reform litigation with reverential articles and reports.

The reforms obtained through institutional reform litigation, however, look quite different from their promise. Nina Bernstein, a reporter who covered child welfare issues for the *New York Times*, began to wonder what had happened to Shirley Wilder, the plaintiff in Marcia Lowry's case. The result of her research is *The Lost Children of Wilder*, published in 2001. Bernstein traced Shirley from birth and placement in the state institution at Hudson, New York, to her death from AIDS on January 17, 1999, at thirty-nine years of age —a result of a life of prostitution and drug addiction. Shirley had given birth to a son, Lamont, in 1974, the year after the lawsuit was filed, but was unable to take care of him. From age three Lamont, like Shirley, lived in a series of unsuccessful foster care homes. In 1995, when he was twenty-one, Lamont too had a son who in turn also fell into the city's foster care and child protective system. Shirley, her son, and her grandson all suffered in the same inadequate system. Despite the heroic efforts of public interest attorneys, repeated attention by family court judges, and supervision by powerful federal judges who imposed detailed, corrective court orders drafted by experts, things did not get better for the thousands of children passing through New York City's child welfare system between 1973 and 1995.

Wilder's failure is not unusual. In the much litigated case of the schools in Kansas City, Missouri, for example, the court forced massive expenditures to improve the quality of education. Nonetheless, the quality remained so low that the Missouri State Board of Education revoked the school district's accreditation because of poor teaching and inadequate educational results.[8] In a lawsuit challenging mismanagement in the District of Columbia's foster care and child protective programs, a federal judge in 1995 directed that the programs be run by a neutral receiver.[9] Six years later the plaintiffs complained that the agency under the receiver was no better than before. The court returned the agency to the control of the district's government.[10]

Scholars and commentators from across the political spectrum have documented the limited success of democracy by decree.[11] Some of these studies were published before the entry of the *Wilder* decree. In the most recent full-scale study of institutional reform litigation by scholars, the authors, who are strong proponents of court-led reform, conclude that they cannot show that decrees actually do more good than harm because the criteria by which such a determination could be made have not been established.[12]

Institutional reform litigation nevertheless remains the first choice of many judges and people bent on improving government. It is so ingrained in the public consciousness that any criticism is met with disbelief. After hearing us describe a particular litigation involving public education, one of our friends said, "I'd still rather have judges run the program than the board of education." It did not matter that the judicial control had lasted twenty-one years and had not come close to meeting its goals.

Institutional reform litigation is held in high esteem despite its shortcomings because of misperceptions. One misperception is that judges control institutional reform litigation. People overlook the failures because they respect judges more than they respect state and local politicians. Judges, it is thought, have the wisdom, intelligence, and good intentions needed to put things right, or at least they have a better chance of doing so than politicians. Yet the truth is that most decrees are not the work product of judges. Instead, judges routinely sign without change decrees negotiated by plaintiffs' and defendants' attorneys, and these negotiators have strong incentives to settle rather than defend or prosecute the litigation. State and local officials, wishing to avoid embarrassment for faults in a governmental program, are glad to consent to a detailed plan, even when written in large measure by plaintiffs' attorneys. Plaintiffs' attorneys, wishing to advance causes they hold dear, are glad to get the power to dictate. Judges, wishing to avoid personal responsibility for solving thorny policy problems, put their imprimatur on the results of the negotiations.

These decrees usually do not closely or sometimes even approximately track the law but rather are deals that, like others in politics, reflect a welter of motives. What programs will look good to the public? Can controversial actions be deferred until after the next election? What will pry more money out of the legislature for a favored program? What do the experts say now? These are considerations of the moment, yet the decrees last for decades. Mayors and governors must continue to obey the decree because deviating from it is a crime, and getting it modified in light of experience, the changing opinions of the experts, or the changing wishes of voters requires the acquiescence of plaintiffs' attorneys. The constitutional and statutory powers of elected officials are eroded in favor of a negotiating process between plaintiffs' attorneys, various court-appointed functionaries, and lower-echelon officials. This group, which we call the *controlling group*, works behind closed doors to draft and administer the complicated decrees.

Consent decrees transfer power not from politicians to a judge but from one political process to another. The winners are the powerful and the knowledgeable. Members of Congress, seeking to please constituents, enact statutes that mandate idealistic goals and then make them enforceable in court. Because the goals are unrealistic, it is the controlling group in negotiating the decree that decides the extent to which the goals will be attained. Mayors and governors gain, too. They jettison responsibility for failed programs and end-run participation and oversight by state and local legislatures. Public interest advocates gain as well. They wield the power of office without running for office. Journalists and professors, who believe in principles and plans more than the tugging and hauling of politics, applaud the high ideals of the statutes and decrees but blame the failures on others or circumstances.

This is democracy by decree, and it often leads to unfair or unwanted results. Lawyers for homeless citizens might, for example, obtain a decree to improve homeless shelters, but their homeless clients may prefer other services and detest shelters because they are dehumanizing.[13] Lawyers for prisoners obtain a decree requiring the closing of an old jail and construction of a new one on an island, but many prisoners and their families prefer the old jail because its in-city location permits easier visits.[14] Lawyers for African Americans obtain a decree calling for special help for African-American children but oppose letting lawyers for Chinese-American children who will be disadvantaged by the decree intervene in the litigation.[15] Lawyers for an environmental group obtain a court order forcing a local government to spend its scarce capital funds to meet a clean water act requirement that has limited environmental benefit but that causes the local government to delay other capital improvements that have greater environmental benefits.[16]

Courts did not always let themselves be used to make public policy, even though judges have long held elected officials to the rule of law. That generally meant ensuring *compliance* with the law, rather than dictating *how to comply* with the law. The difference is critical because when courts dictate how to comply with the law, they assume the responsibility that mayors, governors, and legislators should shoulder.

Judges left policy-making powers to elected officials for a powerful reason—democracy. The Revolutionary War slogan "No taxation without representation" stood for the broader proposition that government policy making should be in the hands of officials who are politically accountable to the voters. It is for this reason that our federal Constitution requires states to have a "republican form of government" and that state constitutions give voters the power to elect mayors, governors, and legislators. Judges have a narrower job—to enforce the laws, including constitutional law, that elected officials adopt. Judges who go beyond what is necessary to enforce the law usurp the policy-making function of elected officials and deprive voters of their constitutional right to a democratically accountable government.

States and cities cannot be run effectively through court decrees that are as thick as phone books. When judges impose such decrees, it is the voters who lose. They lose the ability to hold elected officials accountable for the performance of governmental institutions.

But what about all those people whose voices might not be heard because of poverty, ignorance, or disability? Without institutional reform litigation protecting them, won't they be left behind? We think not. Many voices previously not heard find powerful expression today in the elected and executive branches of state and local government as evidenced by the wide diversity among mayors, governors, legislators, and appointed officials—a success partly attributable to the nation's voting rights laws. Institutional reform litigation has, in any event, proved much less successful than its proponents admit, undermining the claim that people will be underserved without it. The goals it seeks, such as an appropriate education for all children with disabilities or a safe home with a family for all abused children, are valid and humane goals for a just and caring society. But when responsibility for achieving these goals shifts from the legislative and executive branches of government to the judicial branch, profound disadvantages appear, both for society in general and for democracy in particular.

Institutional reform litigation often fails because finding a violation of law to gain a legal hook for a lawsuit reveals little about what should be done to make the program run better. In *Wilder* the malaise in the city's foster care program stemmed from not only deplorable discrimination but also deep-seated problems of policy, management, and resources, as well as the monumental complexity of the undertaking, for which there were no simple solutions. Court processes aimed at eradicating clearly defined illegalities, such as separate school systems for whites and blacks, are ill-equipped to manage governmental programs which require choosing among lawful options, allocating limited resources, and dealing with unexpected circumstances and unwanted side effects. The result is that decrees regularly fail despite the intelligence, expert advice, and good intentions that go into them. Yet judges cannot give up once they have accepted responsibility. Nor can plaintiffs' attorneys. Confronted with failure, judges induce the parties on pain of contempt to draft yet another plan to be incorporated into yet another order. And so it goes.

Many believe that institutional reform litigation has been throttled by the Supreme Court under Chief Justices Warren Burger and William Rehnquist. Press coverage of Supreme Court decisions reads like a series of obituaries.[17] Legal scholars ask us why are we writing a book on something that is over and done with. Our answer is that academic interest may have waned, but the incidence and effect of institutional reform litigation have not.

The Supreme Court, for example, in several recent cases cited the Eleventh Amendment to bar private citizens from suing a state, but that does little to slow institutional reform litigation.[18] The amendment does not restrict lawsuits against cities, counties, or school boards, which are the governmental entities that deliver most social programs. Nor does it bar lawsuits against governors and other state officials when the relief sought is a court decree rather than money damages. Marcia Lowry in 1973 made Jule Sugarman the main defendant in *Wilder*. Sugarman at the time was the New York City commissioner responsible for foster care. Nothing the Supreme Court has done since would prevent someone filing a similar lawsuit today.

The Supreme Court's opinions in any event have been utterly overshadowed by congressional enactments over the past thirty years that make it easy to prove a statutory case against state and local defendants. When Lowry filed *Wilder* in 1973, for example, she relied primarily on the U.S. Constitution. Today, she would rely on the Adoption Assistance and Child Welfare Act of 1980 and its many amendments.[19] This statute conditions receipt of federal funds on accepting federal standards. Its availability has spawned foster care litigation in federal court in at least thirty-four states.[20] Other federal statutes cover a wide assortment of society's goals concerning the environment, child care, education, and health care and ending discrimination based on age, sex, race, disability, and more. Each of these federal statutes authorizes judges to enter decrees against state and local officials. New decrees get issued, piling up on the old, few of which are actually terminated.

Our criticism of institutional reform litigation is different from that which was prevalent in the 1960s and 1970s when the judiciary's new power over state and local government sparked great controversy.[21] Most of that discussion concerned whether the courts were correct in discovering new rights in the Constitution. We express no opinion on how to interpret the Constitution. Our objections focus on how courts remedy violations rather than on how they define constitutional rights.

The judiciary has failed to adopt a set of rules effective in limiting the availability, scope, and duration of decrees against government. Judges as a result become embroiled in problems they cannot solve and so become part of the problem. It is time to put the remedial decrees issued in institutional reform litigation on a footing that will let judges know when it is appropriate to use them and when it is not, and to direct them to use alternatives that will be more effective and more democratic. This is the mission of this book. It proposes limits that the courts can impose on themselves or, failing that, the legislature can impose on them. The aim is not to stop the courts from enforcing rights but to draw a line between the work of courts—to enforce rights—and the work of elected officials—to make policy and manage operations. Judges are right to protect the injured by enforcing rights, but they must also preserve democratic accountability and the flexibility of elected officials to respond to the wishes of voters.

CHAPTER 1

How Courts Came to Govern

At 7:53 A.M. on December 7, 1941, Japanese bombers struck U.S. naval bases on Oahu, Hawaii, killing 2,403 U.S. military personnel and citizens. Not included in the official casualty count but nonetheless a victim of the attack was an evil fellow named Jim Crow.

World War II put soldiers of diverse skin colors in motion around the country. Northern whites witnessed segregation in the South, and southern blacks experienced the freer, but still deeply flawed, ways of the North. The blood they shed overseas was all the same color. The common enemy, Adolf Hitler, exemplified the evil in the claims of racial superiority that gave Jim Crow life. The war called into question the governmentally imposed second-class status of blacks. The cultural tide was turning, as became clear when President Harry S. Truman ended official segregation in the military in 1948.

Although most southern whites still believed in segregation, they were on a collision course with history. Northern businesses, which controlled the lion's share of the nation's investment funds, were reluctant to invest in the Deep South, leaving it an economic backwater. Segregation was also increasingly indefensible in the world arena. Great Britain ceded independence to India in 1947, formally shrugging off the "white man's burden." In the Cold War struggle of imagery and ideas with the Soviet Union, Jim Crow was a dangerous embarrassment to the United States.

Segregation was doomed, but just when and how it would end was not foreordained. Nor was it fated that Thurgood Marshall and his colleagues working with the NAACP Legal Defense Fund would play the pivotal roles they did.

Massive Resistance

Marshall and others who mapped the litigation campaign to end school segregation began without power. The African Americans among them had been brought up in a society that threatened to lynch those who protested their subservient status. Nonetheless, they litigated throughout the South in the late 1940s and early 1950s, with no assurance that they would win. The only certainty was that they would have to bear daily indignities, such as having to eat their lunches huddled in a car because no restaurant would seat them.

Finally, in the 1954 case of *Brown v. Board of Education,* the Supreme Court handed down the decision for which Marshall and his colleagues had so long striven.[1] The Court declared school segregation unconstitutional. It took considerable courage for Chief Justice Earl Warren and his colleagues on the bench to issue this unanimous, politically charged, precedent-breaking decision.

Yet *Brown* itself made hardly a dent in segregation. Southern politicians launched a counterattack. Citing constitutional theories reversed by the Civil War, they claimed the right to disregard Supreme Court decisions with which their white constituents disagreed. To keep African Americans out of the schools and "in their place," these officials organized what they termed "massive resistance." They blocked schoolhouse doors, declaring, "Segregation today, segregation forever." Sheriffs used cattle prods on peaceful demonstrators. Governors egged white mobs into action—and it appeared for a while that the mobs might win. Some federal judges abetted the resistance; those who tried to enforce the law got only grudging support from Presidents Dwight D. Eisenhower and John F. Kennedy. For a while, the "massive resistance" threatened to nullify the Supreme Court's decision in *Brown.*

Backlash in the South produced a counter-backlash in the rest of the nation. Television, a new force in American politics, brought the mobs defending "The Southern Way of Life" into America's living rooms. As Professor Alexander Bickel of Yale Law School wrote in 1962:

> Here were grown men and women furiously confronting their enemy: two, three, a half dozen scrubbed, starched, scared, and incredibly brave colored children. The moral bankruptcy, the shame of the thing, was evident. . . . There was an unforgettable scene, for example, in one CBS newscast from New Orleans, of a white mother fairly foaming at the mouth with the effort to rivet her distracted little boy's attention and teach him how to hate. And repeatedly, the ugly spitting curse, NIGGER! The effect achieved on an unprecedented number of people with unprecedented speed, must have been something like what used to happen to individuals (the young Lincoln among them) at the sight of an actual slave auction. . . . Mob action led to the mobilization of northern opinion in support of the Court's decision—not merely because the mob is disorderly, but because it concretized the abstraction of racism. . . . One of those supreme occasions had been brought about when a decisive reprise is open to the political branches; it was for them to make the Court's decision their rule of political action, or not to do so, and thus to make or break the decision itself. The political branches . . . had independently, on their own responsibility, to speak their moral approval of the Court's decision, to support it by drawing on their own resources, and to act in pursuance of it. This was one time when hiding behind the judges' skirts would not do. The political institutions had a decision of their own to make.[2]

Congress and the president decided in favor of equal rights because the electorate, shocked by these ugly images, demanded it. In 1964, they began enacting antisegregationist statutes with teeth. Instead of passing the buck—instead of telling federal agencies to pursue a melange of goals designed to please everyone—elected officials straightforwardly outlawed the practices that kept African Americans out of schools and voting booths. To ensure that these new laws were obeyed, Congress gave the Department of Justice the authority, funding, and political backing it needed to sue in the name of the United States. The Department of Health, Education, and Welfare was meanwhile instructed to cut off federal money to school districts that failed to desegregate.

Brown v. Board of Education and the ten years of litigation that followed produced hardly any practical change in the field, but what Congress did beginning in 1964 brought massive change.[3] With *Brown*, the Supreme Court had not so much imposed its values on society as called the question of whether Jim Crow should live on. Society answered by coming down decisively against racism.

Southern politicians hollered "states' rights." This principle—that national government should stay out of the affairs of state and local governments and that also goes by the name *federalism*—has validity but was a loser in the context of desegregation. Federalism had never stopped federal judges from protecting other constitutional rights, and the Supreme Court had decided that school segregation violated the Constitution. State elected officials who asserted states' rights were temporarily popular in their own districts but were soon overwhelmed by the social forces sweeping the country. America in the end honored the judges who enforced desegregation decrees as strong and wise and visionary. These assertive judges and the civil rights lawyers who appealed to them were the heroes of the day.

Yet federal courts did more than stop constitutional violations in the desegregation cases. Ongoing resistance to compliance with the law forced federal judges to undertake the policy-making work of school boards and, later, prison wardens. Understandably, the judges wanted the institutions under them to become not only legal, but *better*. From the death of Jim Crow, there was thus born a revolutionary idea: that courts could and should reform state and local governments.

Congress Cashes In

The image of state and local officials as villains in need of judicial correction began with the South but spread to officials across the country during the era of antiwar demonstrations and urban riots. In the resulting culture, mayors and governors came to be considered part of the problem rather than the solution. Local politics that set priorities through democratic tugging and hauling reflected, many young lawyers thought, the basest instincts of society. They wanted to use the courts to improve society just as the heroes of *Brown* had done before them. Marcia Lowry, who filed the *Wilder* case, was one of them. We were, too.

In the late 1960s, with southern segregation on the run, the moral spotlight turned to poverty and the environment. Books such as Michael Harrington's *The Other America* (1962) and Rachel Carson's *Silent Spring* (1962) made the public aware that poverty and pollution, like racial segregation, were the unfinished business of the American dream. As with racial segregation, national leaders blamed these failures on state and local officials.

Congress responded to these new challenges by creating statutory rights enforceable in federal court against state and local governments. Before *Brown*, Congress had created few such rights. Congress, to be sure, had vastly increased national regulation of society in general and business in particular, but it had largely exempted state and local governments or gave them separate, more lenient treatment. The chief way in which Congress influenced state and local governments was by giving them money with strings attached. The strings were in the main aimed at getting state and local governments to spend the federal money for its intended use—highway money for highways, housing money for housing—and were not aimed at using the federal purse for regulating state and local governments. State and local officials sometimes complained that spending conditions were too complex or constricting, but enforcement was generally by the federal agency, which might negotiate a plan to achieve eventual compliance but almost never would turn off the money tap.

In addressing the civil rights challenge, Congress adopted a different strategy. Faced with defiance from elected state and local officials, Congress opted to act primarily through federal agents, especially U.S. marshals, federal voting inspectors, Department of Justice attorneys, and federal judges. Congress followed a similar pattern in President Lyndon B. Johnson's 1965 War on Poverty, in which federal officials worked directly with local poverty organizations rather than through existing state and municipal channels. This was the concept of maximum feasible participation, which proved disastrous, as so brilliantly narrated in Daniel Patrick Moynihan's *Maximum Feasible Misunderstanding*.[4]

As the Voting Rights Act started to make states in the South more responsive to African Americans, Congress reverted to its more traditional means of getting its way: it tied federal money to federal standards. This well-worn strategy had the great advantage of interposing states and cities as buffers between the federal government and the beneficiaries of the social programs and also allowed Congress to observe the niceties of federalism.

Congress increasingly used spending conditions to regulate how states and cities ran programs that they had long funded and operated on their own. Governors and mayors had little choice but to comply, as leaving federal funds on the table would be political suicide. This *fiscal federalism* or *regulatory federalism*, as it came to be called, was the tool by which the federal government imposed national standards on traditional state programs such as education, welfare, medical assistance, water quality, and highway construction.[5]

Although our topic is court management of state and local governments, not fiscal federalism, fiscal federalism is an essential ingredient in how courts came to govern. Fiscal federalism called for a new governmental lineup. The federal government assumed the senior role of setting standards on how and when states and localities would deliver services. To get the federal money, governors and mayors had to promise to dance to the federal tune.

But who would make sure that the governors and mayors delivered on the promises they gave to secure the federal money? Answer: the courts. They stood at the ready. Judge Skelly Wright of the District of Columbia Court of Appeals expressed in 1971 the spirit of the times: "Our duty, in short, is to see that important legislative purposes, heralded in the halls of Congress, are not lost or misdirected in the vast hallways of the federal bureaucracy."[6]

Members of Congress, quick to perceive changes that work to their advantage, latched on to the courts' willingness to supervise state and local governments as a way to crown themselves with the heroic mantel of rights-bestower. The prospect of legislating popular generalities and leaving them to be fleshed out by the courts was especially enticing. After all, what makes the work of elected politicians hard—and makes reelection even harder—is the clash of interests. For one example, those who want factories to reduce pollution clash with management, shareholders, customers, and employees, all of whom have an interest in avoiding the expense of pollution control. Politicians who dare enact rules resolving such clashes often come away feeling that they made more enemies than friends. If the policy-making burden were shifted to the courts, national legislators could have their cake and eat it, too. They could take credit for bestowing rights while lawyers and judges forced state and local officials to shoulder the blame for the costs. The state and local officials would have to impose the higher taxes, tougher regulations, or service cuts needed to comply with the federal mandates. This ploy came to be known among political types as the *unfunded mandate*.

Starting with the 1970 Clean Air Act, Congress gave everyone a *right* to healthy air. Who had the corresponding *duty* to clean it was not specified.[7] The federal lawmakers passed that buck to the elected branches of state and local government by setting up an elaborate process in which state and local officials would have to decide who had to reduce their emissions and how much. To deflect the charge that this new right to clean air was not just hot air, the act authorized citizens to sue in court. The courts, not Congress, became the place where clean air policy would be made.[8]

The state and local officials were not to blame for the dirty air, or no more to blame than Congress, but that was beside the point. Congress acted as if state and local officials were to blame, even though state and local officials had already done far more to reduce pollution from factories than the federal government had done or would do in the next decade.[9] On the theory imported from the civil rights desegregation model that states and cities failed the people, Congress, in the words of the Supreme Court, took "a stick to the States" in the 1970 Clean Air Act.[10]

The opportunity for political profit was irresistible. Legislators began to make names for themselves by searching out appealing causes and then turning them into statutory rights enforceable in federal court against state and local government. As former New York City Mayor Edward I. Koch explained why he, as a member of Congress, had voted to create a right to public transportation for people with disabilities: "I voted for that. You'd be crazy to be against that. When you are a member of Congress and you are voting a mandate and not providing the funds for it, the sky's the limit."[11]

Thus, from the mid-1960s to the end of the 1970s, Congress went from regulating state and local governments hardly at all to regulating them in detail. The list of exactions imposed since the 1970s is staggering, as Figure 1.1 indicates. In statutes enacted between 1970 and 1991, Congress preempted more states' laws than it had from 1789 to 1969.[12] A federal commission concluded in 1996 that more than 200 separate federal mandates involving 170 federal laws reached "into every nook and cranny of state and local activities."[13] A study of reported federal court decisions for the year 1994 found that more than 3,500 judicial opinions arose under more than 100 separate federal laws involving state and local governments.[14] Another study found steady growth of special education litigation following passage of the federal statute in 1975.[15] Public policy issues that had once been decided in the political branches, mostly at the state and local levels, were now affected, if not controlled directly, by federal rights enforceable in federal courts.

This mass production of rights became possible because of a series of basic structural changes in American politics. For one, the U.S. Senate no longer protected the states. Before adoption of the Seventeenth Amendment to the Constitution, ratified in 1913, U.S. senators were elected by state legislatures, not the voters directly. The old system for electing senators, whatever its demerits, tended to protect state and local governments from the predations of officials in Washington.

Another obstacle disappeared with the New Deal. The Supreme Court had previously stopped Congress from extending its reach beyond powers enumerated in the Constitution such as providing for the national defense, regulating interstate commerce, or enforcing constitutional rights. Frustrated by narrow interpretations of these powers, President Franklin D. Roosevelt attacked the Supreme Court, which had the effect of freeing Congress to tackle practically any issue it wished.

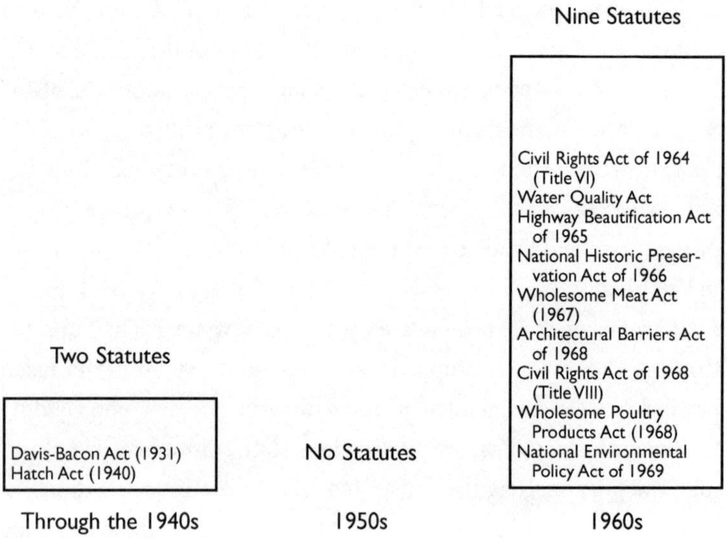

Nine Statutes

Civil Rights Act of 1964
(Title VI)
Water Quality Act
Highway Beautification Act
of 1965
National Historic Preser-
vation Act of 1966
Wholesome Meat Act
(1967)
Architectural Barriers Act
of 1968

Two Statutes

Civil Rights Act of 1968
(Title VIII)
Wholesome Poultry
Products Act (1968)
National Environmental
Policy Act of 1969

Davis-Bacon Act (1931)
Hatch Act (1940)

No Statutes

Through the 1940s   1950s   1960s

Figure 1.1. Major federal statutes regulating state and local governments.
(See the appendix for descriptions of the statutes and methodology.)

Twenty-five Statutes

Occupational Safety and Health Act (1970)
Clean Air Act Amendments of 1970
Uniform Relocation Act of 1970
Equal Employment Opportunity Act of 1972
Education Amendments of 1972 (Title IX)
Federal Water Pollution Control Act Amendments of 1972
Federal Insecticide, Fungicide, and Rodenticide Act (1972)
National Health Planning and Resources Development Act of 1974
Rehabilitation Act of 1973
Endangered Species Act of 1973
Flood Disaster Protection Act of 1973
Emergency Highway Energy Conservation Act (1974)
Age Discrimination in Employment Act (1974)
Fair Labor Standards Act Amendments of 1974
Family Education Rights and Privacy Act of 1974
Safe Drinking Water Act of 1975
Age Discrimination Act of 1975
Education for All Handicapped Children Act (1975)
Coastal Zone Management Act of 1972
Resource Conservation and Recovery Act of 1976
Marine Protection Research and Sanctuaries Act Amendments of 1977
National Energy Conservation Policy Act (1978)
Natural Gas Policy Act of 1978
Public Utilities Regulatory Policies Act of 1978
Surface Mining Control and Reclamation Act of 1977

1970s

Twenty-one Statutes

Voting Rights Act Amendments of 1982
Surface Transportation Assistance Act of 1982
Social Security Amendments of 1983
Highway Safety Amendments of 1984
Voting Accessibility for the Elderly and Handicapped Act (1984)
Child Abuse Amendments of 1984
Hazardous and Solid Waste Amendments of 1984
Consolidated Omnibus Budget Reconciliation Act of 1985
Handicapped Children's Protection Act of 1986
Safe Drinking Water Act Amendments of 1986
Education of the Handicapped Act Amendments of 1986
Emergency Planning and Community Right-to-Know Act of 1986
Asbestos Hazard Emergency Response Act of 1986
Commercial Motor Vehicle Safety Act of 1986
Age Discrimination in Employment Act Amendments of 1986
Water Quality Act of 1987
Civil Rights Restoration Act of 1987
Drug-Free Workplace Act of 1988
Fair Housing Act Amendments of 1988
Lead Contamination Control Act of 1988
Ocean Dumping Ban Act (1988)

1980s

Twenty-one Statutes

Americans with Disabilities Act (1990)
Cash Management Improvement Act of 1990
Clean Air Act Amendments of 1990
Education of the Handicapped Act Amendments of 1990
Older Workers Benefit Protection Act of 1990
Social Security: Fiscal 1991 Budget Reconciliation Act
Individuals with Disabilities Education Act Amendments of 1991
Intermodal Surface Transportation Efficiency Act of 1991
Juvenile Justice and Delinquency Prevention Amendments of 1992
Rehabilitation Act Amendments of 1992
Family and Medical Leave Act of 1993
National Voter Registration Act of 1993
Brady Handgun Violence Prevention Act of 1993
Religious Freedom Restoration Act of 1993
Improving America's Schools Act of 1994
Safe Drinking Water Act Amendments of 1996
Personal Responsibility and Work Opportunity Reconciliation Act of 1996
Adoption and Safe Families Act, 1997
Individuals with Disabilities Education Act Amendments of 1997
Foster Care Independence Act of 1999
Ticket to Work and Work Incentives Improvement Act of 1999

1990s

Congress, however, did not mass-produce mandates against state and local governments until the 1970s because the argument that Washington should stick to truly national issues continued to have political force. That argument fell into disfavor after southern segregationists invoked states' rights for an ugly purpose.

National political parties had also protected state and local governments by knitting federal legislators, governors, and mayors from the same political party into close coalitions. After Watergate and the resignation of President Richard M. Nixon in 1974, political parties lost much of their power. Just as presidential politics have changed, so too have congressional politics. Working one's way up the party hierarchy is no longer the only path to status in Congress. Many legislators make names for themselves by searching out appealing causes and turning them into statutory rights enforceable against state and local officials in federal court.

State and local governments were slow to oppose federal mandates, and when they did they often failed. Paul L. Posner, in his study of unfunded mandates, explained why.[16] National interest groups often have more influence and relevance to the ambitions of members of Congress than do officials from their own state. When issues erupt, enthusiasm for action sweeps over Congress, exciting political entrepreneurs to make the issue their own. Advocates for the new initiative emphasize benefits and hide costs. State and local officials cannot easily oppose new federal programs aimed at helping constituents, and may even be co-opted into supporting a mandate in order to get a larger share of federal funds. Even when some oppose mandates, they have little success because the price of mandates is paid by everyone and therefore is the particular concern of no one. The national media also work against state and local opposition to mandates. Television especially has the capacity to universalize current ideas and to make famous those political leaders seeking to create national standards. In addition, until recently, most members of the media grew up during the civil rights era and came to believe that the assumptions of that period were universally applicable to all policy issues. They are swept along with everyone else.

The Rise of Public Interest Law

Every spring in the half century since *Brown v. Board of Education,* many of the thousands of new law school graduates begin their legal careers dreaming of becoming heroes asserting rights in court or creating them in Congress. We ourselves felt these aspirations. One of us (Schoenbrod) began his legal career as a law clerk for one of the heroes who argued *Brown* in the Supreme Court, Judge Spottswood W. Robinson III. Both of us worked in the 1970s as public interest attorneys in one of the premier advocacy organizations, the Natural Resources Defense Council.

Public interest attorneys were near cousins of civil rights attorneys such as Thurgood Marshall. We sought changes that went beyond constitutional rights such as freedom of speech. Our work extended to all social concerns, from poverty and the environment to prisons, consumerism, women's rights, education, and health benefits. We would stand up to landlords, big corporations, and municipal officials. Public interest attorneys sought to provide legal representation to interests that historically had been underrepresented.[17]

Specialty law centers sprouted up. When *Brown v. Board of Education* was decided, the only cause-oriented lawyer groups were the American Civil Liberties Union and the NAACP Legal Defense Fund. Building on these models, the Ford Foundation funded the first recognizable public interest law firm, a community office in New Haven, Connecticut, in 1963. That same year a similar organization, Mobilization for Youth, set up shop on New York City's Lower East Side. Favorable publicity for these two new groups—and support from the organized bar—led to the creation of the federal legal services program as part of President Johnson's War on Poverty. By 1967, the Office of Economic Opportunity had funded three hundred local legal services organizations and a dozen national law reform centers to focus on test cases and legislative change in particular areas such as education, health, consumer law, housing, welfare, and economic development.[18] Private, nongovernmental public interest law firms also appeared, among them the Environmental Defense Fund, the Natural Resources Defense Council, the Center for Law and Social Policy, the Children's Defense Fund, Public Advocates, and the New York City Legal Aid Society's Prisoners' Rights Project. Critical to the growth of these centers was the fact that the Internal Revenue Service decided in 1971 that public interest litigation was a charitable activity deserving tax-exempt status. This brought money and legitimacy.[19] Although public interest law continued to cause controversy, it had become part of the legal terrain.

The new federal standards for states and localities empowered us and our public interest colleagues. Federal statutes and federal regulations allowed recent law school graduates to steamroll statehouses and municipal councils throughout the land.

Our power depended on our ability to enforce the standards in federal court. If enforcement were solely by federal agencies and not also by federal courts, the agencies could bend the standards in response to political pressure brought by mayors and governors. We insisted instead on rights enforceable in court by us. Desegregation was always the analogy. With public interest attorneys on the case and the doors to the federal courthouse open, what ought to be done would be done, or so we argued. Politically, this translated to a demand that the public interest bar be accepted as "private attorneys general" to enforce federal laws whenever the federal government failed to do the job. We in the public interest bar amended the pyramidal relationships first envisioned by Congress. Under our amendment, the federal government remained as regulator on the top setting the standards, with states and localities at the bottom mandated to comply with the federal standards. In the middle, however, as the chief enforcers of the standards, would be the private "public interest" attorney.

The demand that private attorneys be given public power was most famously answered in the citizen suit provision first incorporated in the Clean Air Act of 1970. As proposed, the act would have made federal officials solely responsible for assuring that the states complied with federal standards. This did not sit well with environmentalists and led to discussions between David Sive, a founder of the environmental public interest bar, and Tim Atkinson, general counsel to President Nixon's Council on Environmental Quality. The environmentalists of the era analogized environmental rights to constitutional rights. They drafted a proposed amendment to the Clean Air Act that allowed private citizens to enforce federal standards and, if successful, to win court-awarded attorneys' fees paid by the loser. This citizen suit provision was inserted into the pending bill and passed Congress without attracting much attention. Similar citizen suit provisions were later inserted in succeeding environmental statutes as well as many nonenvironmental statutes, such as the Americans with Disabilities Act.

The citizen suit provision in its many forms created a powerful tool that linked two of the most potent ideals in the American canon: (1) the right of the individual to lawful treatment by government and (2) the moral authority of courts to condemn illegality. While these noble ideals got their pedigree in the enforcement of constitutional rights, the legislators in Congress now had a way to mass-produce statutory rights against states and localities. In this process, national legislators became heroes; so did federal judges and public interest attorneys. Heroes in Congress proclaimed new rights, hero-judges enforced the new rights against the law-breaking state and local officials, and hero-attorneys guarded the new rights.

The Courts Go with the Flow

There was a time as late as the mid 1970s when it was still doubtful whether judges would assume managerial control of government programs except when necessary to remedy egregious violations of civil rights. In our careers at the Natural Resources Defense Council, we saw the courts move from reluctance to enthusiastic embrace of their new role. In the early 1970s, we sometimes lost cases because judges felt that it was inappropriate for private plaintiffs to micromanage state and local governments. By the end of the 1970s, we were winning these cases and negotiating lengthy consent decrees that bind such governments to this day.

Take, for example, our own efforts to improve the mass transit system in New York City. Our first efforts began with a 1973 noise pollution lawsuit brought in the name of children trying to learn in an elementary school adjacent to an elevated subway track. We asked the Transit Authority to reduce subway noise so that children could learn and employees and riders would not suffer hearing loss. The state high court dismissed our suit.[20] That noise standards were violated was beside the point, the judges ruled, because courts could not correct the violations without enmeshing themselves in public administration. The decision—which, at the time, we thought wrong—was one of the last times that New York State courts stuck to the traditional concept that they should not control policy.

But subway noise was only one symptom of a deeper crisis. Public transit was fighting a losing battle against the private car. Cities had failed to maintain their transit systems, and the systems were falling apart. Unwilling to raise fares, to postpone union wage increases, or to raise taxes, politicians held down costs by "deferring" maintenance. Although cities sought help from Washington, Congress never delivered much for public transportation.

Congress, however, had promised clean air—and auto congestion produced pollution. Here was a legal hook, which proponents of public transit could use to regain the initiative. If subways ran better, fewer people would drive cars; less traffic would mean cleaner air.

New York took the right to clean air seriously. Governor Nelson A. Rockefeller and Mayor John V. Lindsay agreed on a clean air plan that included bridge tolls to fund transit improvements. But the officials who succeeded Rockefeller and Lindsay hesitated to impose tolls because tolls would be unpopular with motorists.

Relying on Congress's declaration that citizens had a right to clean air, we decided that we would be the ones who would enforce that right in the New York courts. In 1975 we went to federal court in Manhattan to force the state and city to implement the clean air plan, including tolls. U.S. District Court Judge Kevin T. Duffy refused to enter an injunction on the grounds that it would enmesh him in public policy decisions that should be left to elected officials. We appealed to the court of appeals to discipline Judge Duffy by ordering him to enforce the law. The appeals court ordered him to do so, pointing out that Congress had expressly given citizens a right to healthy air and had specifically authorized citizens to vindicate violations of that right in federal court. Judge Walter Mansfield wrote that "Congress made clear that citizen groups are not to be treated as nuisances or troublemakers but rather as welcomed participants in the vindication of environmental interests."[21]

What happened next was an exercise in pure politics. Legislators, who had been only too happy to announce a general right to clean air, backed off when they heard complaints from constituents. Judge Duffy's decision had shown that Congress was the ultimate source of the bridge-toll requirement. Once that became clear, the city's representatives in Washington wrote tolls out of the Clean Air Act. Led by Daniel Patrick Moynihan in the Senate and Elizabeth Holtzman in the House, Congress outlawed both our lawsuit and Governor Rockefeller's decision favoring tolls. When we asked the congressional leaders how the state should meet Congress's clean air standards without bridge tolls, they would not say.

The legislators in Washington usually escape personal blame for the consequences of the rights they impose because the costs of honoring rights typically fall on the public generally and not some discrete group such as those who commute into Manhattan by car. Consequently, legislators rarely reconsider the rights they bestow. That leaves the courts free to enforce the rights as originally enacted. With the supreme legislature in the land positively commanding the courts to lead the way, many judges marched forward into policy making, and did so openly, even self-righteously. The assumption, borrowed from the days of massive resistance to school desegregation, was that if state or local government failed to honor the new rights, the reason had to be official resistance.[22] But official resistance seldom is the cause. Unlike the officials in the old South who resisted the goal of desegregation because their white constituents opposed it, state and local officials today favor the goals of the new rights because their constituents support them. The problem for the officials and for the courts is that the same constituents often oppose the measures needed to translate the goals into reality.

Seeds of Doubt

Lawyers today have grown up in a culture believing that many of the improvements that people want come only through judicially enforceable rights. But long before democracy by decree, citizen advocates and public officials worked for reform in other ways. They organized, petitioned, voted, testified, and appealed to public opinion and state and local legislatures.

Believers in democracy by decree argue that political progress is not fast enough or cannot be trusted. We thought the same when we were public interest lawyers, but we were wrong. Looking back, we see that our own accomplishments came chiefly from politics as usual, not democracy by decree.

Our court victories did little to clean the air, and our successes were mostly at the sufferance of society. Although we lost the subway noise lawsuit in the courts of law, we ultimately won through politics. The worst of the noise came from flat spots on subway car wheels. Once a steel wheel gets even a little out of round, the wheel skids on the flat spot whenever the brakes are applied, making the flat spot larger. Without proper maintenance, the enlarged flat spots bang like hammers when the train runs at normal speed. Our lawsuit was rejected, but the political pressures we set in motion forced politicians to find ways to bring the wheels back into round.

Congress got rid of the bridge tolls, but, working with Mayor Koch, the City Planning Department, and the Transit Authority, we published a book in 1978, *A New Direction in Transit,* that showed how to make the transit system reliable.[23] All New York newspapers endorsed our plan, which laid the groundwork for the state to develop a series of capital programs that over time largely transformed New York City's public transportation system at a cost so far of more than $20 billion.

Our Clean Air Act victories in the courtroom produced very little improvement in air quality. The lengthy court orders ultimately imposed on New York City regulated how it assigned police, controlled traffic, and permitted the operation of parking lots, but in general only marginally affected air quality.

We had aspired to be like Thurgood Marshall. Instead of the constitutional right of equality that Marshall fought for, we relied on the congressionally declared right to clean air. The federal courts backed us with orders and favorable decisions, including one from Marshall himself sitting as the circuit justice. After a memorable argument in his chambers in the Supreme Court building in Washington, Justice Marshall wrote a decision denying Mayor Abraham D. Beame's request to stay Judge Duffy's toll order pending an opportunity for the mayor to present the city's case to the full Supreme Court. The city never needed that hearing, however, because Congress eliminated the city's bridge-toll requirement that same summer.

The public interest bar oversells the ability of courts to reform society. People are prone to mistake the doings of heroes, including the heroes of *Brown v. Board of Education,* for the whole of history. As Leo Tolstoy wrote in *War and Peace,* "in historic events, the so-called great men are labels giving names to events and like labels they have but the smallest connexion with the event itself."[24] Tolstoy was arguing that the French invasion of Russia in 1812 was not caused by the great men on the scene—Emperor Napoleon and Czar Alexander—but rather had "myriads of causes": "The deeper we delve in search of these causes the more of them we find; and each separate cause or whole series of causes appears to us equally valid in itself and equally false by its insignificance compared to the magnitude of the events. . . . The actions of Napoleon and Alexander, on whose words the event seemed to hang, were as little voluntary as the actions of any soldier who was drawn into the campaign by lot or by conscription. . . . The higher a man stands on the social ladder, the more people he is connected with and the more power he has over others, the more evident is the predestination and inevitability of his every action."[25]

Similarly, the prime causes of the death of Jim Crow were not the heroes, as heroic as they were, but the forces that led society to want to extirpate that disease from the body politic. The courts played a vital role. *Brown v. Board of Education* forced society to decide whether it wanted to honor its higher principles. When society answered "yes," courts were needed to impose remedies on recalcitrant officials, such as the governors who blocked the schoolhouse door.

Yet, on balance, the courts rode the wave of history rather than set it in motion. Seen from this broader perspective, the heroism in the courthouse is no less heroic, but of a different nature. Thurgood Marshall, Earl Warren, and their colleagues did not command their country to stop segregation, but they did diagnose the disease and recommend a cure. In the end, the cure came from society, not from the courts. Judge Spottswood Robinson told one of us not long before he died: "We weren't the heroes. The heroes were our clients. We came and went, but they had to stay and face the intolerance every day."

The basic premise of democracy by decree is that government can be made more compassionate only if judges impose their will on elected officials. Although dubious on many scores, that assertion has popular appeal precisely because most people want a compassionate government. The same voters elect both the members of Congress and state and local governmental officials. Why then should the federal officials be the more compassionate?

The battle to overthrow segregation is not the right model for all interrelationships between federal and state and local officials. By extrapolating that battle to a whole host of newly minted rights, we have created a new governmental lineup in which one set of officials at the federal level largely escapes accountability for the costs of the laws they pass and another set of officials at the state and local levels lacks the power to balance the costs of implementing the federal statutory rights against other competing priorities. Perhaps federal officials should impose mandates on state and local governments.[26] This is not a question we address. Our focus is on what happens in the twenty-first century after Congress has spoken and judges are asked to empower a controlling group to manage and supervise institutions of state or local government.

Congress, whatever the limits ultimately imposed under the federal Constitution, should be sensitive to the consequences of the mandates it proposes. It does not have to be, however, because of democracy by decree. Through democracy by decree, the courts exonerate the politicians in Washington from blame for the messes they create by commandeering state and local governments and thereby assuming the power to make policy.

CHAPTER 2

How Congress Creates Rights
A Case Study

Courts justify their remedial decrees against state and local governments by pointing to violations of rights that Congress has created. Courts also parry charges that their decrees undercut democratic accountability by noting that Congress can get rid of the decrees by amending the statutory rights. This chapter shows how Congress created one right—the right to curb ramps—and later dealt with pleas from mayors to amend that right.

The Humble Curb Ramp

Curb ramps appeared on the public radar screen during the 1960s in New York City.[1] With the city hemorrhaging manufacturing jobs, the government asked the remaining firms how it could keep them. Garment manufacturers replied that curb ramps in Manhattan's garment center would help. Curbs were a barrier to the wheeled racks used to move garments from specialist to specialist. The city started to install what it called "carriage ramps."

Curb ramps in the garment center caught the attention of parents with baby carriages and veterans using wheelchairs who asked for them to be installed elsewhere. The city began to do so in the mid-1960s. No mandate was necessary because local politicians wanted to please voters.

New York City has 160,000 intersections. In thirty-five years of effort, it had managed to ramp half of them. If it continues to spend on ramps at the current rate, roughly $32 million a year, the job will take a century to complete. Progress is slow partly because traffic signals, fire alarm boxes, underground utilities, or vaults make some street corners much more expensive to ramp than others. Narrow sidewalks lack the space for a ramp engineered the standard way. A poorly engineered ramp stops the flow of water, causing a puddle in summer and an icy hazard in winter.[2] Although an easy sidewalk corner costs about $2,500 to ramp, a difficult one can cost up to $200,000.

This reality was forcibly brought home to a prominent state legislator representing a Manhattan district several years ago. Thinking to sponsor new curb ramps in his Manhattan district, he secured a special state appropriation of several hundred thousand dollars for ramp construction. When he discovered that any one of the remaining intersections without ramps in his district would consume his entire appropriation, he changed his mind. Instead, he used the money for other local projects that had greater political payoff.

Curb Ramps Become a Federal Right

Curb ramps were too desirable a benefit for federal officials to ignore. In 1973, in response to lobbying by advocates for people with disabilities, Congress enacted a simple law that broadly required recipients of federal funds not to discriminate against handicapped people in any federally funded program.[3] Congress did not mention curb ramps in the statute but left it to each federal agency running a grant program to specify how recipients of funds would meet the new requirement. In response, the U.S. Department of Transportation in 1977 called for curb ramps to be included in *new* highway projects financed by the federal government. This requirement caused few problems because installing ramps in new construction adds little cost. Many, perhaps most, cities would have done about the same without the federal requirement.

In 1990 Congress granted broad new rights in the Americans with Disabilities Act (ADA).[4] Congress did not mention curb ramps in this statute either, but it did specifically ban architectural barriers to government services, and at least one of the key legislative documents portrayed rampless curbs as a barrier to the use of sidewalks. Congress designated the Department of Justice as the federal agency that would dictate what must be done about architectural barriers. The department announced on July 26, 1991, that all states and localities must install ramps that meet federal engineering guidelines. A curb ramp could have no more than a one-quarter-inch front lip and a maximum slope of one inch per foot, among other stringent requirements. Curbs at all intersections in the nation had to be ramped in under four years, by January 26, 1995, with all priority curbs ramped sooner.[5] The only exceptions allowed had to be based on a showing that ramping a particular curb would fundamentally alter the service provided or result in undue financial or administrative burdens.

The right to curb ramps immediately put local officials in a political and legal pickle. Many curb ramps already installed did not meet federal standards, and the time set for ramping old curbs was so short that most large cities could not possibly meet the deadline. City officials would inevitably become lawbreakers vulnerable to charges that they discriminate against the disabled. Federal courts issued orders against Memphis, Tennessee (1999); Charleston, West Virginia (1998); Toledo, Ohio (1998); Manhattan, Kansas (1994); and Philadelphia, Pennsylvania (1993).[6]

Congress Is Asked to Reconsider

As the 1995 deadline for installing ramps at all intersections drew near, the mayors went back to Congress, the ultimate source of this impossible requirement. Congress offered no relief. When statutes confer rights on targeted groups such as the disabled that are to be paid for by the general public, it is hard for Congress to change its mind. Congress has difficulty standing up to any focused lobby, and few lobbies in Washington are as powerful as that for the disabled community.

The upshot of the mayors' appeal was that on March 24, 1995, a bipartisan group of five prominent senators (Tom Harkin, Bob Dole, Edward M. Kennedy, Orrin G. Hatch, and John McCain) jointly signed a letter to Attorney General Janet F. Reno petitioning her to grant the nation's cities five additional years to complete priority curb ramps and ten years for the remainder. The senators presented themselves as "strong supporters of the ADA and its fundamental principle that access is opportunity for people with disabilities." With their bona fides thus protected, the senators continued that they had "heard that curb cuts are a unique, significant capital expense, and believe that our intent would be more properly fulfilled over a longer period of time." The five senators asked the Department of Justice to adopt "this policy change as soon as possible, consistent with all laws and ethical guidelines."[7]

The letter shows how little Congress wanted to be involved with adjusting the absurdly tight time schedule that made lawbreakers out of local officials across the country. Congress did not need the agency to adjust the deadlines, and the agency could not readily grant the senators' request. The deadlines were a product of the statutory instructions that Congress gave the agency. Senators and representatives had been elected precisely for the purpose of taking responsibility, but voting to weaken a deadline, even an impossible one, would have placed them in the awkward position of weakening what they had previously declared to be a civil right that benefited a powerful lobby. Thus the senators ducked a legislative solution in favor of appealing with a wink to the attorney general.

Attorney General Reno winked back. On November 27, 1995, she published a formal notice that the Department of Justice was considering extending the deadline just as the senators had proposed.[8] The department made no argument of its own for the change nor did it mention that its 1995 deadline could not possibly be met in any significantly built-up urban area in the country. And that was the end of the matter. The department never put the proposed regulation in final form. The senators' letter was only a sop to the mayors, and the department's proposal was only a sop to the senators.

The original regulation, which today remains on the books fully enforceable in federal court, requires all cities in the country to have added ramps to existing curbs (except where they can prove hardship) by January 26, 1995—a date long gone. Almost every city is late, is out of compliance, and, where plaintiffs are inclined to sue, is a sitting duck for a lawsuit for which there is no defense.

Curb Ramps and the Campaign against Unfunded Mandates

By the early 1990s mayors and governors, finding that they tend to lose when they object to particular unfunded mandates such as curb ramps, decided to make an issue of unfunded mandates in general. Democratic and Republican officials joined the campaign, and it struck a responsive chord with voters. By 1994 getting rid of unfunded mandates was a key part of the Republican "Contract with America." Although individual mandates had been popular, unfunded mandates collectively had become unpopular. In 1995 Congress passed the Unfunded Mandates Reform Act.[9] President Bill

Clinton in signing the bill stated: "Today we are making history. . . . We are recognizing that the pendulum had swung too far [toward Washington], and that we have to rely on the initiative, the creativity, the determination, and the decisionmaking of people at the State and local level to carry much of the load for America as we move into the 21st century."[10]

The act made it harder, but not impossible, for Congress to enact new statutes imposing unfunded mandates but left previously enacted mandate statutes such as the ADA on the books. Rather than reconsider these old statutes itself, Congress instructed an obscure federal think tank, the Advisory Commission on Intergovernmental Relations (ACIR), to report to Congress on which existing federal statutes should be changed.

The ACIR, a tiny, nearly invisible federal agency, had been created in 1960 to provide a forum for discussing the relationship between the federal government and states and localities. Its small, industrious staff had turned out hundreds of studies over the nearly four decades of its existence. The commission itself was a star-studded group of senators, representatives, cabinet heads, governors, mayors, county heads, state legislators, and prominent citizens selected to speak for a wide array of interests.

In response to the command in the Unfunded Mandates Reform Act, the ACIR staff reviewed the length and breadth of federal statutes, surveyed state and local officials for their concerns, and identified more than two hundred federal statutes and regulations imposing enforceable duties on state and local governments. The ACIR decided to concentrate on mandates that required state and local governments to expend substantial amounts of their own resources in a manner that significantly distorted their preferred spending priorities. It further narrowed its focus to mandates imposed as conditions for accepting federal funds that states and localities could not realistically refuse, that abridged historic powers of states without significantly advancing nationally important goals, or that imposed compliance requirements that were difficult or impossible to meet. The result was a list of fourteen specific statutes that met ACIR criteria for elimination or modification, among them the ADA, the statute that had spawned the curb ramp mandate. The ACIR cited the difficulties that state and local governments experienced in meeting the accessibility requirements of the ADA by January 26, 1995, and recommended that Congress ease the deadline, increase flexibility, make the federal government pay compliance costs, and eliminate private lawsuits.[11]

On January 24, 1996, the ACIR released its draft report for public review in conjunction with the winter conference of the U.S. Conference of Mayors. At the press conference Mayor Edward G. Rendell, the Democratic mayor of Philadelphia and a member of the ruling board of the ACIR, singled out the curb ramp requirement. Because of the federal curb ramp right, he said, a federal court in a private lawsuit had ordered Philadelphia "to make 320,000 'curb cuts' for wheelchairs at 80,000 intersections at a cost of $180 million over two years when the city's entire capital budget was only $125 million." He added that "if the federal government wants us to make 320,000 curb cuts in two years, they should pay for it, or let us do it our way."[12]

The ACIR's draft report, a full-bore attack on unfunded mandates and federal intervention in state policies, recommended that Congress should end lawsuits by individuals against state and local governments to enforce federal mandates. Only the federal agency responsible for enforcement of a law should be permitted to sue state and local governments. The ACIR recommended that the federal government impose fewer detailed procedural requirements, stick to research and technical advice, allow state and local governments to comply with mandates in ways that best suit their own needs, and assume greater responsibility for paying for mandates. In short, the draft report called for changing the role that senators and representatives had carved out for themselves as heroes bestowing rights and instead return huge chunks of authority back to the states.

The ACIR, with exquisite bad luck, issued the draft report to wide publicity just when the proponents of mandates had regrouped and Newt Gingrich, their chief opponent, was setting world records for political ineptitude.

President Clinton, so supportive in 1995 when he signed the Unfunded Mandates Reform Act, reversed himself. The White House and every federal agency involved attacked the ACIR report. Leading an extraordinary series of personally signed letters, Marcia Hale, a White House aide and a member of the ACIR, broadly criticized the report and listed as of particular concern recommendations to modify the ADA and to eliminate private lawsuits. Attorney General Reno wrote that the ADA was "both flexible and reasonable" and offered as an "example of the inherent flexibility in the ADA" the curb ramp requirement. She added that she had just proposed to relax the curb ramp requirement in response to concerns by members of Congress. Robert Reich, secretary of labor, defended applying wage, worker safety, and family leave laws to state and local governments. He wrote that "the report's recommendations on labor standards would seriously *erode* intergovernmental relations and irrevocably *harm*" workers (emphasis in original). Carol M. Browner, administrator of the Environmental Protection Agency, defended environmental mandates, writing that the draft report "would dramatically compromise public health and environmental quality." Other letters came from the Department of Education, the U.S. Equal Employment Opportunity Commission, the Department of Transportation, and the Department of the Interior.[13]

The ACIR wilted. On July 23, 1996, the ACIR ruling board met in a rump session and voted down its own report. Fifteen members had previously voted to release the draft with only three opposing. Just a few months later, thirteen voted against the report with only seven in favor. Mayor Rendell, the vocal advocate for the draft report and of easing curb ramp requirements, was among those who switched from yea to nay.

This did not satisfy Congress. Not wanting to hear a message that it had expressly asked the ACIR to deliver, Congress literally killed the messenger. Republicans, who play the mandate game as cavalierly as Democrats and who were looking for agencies to eliminate as part of their effort to reduce the size of the federal government, put the ACIR at the top of the list to axe. Democrats were only too happy to agree. Friends accumulated by the ACIR over forty years of solid research ran from it like it was a disease carrier. With a budget of less than $1 million, the ACIR was not even a fly speck on the federal budget but could be added to the body count of agencies that legislators could claim to have eliminated.[14] Congress defunded the ACIR. When we looked for traces of it in 1998, we found that its office was locked, its telephones removed, and its files, including those on mandates, were scattered, warehoused, or lost.

Learning from the Curb Ramp Saga

It is possible to argue that American cities were remiss for not including curb ramps in their sidewalks from the beginning, but it is not possible to argue that the federal government led the change to get them included. Change started at the local level.

It is also possible to argue that cities should spend more on curb ramps. Thirty-two million dollars is not a large sum in New York City's budget, but New York City has a long list of acute needs and high taxes. More money for curb ramps has to come from somewhere, and $32 million a year buys a lot, even in New York City. With the same money, the New York City Department of Transportation could annually fill every pothole in the streets, thereby preventing the accidents and injuries they cause. How much to spend on curb ramps is a question of priorities. Not even the lobby for people with disabilities argues that all the intersections should have been finished by 1995.

It is also possible to argue that individuals should have the power to enforce their rights in court. We agree. If something is our individual right, federal bureaucrats ought not to be able to take it away by nonenforcement. The critical question is which of our desires should be rights.

It should *not* be possible for judges to tell state and city officials with a straight face that if they do not like the mandates, they can get them changed. In the abstract, that might seem like a logical response to the difficulty a state and local government might have in meeting one-size-fits-all national standards. But amendments by Congress moderating rights are rare. As with the curb ramps, senators would rather write letters than vote in the face of conflicting demands.

It is also *not* possible to argue that Washington does a fair job of deciding which of our desires should be made rights against state and local governments. The political deck in Washington is stacked toward creating rights enforceable against state and local governments and to announcing those rights without full regard to the costs and difficulties of implementing them. Governors, mayors, and other local officials, no matter how good their intentions, inevitably become lawbreakers. This is not news. Anyone who follows politics knows it. But it is an essential part of the backdrop to our topic, which is what happens when public interest attorneys bring state and local officials before the bar of justice in federal court.

CHAPTER 3

How Courts Enforce Rights
A Case Study

We now turn attention to what happens when public interest lawyers go to court to enforce federal rights against state or local government. Compliance with the curb ramp mandate is too uncomplicated to give a good sense of how such court enforcement typically works, so we describe a case to enforce a more complicated mandate: the right to special education.

Special education encompasses an extensive and expanding array of programs for coping with disabilities that range from stark, catastrophic physical and mental handicaps to the newer and vaguely defined categories of learning disabilities. In 1975, by overwhelming votes, Congress created a federal right to special education in the Education for All Handicapped Children Act.[1] Its rationale was that the federal government should share the huge financial burden of providing special education to the estimated eight million handicapped children in need of it. Congress promised to pour federal special education money into state treasuries until the federal share reached 40 percent of the total cost. To receive this money, or for that matter to keep on receiving federal education grants of any kind, states would have to agree to meet new federal standards for special education, enforceable in federal court. Faced with an offer they could not refuse, every state agreed.[2]

The new right to special education required that all handicapped children receive a "free appropriate public education," a compact phrase that the act defined extensively in terms of content, process, and parental involvement. Each state must provide, at public expense, programs (such as speech therapy and appropriate curricula) and related services (such as transportation and medical technician support to accommodate classroom attendance) in sufficient quantity to enable every child with a disability to have an individually tailored, expertly written, and parentally approved educational program, which to the extent practical must occur in a regular classroom with nonhandicapped children.

Because local school boards had difficulty complying with the federal standards, parents and advocates for children have brought many lawsuits in federal courts. One of those was *Jose P. v. Ambach*, filed in February 1979.[3] Just three months after filing, U.S. District Court Judge Eugene H. Nickerson ruled that the New York City Board of Education was in violation of the federal law. That was the easy part. The hard part was curing the violation. Twenty-four years later, the New York City schools are still in violation despite continuous, detailed supervision by the federal court. We tell the story of *Jose P.* to illustrate how federal court supervision of state and local governments works.

Jose P. v. Ambach

On February 1, 1979, John Gray, a young public interest lawyer at the Brooklyn Legal Services, filed a seventeen-page complaint alleging that New York City's public schools violated federal and state special education laws. Lead plaintiff Jose P. (his last name abbreviated to protect his anonymity) was fifteen years old, lived in Manhattan with his mother, and had been diagnosed as deaf, mute, and spastic. He had recently arrived from Puerto Rico, where he had received no education. In October 1978, Jose P.'s mother notified the New York

City Board of Education of Jose P.'s condition. Three months passed and the board still had not given him an appointment for the initial evaluation leading to placement in an appropriate educational setting. The complaint asserted that his situation reflected a systemic failure to screen and place handicapped students and asked the federal court to direct the board of education to meet its federal and state obligations.

Lead defendant Gordon Ambach was the New York State commissioner of education. He was named a defendant because the state had accepted federal special education money, making all schools in the state subject to the federal standards. The most important defendant, however, was Frank J. Macchiarola, chancellor of the New York City school system. He had taken office only seven months before the complaint was filed and as a result had assumed responsibility for curing the city's violation of the federal right.

Macchiarola faced a staggering task. Not only Jose P. but another fourteen thousand city children awaited evaluation and placement. How could it be that New York City, a mecca of liberal politics, was so much out of step with national standards enacted almost unanimously and across party lines? Indeed, how could it be that the whole country failed to serve children in need of special education when the same country had elected the Congress that created the right?

Actually, the states were not as backward as Congress portrayed, nor was Congress as advanced as it pretended in 1975. The same public sentiment that prompted Congress to act had long before prompted state and local governments to try to provide education for children with disabilities. States in general recognized and accepted their responsibility but had yet to meet it. New York State, for example, reformed its education law in 1917 and again in 1957 to include children with disabilities. Competition for funds, a lack of understanding of needs, and the absence of an accepted consensus on the best strategies left many children poorly served or not served at all. With increasing prosperity and understanding, however, states across the country made significant progress. Between 1965 and 1975, the ten years immediately before Congress created the federal right, forty-four states had enacted or amended their statutes to improve special education.[4]

Money remained a barrier. State and local education officials came to believe that the solution lay in increasing federal aid that, for special education, had begun in 1965 with demonstration projects and teacher training. State education officials joined with the advocates for children with disabilities in lobbying Congress for federal funds. Congress promised in 1975, when it enacted the federal right, to step up its grants to the states in stages until, by 1982, the federal government would pay 40 percent of the special education costs.[5] That was the promise that got the states to accept the federal standards.

As part of the bargain Congress granted the advocates' demand that it create a federal right to special education enforceable against states and localities in federal court. But the basis for the demand—a statistic produced by a federal agency that fully half of the handicapped children were not receiving special education—was misleading. The states were serving approximately 80 percent of the handicapped children as that term had traditionally been understood— still not good enough, but far from the 50 percent statistic that suggested indifference. That statistic came from inflating the estimates of the total need to a level never reached even to this day and by counting among the children unserved those who suffered from a learning disability or emotional disturbance.[6] Educators at the time had only recently begun to recognize many of these children as having disabilities, and few clear definitions, or recognized solutions, existed.

In response to an inflated estimate of little understood needs and under cover of a promise of generous federal aid down the road, Congress did not strain itself to think through a realistic solution. Federal standards were adopted wholesale from a decree entered by a federal court three years earlier in Philadelphia.[7] Following the pattern typical of state officials, Pennsylvania's governor and attorney general had chosen not to defend Pennsylvania's special education programs and instead consented to a lengthy decree that pleased plaintiffs and their experts. The decree effectively replaced the state's existing special education laws with an amalgam of the latest thinking on special education from academic experts, organizations advocating programs for handicapped children, and parent groups. Pennsylvania's new and comprehensive special education protocols, a product of negotiation rather than a decision by judges or the state legislature, had yet to be proved workable when Congress in 1975 mandated their use throughout the nation.

New York City, for its part, had been making progress, but not nearly enough. The beginnings of its program were small indeed. In 1959, it had only eight special education classes. By 1970, it had 184. These classes and other special education programs served 22,690 students. The board used boroughwide panels, each composed of nine experts, to evaluate students and recommend placements.[8] By 1979, the year *Jose P.* was filed, city efforts had more than doubled again. New York City provided special education services for 59,000 children, nearly 6 percent of the 1 million children attending public schools. The growing demand for special education services, however, consistently outran the board of education's capacity to evaluate and place children. With more than 14,000 children, including Jose P., awaiting evaluation and placement, the average waiting time exceeded eight months.

Why had the city, knowing of the federal standards, not done more to save itself from legal peril? In the 1970s, despite the importance of special education, other educational issues preempted the attention of top education and city officials. The same educational bureaucracy that failed to meet the needs of children with disabilities also failed other children. Widespread dissatisfaction with the central administration had led to a drive to wrest control from a central board of education and put it in the hands of community-level school boards to be run, it was hoped, by parents. The result was an epic political fight in which the teachers' union supported central control and liberal educators and minority groups supported decentralization.[9]

Then, in 1975, New York City discovered that it was teetering on the brink of bankruptcy. It had overspent for so long and by so much that it could not borrow. Debts were coming due faster than they could be paid. To prevent the embarrassing and unpredictable consequences of a formal declaration of bankruptcy, the state took over the city budget and insisted upon painful economies. Tens of thousands of city employees were laid off or furloughed. The subway fare was increased 43 percent. Public schools suffered along with all city services. Between 1974 and 1977 the New York City Board of Education laid off 15,554 teachers and other employees, a staggering 19.5 percent of its full-time workforce.[10] The board also ended or sharply curtailed gym, drama, music, art, libraries, science, and after-school athletics.

In 1975, the same year that New York City slashed all municipal budgets in its long struggle to avoid bankruptcy, Congress passed the Education for All Handicapped Children Act. The fiscal consequences of the act were still not apparent on January 1, 1978, when Congressman Edward I. Koch took office as mayor. As a symbol of the precarious fiscal condition of the city, he rode a public bus two miles down Broadway from his Greenwich Village apartment to City Hall rather than ride in a city limousine. His defeat of the incumbent Mayor Abraham D. Beame represented a mandate to restore fiscal integrity. For 1978, the last budget proposed by his predecessor, New York City schools accounted for 18 percent of the city's expenditures.

Although funded by the city, the schools were not controlled by the mayor but rather by a board of education with seven members, only two of whom the mayor appointed. The board in turn appointed the chancellor, the board's chief operating officer. Mayor Koch had declared education to be a priority of his new administration and wanted an outsider to the city's education bureaucracy to reform the system. It took him six months to find and install a politically suitable candidate for chancellor over the opposition of the teachers' union head, Albert Shanker, president of the United Federation of Teachers. As Koch recounted in his memoirs, Shanker came "into my office and tells me he's going to pick the next Chancellor; the teachers' boss is going to be picked by the teachers' union boss. It's an outrage to the people whose kids are trying to get an education."[11] Koch persisted, ultimately winning by a vote of four to three. On July 1, 1978, Koch's candidate, Frank J. Macchiarola, took over as chancellor.

Macchiarola, whose father had been a city sanitation worker, was a child of the city and a resident of Brooklyn. He was a lawyer with a Ph.D. and had impressive academic and political credentials. Most importantly, he was an outsider to the education bureaucracy and possessed a mayoral mandate for reform.

During his first week in office, special education became an issue when State Commissioner of Education Ambach notified Chancellor Macchiarola that delays in evaluating and placing children in need of special education violated state regulations and could jeopardize federal funding. Then, in that same week, the senior official who had headed the city's special education program for eight years resigned.[12] Macchiarola had wanted six months to decide whether to retain subordinates in their positions, but the head of special

Figure 3.1. U.S. District Judge Eugene R. Nickerson. Judge Nickerson was assigned the *Jose P.* litigation when it was first filed in February 1979 and oversaw
the *Jose P.* consent decree until his death in January 2002. Photograph by Rick
Kopstein.

education demanded an immediate decision, and, when she did not
get it, left. Macchiarola appointed an acting head of special education and ordered a review of the program. The report, completed
five months later in December 1978, laid out in bold relief the program's many deficiencies. With the report in hand, Macchiarola and
Ambach in January 1979 agreed to new measures to improve the
city's performance.

Advocates of special education were disappointed with the new
measures and thought they had the means to get their own way. In
the city's political stew, they were only one pressure group among
hundreds seeking to protect their particular municipal program
threatened by extreme fiscal constraints, but with one major differ-

ence: The Education for All Handicapped Children Act gave them a
trump to play because it made special education a federal right. Only
a month after Macchiarola and Ambach had agreed on new steps to
improve the city program, the advocates of special education filed
their complaint in *Jose P. v. Ambach* in Brooklyn's federal court. The
court clerk randomly assigned the case to Judge Nickerson. Judge
Nickerson (Figure 3.1) had been a superior law student, winning
a clerkship with Supreme Court Justice Harlan F. Stone. Before
his appointment to the bench by President Jimmy Carter in 1977,
Judge Nickerson had made history as the first Democrat to be elected county executive of Nassau County, the suburban Long Island
county bordering Queens. During his tenure from 1962 to 1970, he
championed environmental protection and changes in zoning laws
that opened up housing for the poor and minorities in his affluent,
suburban county.[13] Now, as the judge in *Jose P.*, he would be a
reformer again.

The Federal Court Takes Control

Chancellor Macchiarola wanted time to cure the city's blatant violation of the federal right. Board of education officials quickly placed
Jose P. in an appropriate school and then argued to Judge Nickerson
that he should declare the lawsuit moot. Judge Nickerson declined
and instead certified as plaintiffs not only Jose P. but all the thousands of children awaiting screening and placement.[14]

   The board of education also argued that the federal court should
leave this complicated public policy issue to the state and city education officials and to state courts. The city had previously used
that argument in a case against its special education program filed
in federal court a decade earlier. That case, predating the federal
statute, alleged violations of the federal Constitution. The federal
judges in the prior case decided to abstain because the problem was

complicated and there was hope that the state and city could, without state court oversight, improve the program.[15] Education officials did improve the program, but not enough to meet the subsequently enacted federal standards. In *Jose P.*, the board pleaded that it had steadily increased resources devoted to special education and would continue to do so.

In countering the board's argument that the case was too fraught with policy complications for federal court resolution, plaintiffs' attorneys benefited from a fortunate turn of events. There were actually two very different lawsuits before Judge Nickerson: *Jose P.*, filed in February 1979, and *United Cerebral Palsy*,[16] filed in March 1979.

Michael Rebell was a private Manhattan lawyer who primarily represented parents and teachers in lawsuits against the board of education. For several months Rebell had been developing and drafting his own special education lawsuit on behalf of United Cerebral Palsy that he had planned to file in Manhattan's federal court. News of Gray's Brooklyn lawsuit stunned Rebell. To avoid being left out, Rebell quickly filed his *United Cerebral Palsy* complaint in Brooklyn's federal court with the hope that it would be consolidated with *Jose P.*

The two lawyers had quite different approaches. Gray's *Jose P.* complaint was like a single silver bullet, whereas Rebell's *United Cerebral Palsy* complaint was a broad assault on the board's entire program. Gray represented individual children denied special education services. He limited the *Jose P.* complaint to one narrow, easily proved claim: the city's failure to meet the state's timetable requiring an evaluation of a student's needs within thirty days and placement within sixty days. The city regularly missed these deadlines, with the result that Gray's clients were denied timely services. In contrast, Rebell and his client United Cerebral Palsy took their lead from the comprehensive reforms embraced by the federal legislation. Their lawsuit sought a complete overhaul of special education from start to finish, from identification of a child for evaluation through class assignment, facilities, and outcomes.

The two lawyers met for the first time at the initial *Jose P.* hearing on March 6, 1979, in Judge Nickerson's Brooklyn courtroom. The encounter was far from friendly. Rebell was angry and told Gray that his approach was wrong. Gray was just as perturbed and disliked Rebell's approach. It fell to Judge Nickerson to put the two cases together.

First in time was *Jose P.*, and that is where Judge Nickerson started. The board admitted not meeting evaluation and placement deadlines, and the state conceded its inability to give parents a prompt administrative remedy. With no factual dispute to resolve, Judge Nickerson on May 16, 1979, granted Gray's motion for a preliminary injunction on behalf of all the children waiting for evaluation and placement. He wrote that the board's failure to meet the deadlines "appears to be due not only to the bureaucratic infrastructure involved in the evaluation and placement process, but perhaps also to factors not entirely within the control of the Board. . . . It is said that there is difficulty in initially locating handicapped children, failure of parents to bring children to scheduled appointments, frequent rejection of offered placements by a child's parents, and difficulty in recruiting adequate qualified teaching and administrative personnel and obtaining sufficient classroom space."[17]

By expanding the problems of evaluation and placement presented by *Jose P.* to implicate other aspects of special education, Judge Nickerson became in effect the chief federal official in charge of enforcing the federal right to special education in New York City, a task fraught with policy and resource choices. His management solution for handling this assignment was to create an extrajudicial process, more legislative than judicial, overseen by a "special master," whom he would select. Quoting language from an earlier segregation case, he wrote: "This type of 'polycentric problem . . . cannot easily be resolved through a traditional courtroom-bound adjudicative process.' . . . The court finds this to be the type of exceptional case requiring appointment of a special master."[18]

For special master, Judge Nickerson chose Marvin E. Frankel, a distinguished former federal judge and former law professor at Columbia. Frankel lacked special education credentials but knew something of the city's schools from having presided over a case against the board of education on bilingual education. He had only recently resigned from his lifetime appointment as federal district judge to become an active practitioner at a large Manhattan law firm. While on the bench he had earned a reputation for his intelligence and humor, his inclination to talk out issues as if he were still a professor teaching a law school class, and his ability to induce reasonable solutions to litigation problems. As special master, Judge Frankel was to be paid by the city at the same high regular hourly rate that he charged his commercial clients.

Given Judge Nickerson's sweeping order in *Jose P.*, handling the *United Cerebral Palsy* case became easy. On August 13, 1979, Judge Nickerson wrote that Special Master Frankel's mandate was broad enough to reach issues raised by the *United Cerebral Palsy* complaint. The justification—efficiency—skirted the fact that the court had not actually decided that the city had violated any duty other than the narrow one of failing to meet evaluation and placement deadlines. By consolidating the two cases, Rebell and his clients were able to skip directly to the remedy stage without ever showing how and in what ways the city was in violation of federal standards. It was like *Alice in Wonderland:* verdict first, trial later—except there never was a trial.

In October 1979, as negotiations under the supervision of the special master for a remedial order heated up, another plaintiff group, the Puerto Rican Defense Fund, filed a third complaint, this time on behalf of Hispanic children with disabilities and limited English proficiency—a category of children who allegedly were either overclassified as needing special education or, when assigned to special education, found an inadequate number of educators who could speak Spanish.[19] The special master on his own accepted them into the negotiations, and in December 1979, Judge Nickerson formally consolidated their complaint with *Jose P.* The three groups each retained separate counsel: John Gray and his colleagues for Jose P., Michael Rebell and his colleagues for United Cerebral Palsy, and the Puerto Rican Defense Fund for the Hispanic plaintiffs.

Still more education advocates clamored to join the case. The Public Education Association, active in New York City since 1895, demanded to participate. Advocates for Children of New York, a newer education watchdog group that came into existence during the fiscal crisis, also asked to be included. Judge Nickerson welcomed both groups into the litigation, granting each the status of amicus curiae (Latin for "friend of the court"), an appellation that judges bestow on those who are not full parties to the case but are nonetheless allowed to participate in some limited way. Amici curiae (the plural form of the phrase) usually do little more than file a legal brief, but Judge Nickerson gave his amici far broader rights. He authorized them to participate in all phases of the development of the remedial order, including full participation in meetings and hearings before the special master and the court. Still other advocates were informally invited to join the discussion. These included the Association for the Help of Retarded Children; the Legal Aid Society Juvenile Rights Division; the United Federation of Teachers; the Handicapped Person's Legal Support Unit, U.S. Department of Health, Education and Welfare; and two parents of children with disabilities who had expressed interest in the proceedings.[20]

Plaintiffs, amici, and invitees reflected a rather narrow segment of public opinion. Each of these organizations staked out education as its particular interest, held similar views on it, and was generally represented by full-time public interest attorneys of like mind. In the contest for New York City's resources, this faction now had the upper hand.

The Consent Decree

Judge Nickerson gave the special master the extraordinary power to decide what was "appropriate" to "provide the requisite public education to handicapped children in New York City." He authorized Special Master Frankel to hold hearings and consult with the parties, outside experts, and others, including parents, community groups, and private organizations that provide services to handicapped children. The special master could conduct informal working sessions with trial counsel and officials of the various concerned public and private agencies. He could also consult privately with whomever he wished as long as he later informed counsel of the meetings. He could hire legal, administrative, and clerical aides and would have full access to all reports, statistics, and studies "about all phases of the school system and services." The city and the state were to provide full professional, technical, and other assistance required in familiarizing Special Master Frankel with the school system and "the various problems to be solved in providing free appropriate public education to handicapped children."[21]

Although laden with elaborate powers and duties, Judge Frankel adopted a more conventional strategy. He preferred that the parties agree on a plan and he set out to get that agreement. "After all," he recollected in a 1999 interview, "my assignment was to obtain a decree on consent."[22]

Special Master Frankel asked the parties and amici to exchange information. After a cooperative start, the discussions fell apart as the parties found little common ground. Then a new personality entered the talks. Since his first week in office when the head of special education had resigned, Chancellor Macchiarola had operated with an acting director of special education. On July 5, 1979, after a year's search, Chancellor Macchiarola finally was able to hire a permanent director of special education, Dr. Jerry Gross. Gross had run the Minneapolis special education program and in that capacity had given important testimony in the congressional hearings leading to adoption of the Education for All Handicapped Children Act of 1975.[23] He left Minneapolis to head a special education program in Illinois and was, at the time Macchiarola selected him, the president-elect of the Council of Administrators of Special Education.

In September 1979, just two months into the job, Gross recommended to Chancellor Macchiarola a radical new approach in which decisions about individual children would be made in the local school rather than centralized under the borough committees. Each of the one thousand schools in the city system would have its own three-person professional team made up of a psychologist, a social worker, and a special educator who, in conjunction with the school principal, a guidance counselor, and the regular classroom teacher, would evaluate and recommend placement of the child.

Gross's program was revolutionary. It called for New York City to turn both the goals and structure of its special education program upside down. The old, top-down system gave the final say on placements to borough-level committees that categorized each child's needs and dictated educational assignments. The new system reflected a wholly different philosophy. As demanded by Congress, it avoided categorization in favor of mainstreaming all students and commanded that decisions on assignments be participatory. Congress had given new and powerful procedural rights to parents that made them full participants in the educational placement decision and had further directed that special education placements be integrated rather than separated whenever possible. Gross's program embraced and embellished all these new federal policies, but this merely papered over the profound organizational tremors and educational questions that the proposed program set off.

Despite the uncertainty of the untried program, plaintiffs and amici embraced it. They insisted, however, upon specific deadlines and resource commitments, explicit procedural rights to ensure full parental participation, and regular reports to them so that they could monitor performance and, if necessary, get the court to hold defendants to the program. An institutional change of this dimension would take time, and the attorneys for plaintiffs and amici intended to be there the whole time watchdogging performance every step of the way.

Chancellor Macchiarola also endorsed the Gross Program but soberly cautioned the board of education not to consent to a court order because its ability to comply depended on financial support from the city and state. New York City in 1979 had not yet emerged from its fiscal crisis, and the proposed 1980 school budget, announced in November 1979, projected a large deficit. The board, Macchiarola warned, might agree to a program with heavy costs, but funding pressures could later force hard choices to be made. In a legal straddle, the board voted to accept the Gross Program and to allow it to be submitted to the federal court as the board's plan but refused to state that it consented to the decree. The board hoped that the absence of its formal consent would allow it to make future adjustments.

In an interview in 1999 Macchiarola reflected on his decision twenty years earlier to go with the Gross Program: It was produced by the best expert in the field who had been hired precisely to come up with a new program; it keyed off federal requirements; and no one else advanced a better idea. The board needed a new program for itself, for the state, for its federal funding, and for the court. The program had not been tested and was elaborate, but these were merely cautions, not reasons for no action.[24]

Jeffrey Glen, one of the lawyers who negotiated the agreement for the city, gave another interpretation of the board's thinking. Rather than fear the budget effect of the order, education officials welcomed being bound by the decree because it converted a voluntary program with large staffing requirements into a mandatory one that the city had to fund.[25]

On December 5, 1979, Special Master Frankel filed a report recommending to Judge Nickerson that he approve the proposed forty-seven-page remedial order based on the Gross Program. Frankel stated that it had been worked out by the parties with "relatively minimal participation by the special master." He discounted the board's reservations because all parties, he stated, understood that time and experience might warrant modification, and he advised Judge Nickerson to treat the board's position as supportive of the order. Frankel heard no evidence, made no factual determinations, and did not consult experts on his own, nor did he seek opinions from community groups or organizations other than the relatively limited segment represented by the parties, amici, and invitees. In reflecting on the basis of his recommendation years later, Frankel said that in an important sense when matters are of such a complex nature, "you rely on the parties. In the end I felt that it was a workable arrangement."[26]

On December 14, 1979, Judge Nickerson, without an opinion or additional comment, signed the consent order without change. The *Jose P.* case was still less than one year old.

The Controlling Group

The *Jose P.* decree shifted power dramatically. It transferred control of special education from the board of education and elected officials to the federal court. Instead of exercising that power personally, Judge Nickerson pressured the parties to work by consent. Power previously exercised by high-level government officials went to those around the negotiating table. Chief among them were the lawyers representing the plaintiffs and amici because of their command of the arcane terms of the decree and their ability to haul the board of education before the special master and the judge.

The court had in effect dropped a major educational policy concern into private hands and told them to work out the special education programs for the city. To be sure, board attorneys and staff members also participated in the negotiations, but not precisely as adversaries. They got a share of the power, and special education administrators had a parallel interest in increasing the resources devoted to their programs.

Those sitting at the negotiation table in cases against state and local governments are, collectively, in our terms, *the controlling group.*

The board of education's major obligation under the consent decree Judge Nickerson approved on December 14, 1979, was to submit two mega-operational plans, the January Plan and the April Plan, that would breathe life into the Gross Program. Coming up with these plans proved far more difficult than coming up with the decree. The decree, like the platform of a political party, stuck mostly to shared objectives. The January and April plans would in contrast have to face hard choices about budgets and operations. As Michael Rebell, the attorney for United Cerebral Palsy, later wrote, the Gross Program "did not constitute a proven educational system that could be fully implemented over time if sufficient resources were provided. Rather, it was an imaginative proposal for beginning a structural reform process whose direction and substance would be subject to ongoing reformulation."[27] The first steps in that process were the January and April plans.

The controlling group met often, sometimes in subgroups, other times in full. Usually, both lawyers and educational professionals attended. The special master generally was not present. Rebell described the process in purely managerial terms. "As feedback was obtained on problems arising in the field," he wrote, "the parties drafted provisions in the follow-up documents that would deal with these realities. In working through their concerns, the parties often agreed on entirely new organizational approaches, with new deadlines and resource commitments that would then supersede the original agreements."[28] When they could not agree, the controlling group submitted lists of disputed issues to Special Master Frankel, who mediated compromise.

Professor Joseph Viteritti, who closely followed *Jose P.* as a member of Chancellor Macchiarola's staff and then as an academic, saw the process differently. With certainty in the law, but enormous uncertainty in education practice, plaintiffs' lawyers gained the upper hand over educators. Viteritti summarized the resulting dynamic in a single sentence: "The lawyers would make education decisions, and the educators would say, 'we can live with that.' "[29]

The remedial decree signed in December 1979 specified that the plans were to be completed in January and April 1980. That schedule "was never perfectly realistic" Special Master Frankel later wrote.[30] The January Plan was not approved until January 9, 1981, a year behind schedule, and the April Plan on September 1, 1981, a year and a half behind schedule. Even then, the April Plan was incomplete, with many core issues open to debate for years.

The plans produced by the controlling group constituted a collection of detailed directives for every aspect of special education from staffing to teaching and collecting data. The two plans with appendices filled 515 pages. Negotiations may have been a process, but the result was not. It was a written set of duties and deadlines with intermediate milestones, all backed up by the court's power to hold the defendants in contempt.

Judge Nickerson played an even smaller role than did Special Master Frankel in developing the January and April plans. He did not set the agenda, propose solutions, or mediate compromise. He empowered the controlling group, leaving it to decide where to go and how to get there. The lawsuit had started narrowly with tardy evaluations and placements but turned into an open-ended regime. Any educational policy however vaguely related to special education could be included. Plaintiffs and amici, skilled activists who fervently believed that the entire school system needed reform, pushed for the programs that they favored without being strictly tethered to legal requirements. To paraphrase Boss Plunkett, "They saw their opportunity and they took it."[31]

Under constant pressure to agree, the controlling group usually found ways to do so, but not always. A major dispute erupted over "preventive services." The term refers to any action to prevent children from needing special education. It could mean anything from better training for classroom teachers on how to motivate underachieving students, to family counseling, health screening, diet, truancy programs, and more. The term was not mentioned in the statute or the court order and, strictly speaking, was not a legal requirement. It had been discussed, however, in Gross's original program.

In the first and happier stages of their work, the controlling group included preventive services in the drafts of the April Plan. As negotiations continued, however, city budget issues began to surface with the predictable result that board of education officials and city budget directors began to question court-ordered programs not strictly required by law. In mid-1980 the board's projections showed that special education expenses would increase the annual school budget by $74 million. The Financial Control Board, the state's oversight agency that oversaw New York City's budget, projected that the city would experience a $1 billion deficit for the fiscal year beginning in July 1981. The executive director of the Financial Control Board in

August 1980 wrote Chancellor Macchiarola expressing anxiety over the increasing costs of special education.[32] Because neither federal nor state law required preventive services and the court decision covered only children already in need of special education, preventive services seemed a logical place to cut.

Plaintiffs, on the other hand, insisted on retaining preventive services. The plaintiffs' reference point was the bargains made in court proceedings. They were unwilling to make adjustments for financial reasons even when compelled by external fiscal authorities established by the state legislature to oversee the city's budget. For plaintiffs and amici, a bargain was a bargain.

Disagreements among the controlling group went for decision to Special Master Frankel and then Judge Nickerson. Special Master Frankel, first to hear the issue, ruled for plaintiffs, although without any clear legal justification. He acknowledged that there were legal questions because the federal law, the state law, and the court order did not mention preventive services. With the law uncertain, he reasoned, he was empowered to embrace the policy he preferred. Frankel wrote that prevention "is a humane, and very probably economical, course for holding down the numbers of students who find their way into special education programs because conditions not caught earlier have come to be, or to seem, 'handicapping.'" There was no realistic way, he argued, to create "a wall" between the special and regular education programs. Because all parties accepted the educational value and benefits of preventive services, Frankel ruled that it was better policy to have preventive services than not to have them. He brushed aside the board's choice to put its limited resources into complying with legal obligations by saying that all he was deciding was that preventive services were required under the decree; the parties could sort out later when and how they would be provided.[33]

This was exactly the result the board feared. Adding preventive services to the decree would give plaintiffs and amici a mandate to dictate overall educational policy, not just special education policy. The board appealed to Judge Nickerson.

Judge Nickerson, also feeling free to adopt his preferred policy without reference to legal authority, split the difference. He, too, liked preventive services but felt that the board should not be compelled to provide preventive services until its other major obligations were carried out. He left open the fundamental legal question of whether "the proposed preventive services [were] voluntary rather than compulsory under the *wording of the judgment*" [emphasis added]. He continued that plaintiffs have "an obvious interest in preventive services if only to reduce the overload on special education facilities."[34] Preventive services, he ruled in so many words, were within the court's jurisdiction because preventive services might reduce the number of candidates for special education and hence reduce the potential for missing deadlines.

The dispute over preventive services demonstrates how quickly a remedial process run by a controlling group without boundaries can stray from the narrow path of enforcing rules of law into the thicket of policy and management. If preventive services were, for some reason, a right, they could not be ignored until convenient. If they were not a right, they were no business of the court.

As the controlling group wound down the work of drafting the January and April plans, its members began to disagree on other matters. Plaintiffs and amici claimed that the board was not trying hard enough. The board, chafing under the many demands placed on it, claimed that it had set a proper course by agreeing to the plans and that further interventions by the plaintiffs and amici undermined sound educational policy.

With the early harmony deteriorating, Gross, a major player on whom the controlling group relied, left the field. In March 1981, less than two years after his arrival in New York City, he resigned. His program had provided the basis for the consent decree but proved extraordinarily difficult and costly to implement. In addition, he had developed a poor working relationship with the board of education and with Chancellor Macchiarola, who had lost confidence in Gross's ability to manage the program.[35]

Gross's departure resulted in an even more adversarial relationship between the parties. Plaintiffs and amici published reports accusing the board of mismanaging special education and of allowing the backlog to grow despite promises to the contrary. Falling back on an aggressive litigation strategy, they demanded that the board create new programs to help students whose placements in public schools had been delayed—a new summer school and quick placement in private schools at city expense. When the city refused, plaintiffs and amici appealed to Special Master Frankel, who denied the summer program but granted the quick placement in private schools.[36] Judge Nickerson affirmed Special Master Frankel's decisions.[37]

Chancellor Macchiarola Files an Affidavit

Despite its failings, the board did succeed in serving many more special education students. By the 1982–83 school year, three years after Judge Nickerson signed the *Jose P.* order, the city's special education population had grown from sixty thousand to more than ninety thousand children.

As the lawyers in the controlling group skirmished in increasingly bitter meetings and public attacks, Chancellor Macchiarola filed on March 3, 1982, a startlingly personal, thirty-nine-page affidavit to inform Judge Nickerson of what he saw as the adverse effect of the *Jose P.* order.[38] Macchiarola stated flatly that the litigation had actually harmed the children of the school system.

Litigation, Macchiarola wrote, forced attention to an almost numbing succession of specific educational and administrative issues that diverted educators from the education of children. It elevated speed of placement above all other educational values. The mass processing of children with disabilities forced by the order directly conflicted with efforts to educate these children. Although special education was still a new and developing field, the litigation set up an entrenched status quo that was crippling the city's capacity to innovate or modify its approach in light of experience. He pleaded for more time to plan and for more flexibility.

Macchiarola's affidavit was a catalog of questions about the *Jose P.* process and an attack on the assumptions that underlay the plans and programs it fostered. One basic assumption concerned the nature of handicaps found in large urban public school systems. The order and underlying laws treated handicaps as certain or visible, like the deafness and muteness that afflicted Jose P., whose handicap, Macchiarola wrote, was the exception, not the rule:

> Many assume—erroneously—that an educational handicap is a specific, identifiable condition, typically organic, which can be diagnosed and either treated or controlled like a disease. Failure to provide appropriate services to handicapped children is then seen as withholding medicine from the sick. While this understanding of 'handicap' has some applicability for certain traditional categories of handicapped children—the deaf, the blind, the speech-impaired—it is seriously misleading when applied to the broad majority of students with special needs. The handicaps we are most frequently called upon to address—learning and emotional disabilities—are functional and contextual, not clinical, in nature; they are not conditions which a child does or does not have, but relationships between the child and his or her peers, family, and educational environment.
>
> It is vital that the Court understand, and that our agenda be changed to reflect the fact, that the state of the art of evaluation does not permit the consistent and accurate diagnosis of these functional, non-organic handicapping conditions. Handicaps such as learning and emotional disabilities are widely recognized to be ill-defined and poorly-understood. The identifi-

cation of more students in these categories does not indicate greater success in serving the handicapped. It indicates a different judgment, which may or may not be educationally justified, about which students to serve in which ways. (par. 23–24)

Macchiarola went on to criticize the procedures for evaluation and placement developed out of the Gross Program and rigidly required by the court order:

The judgment [in *Jose P.*] has created a bias in favor of special education placement, whether or not that placement is appropriate. Through the judgment, the court has in effect declared to staff, parents, and the public at large that the New York public school system has short-changed handicapped children by failing to identify enough of them and by failing to provide services which, if provided, would work to their benefit. The Court has required City defendants to create an organizational machine which will identify and place greatly increasing numbers of handicapped students, and this machine, once created, has taken on a life of its own. Classroom teachers feel they have an obligation to refer students who are not meeting expected standards of academic or behavioral development. Evaluators feel they have an obligation to identify a handicapping condition that explains the child's difficulties. These tendencies are extremely difficult to arrest. Diagnostic and placement decisions are a matter of judgment, not of science, and it is rarely clear in individual cases what the impact of special education evaluation and placement will be. (par. 29)

Evaluations forced to be made within thirty days, Macchiarola believed, may well be incorrect. They lead to more restrictive assignments within segregated special education classes. For the vast majority of students in the learning disabled category, Macchiarola wrote, the weight of evidence is that special education placement is no more effective, and perhaps marginally less effective, than regular classroom placement.

In summing up his views Macchiarola pleaded for the court to consider the effect of its order:

I have become deeply concerned as the person responsible for education of all the City's children that harm is being caused by the increasing attention focused in this litigation on readily comprehensible questions of quantity, principally timeliness and numbers of students served, at the expense of questions of quality, such as the appropriateness of diagnostic and placement decisions and the educational effectiveness of services provided to different categories of handicapped students. As I see it, the judgment has converted personnel in the field from educators to implementers of legal rules and thereby encouraged inappropriate special education evaluations and placements, fostered a widening administrative division between special education and regular education, and impeded our attempts to make regular classroom programs, the backbone of our school system, more effective in responding to the educational needs of children with learning disabilities. These tendencies, unforeseen three years ago, are inconsistent with the letter and spirit of [the Education for All Handicapped Children Act] and with the growing weight of professional opinion.

I also believe that however closely the judgment may have approximated the best professional judgment at a particular time, it is a mistake to elevate any set of practices and procedures to the level of an inflexible mandate. Such an approach robs the school system of the flexibility it needs to adapt to changing circumstances, increasing practical experience with alternative approaches to implementation, and a constantly growing understanding of the nature and dimensions of the educational issues we face. (par. 17–18)

Macchiarola's affidavit challenged a basic assumption underlying the court order. *Jose P.* followed a remedial strategy that had evolved from school segregation and prison cases in which courts met intense official resistance with minutely specific orders, empowered plaintiffs' attorneys to police the orders, and insisted on rigid compliance with plans and milestones. Macchiarola suggested a different approach aimed also at compliance, but more flexible and more forgiving of the human, political, and institutional realities in managing a public school system of one million students. The parties in

Jose P. were not truly adverse, Macchiarola observed: "[E]ach side, in the final analysis, has an equal claim and an equal obligation to represent the interests of the handicapped children who constitute the class. City defendants are no less committed to serving children with special needs than plaintiffs" (par. 11).

Macchiarola's affidavit received coverage in the *New York Times* but had no effect on the adherence of plaintiffs and amici to the *Jose P.* process.[39] The *Times* quoted Michael Rebell, the attorney for United Cerebral Palsy and the most forceful member of the controlling group, as stating that "if the board feels that the judgment is pressing too hard, the plaintiffs will be happy to sit down, as we have in the past, to deal with these matters."[40] Plaintiffs filed no formal response, and Judge Nickerson, not having been asked for a decision, was silent.

The parties, locked midstream in the *Jose P.* process, could not resolve such widely divergent philosophical approaches to reform. In part, this was because some of the flexibility Macchiarola sought would require Congress to alter the right to special education, which was no more likely than its amending the right to curb ramps. But that consideration did not lie at the core of the plaintiffs' objections since they had readily agreed to adjust statutory and regulatory requirements to tailor the order in the ways they preferred. More at stake was control over the reform process itself, and here the views were so divergent that the parties were bound to clash.

The philosophical differences exposed by the Macchiarola affidavit intensified the confrontational relationship between the parties. As the disputes increased, Special Master Frankel shifted from mediation to formal litigation. He began to hold trial-like hearings in the Brooklyn federal courthouse on failures of the city to meet hiring schedules and on other issues arising out of the placement backlog. On September 7, 1982, he filed a stinging report that rejected the city's claims that its programs were adequate and brushed aside legal arguments that courts generally should defer to the board of education's expertise in fashioning remedies, an indirect rejection of Macchiarola's affidavit. He reminded the board that its job was to comply with the order, pure and simple. Whatever deference meant, it did not mean that the board of education could ignore the order. Exasperated with the board, he wrote:

> The time has come, it is now believed, for defendants either to comply with the judgments or to confront the familiar conse-quences of noncompliance. Unless or until a receiver comes to take over the Division of Special Education, defendants invoke sound principles when they argue that they rather than the Court should be determining the administrative techniques, es-timates, and procedures for complying with their obligations. Demanding respect for their expertise, defendants ought to get it. Promising compliance, they ought to achieve it or face contempt charges. It will be recommended, therefore, that the Court draw stark lines. Let the defendants plan, project, and execute in the exercise of their expert discretion. But let them understand, having been reminded that the mandatory injunc-tion issued long ago, that they do not have the discretion to disobey.[41]

A month after Special Master Frankel's warning, on October 2, 1982, the board moved to be released from the court decree. It had satisfied its primary planning requirements under the 1979 order by completing the January and April plans and was advancing the pro-grams, although as made clear by Macchiarola's affidavit, the city wanted to make many adjustments in the written plans. In addition, it claimed that the waiting time had dropped to within acceptable limits.

Plaintiffs and amici would have none of this. Writing plans and start-up work, they argued, were not enough. The court should not release the city until it had actually complied fully with all federal and state laws, including proof that it successfully prepared Individ-ualized Education Programs (IEPs), mainstreamed students, made facilities accessible, and provided related services, all within the time specified. Plaintiffs and amici also asserted that the city fudged its statistics by delaying the start of the thirty-day clock for evaluating students through use of a screening method not allowed under state regulations. Under the board's rules, a teacher's request did not start the thirty-day clock until the child's parent consented to the evaluation. This consent, according to the board, facilitated a quicker, less formal evaluation process that in many cases solved the student's needs without triggering the exhaustive, full-scale evaluations of the Gross Program. Screening which children were to be evaluated ameliorated two widely acknowledged abuses: classroom teachers who referred discipline problems to special education, and the bias by evaluators toward classifying nonachieving children or children with discipline problems as learning disabled. In addition, many parents disliked school officials unilaterally drafting their children into a process that labeled them handicapped or learning disabled. Parental consent before starting the clock allowed the school principal to avoid parental anger and later delay.

Judge Nickerson rejected the city's request to terminate court supervision. He ruled that the city's delay in starting the thirty-day clock violated state regulations, advised the city to take its case to the state if it wanted to change the rule, and declared that the thirty-day clock started ticking the moment a classroom teacher referred a student for evaluation. Judge Nickerson, in a final, angry coda to his opinion, seconded Special Master Frankel's threat that the city might well be in contempt of court. He asked the special master to review the facts and recommend sanctions and listed eight areas of performance that should be examined.[42]

With Judge Nickerson's decision, the city's effort to escape court supervision ended. The city would remain under strict supervision by the court—in reality, by the controlling group. Judge Nickerson also set in motion formal hearings that could possibly lead to fines and jail time for school officials. Not wanting to risk such sanctions, the board returned to the controlling group for renewed negotiations with attorneys for plaintiffs and amici, who held the keys to the court's mercy. The harder the board tried to escape the controlling group, the more firmly it was in its embrace. The result was that the board agreed to many new obligations, including detailed plans to hire 613 new teachers and 600 psychologists, social workers, or educational evaluators by September 1983.

The Beattie Commission

Chancellor Macchiarola resigned in February 1983, the same month Judge Nickerson rejected his plea for more flexibility and for termination of the court order. He was replaced by Anthony Alvarado, a highly respected educator who was nonetheless forced to resign in 1984 as a result of an inappropriate personal financial arrangement with a subordinate. Chancellor Alvarado was replaced by Nathan Quinones, who served from March 1984 through December 1987. Attorneys representing the city and the board of education came and went, but Michael Rebell, John Gray, and Roger Juan Maldonado, representing plaintiffs and amici, remained.

Dennis deLeon, a lawyer for the city who participated in the controlling group meetings during this period, described attending them as like walking in on "the second reel of a five-reel movie. The other players all knew each other."[43] When city lawyers new on the assignment wanted to know what was going on, attorneys for plaintiffs and amici provided the history.

Under the new chancellors, the controlling group resumed a more friendly motif. They met in regular Thursday sessions, effectively functioning as the board of special education.

In April 1984, a month after Chancellor Quinones took over,

Mayor Koch created his own Commission on Special Education to review special education. The city's programs by then had grown to serve 116,000 children at a cost of $850 million but still did not meet the mandates of *Jose P.* or its own goals. To chair the commission Koch selected Richard Beattie, a successful Wall Street lawyer who had served in the Carter administration as deputy secretary of the Department of Health, Education, and Welfare.

The Beattie Commission confirmed Macchiarola's dark view of the court order's effect. A consultant to the commission, Dr. Jay Gottlieb of the Department of Educational Psychology at New York University (NYU), showed that special education had molted into a program for handling any child who for one reason or another performed at less than expected levels or who caused trouble in the classroom. Eighty-nine percent of all referrals for evaluations were either for poor academic performance in the classroom, bad behavior, or both. Special education was no longer either distinctly special or exceptional, as those terms were commonly understood. The program had come to function as a rapidly expanding and increasingly expensive general education program.

Gottlieb's other major findings were equally disturbing. School psychologists and educational evaluators routinely administered the same battery of tests to every child referred regardless of the reason for the referral. There was no "apparent relationship between reason for referral and the nature of testing that was provided."[44] This discontinuity had little effect on the evaluator's recommendation, however, because the referred children were in fact performing poorly or behaving badly, a conclusion known at the time of referral by the classroom teacher and confirmed by the child's standardized test scores. Gottlieb's observation about testing clarified why virtually every child sent for evaluation was found in need of special education. Acceptance into special education was correlated with the classroom teacher's initial recommendation and previous test scores; the testing done during the course of the evaluation added little to support the finding of learning disability.

The vast majority of children assigned to special education were not, in fact, learning disabled. Gottlieb found that they had neither a 50 percent discrepancy between ability and achievement nor a high intratest scatter of results—two of the defining features of learning disabilities. In other words, they did not meet the standard definition of learning disabled.

Six months later in April 1985 the Beattie Commission issued a final report equally critical of special education under the *Jose P.* process. Picking up the thread from Macchiarola's affidavit and Gottlieb's studies, the commission stated that the major cause of the growth of special education "is the lack of programs within regular education in New York City to help those students who may not be 'handicapped' but are in need of additional assistance. . . . With over thirty students in a classroom, a regular education teacher has little time or opportunity to devote individualized attention to students who do not keep up with the work or who cause disturbances and too few places to turn for help except special education."[45]

The Beattie Commission reported that the board's evaluation and placement workforce of 1,844 professionals (670 social workers, 664 psychologists, and 510 educational evaluators) did nothing but evaluate students for special education.[46] Evaluators spent "too little time . . . observing behavior in the classroom and consulting with regular education teachers. Existing diagnostic tests are not sophisticated enough to be used as the primary method for distinguishing between children with learning disabilities and slow learners."[47] The commission recommended that the city rely more on classroom teachers and school-based educational evaluators and that it eliminate social workers that the Gross Program and the *Jose P.* court order required be included on every evaluation team. This should "decrease scheduling problems and increase both accountability and productivity."[48] The commission also recommended that the board of education hire more reading specialists and counselors to assist in regular classrooms and to provide an alternative for inappropriate reliance on special education.

Distilling its conclusions into an epigram, the Beattie Commission stated that "all children should receive the services they need, but children should not have to be labeled 'handicapped' in order to obtain them."[49]

While the Beattie Commission was still gathering data, the state comptroller issued his own, highly critical audit of the city's special education program. The comptroller's auditors focused on the thirty- and sixty-day rules and confirmed that the city was widely missing its evaluation and placement deadlines (75 and 86 percent of the time, respectively, in the cases studied). These findings represented only cases for which the comptroller's auditors could locate records; in one-quarter of the cases selected the city could not produce the records to audit.

Thus, within a short period, two external audits produced critical reports, but with strikingly different orientations. The Beattie Commission looked at the role special education played in the education system and advocated a major reorientation of the program, whereas the comptroller's audit looked primarily at evaluation and placement deadlines. The two reports led to strikingly different recommendations: the first, to redirect the entire program, and the second, to work harder at implementing the old.

Plaintiffs and amici followed these proceedings carefully and were listed among those who assisted in the commission studies. With the power they possessed under the *Jose P.* decree, however, they did not have to sit on the sidelines waiting for others to act. In July 1986 they returned to Judge Nickerson and demanded additional enforcement of the January and April plans.

Plaintiffs and amici were as sophisticated as anyone about the shortcomings of special education, but the logic of the litigation inevitably drove them to focus on time deadlines. Plaintiffs and amici showed that at best the board completed only 52 percent of all initial evaluations and 33 percent of the bilingual initial evaluations within the magic thirty days. Fault, the plaintiffs and amici contended, lay with the city's refusal to hire sufficient staff. The city, evaluating the same data, replied that the delays were only marginal and that placement actually occurred within sixty-three days for most students despite late evaluations, and that most of the delay was caused by parents.

This was not enough to please the court, which once again ruled that New York City was in violation of the decree and, accepting the solution of the plaintiffs and amici, directed it to hire sufficient staff to end the delays.[50] The city came up with another hiring plan that the plaintiffs and amici again found wanting. Judge Nickerson, drawn into closely examining the city's hiring projections, ruled that the city would still lack the professional resources to meet its projected workload of more than 117,000 annual evaluations. He ordered the city to hire fifty-four professionals in addition to the three hundred it had already agreed to hire.[51]

Job Security for Social Workers

The city planned to hire educational evaluators and psychologists, but, following the recommendation of the Beattie Commission, no social workers. Indeed, the city planned to reduce the number of social workers by attrition.

Alarm bells rang in organizations representing social workers. The New York City chapter of the National Association of Social Workers and the United Federation of Teachers demanded to be heard. The social worker was, they claimed, the "primary advocate of the student's interests" and the only team professional "with the requisite training and experience to assess fully the dynamics of a child's life at home and in school."[52]

The professional mix of evaluation teams, one would think, would be a policy question for the board of education. Federal law did not require social workers. The statute only required that at least one member of the team be trained in a relevant special education skill. Gross in 1979, with the board's assent, opted for top-heavy teams composed of three trained people, not one, and specified that a social worker be on the team. The Beattie Commission, based on seven years of experience with such teams, flagged the three-person team as a major problem, with the social worker providing the least value because most evaluations related to learning disabilities. The Gross Program had, however, been turned into a decree by Judge Nickerson and could not be changed without his approval. With that opening, the social workers saw an opportunity to stop the board by appealing to the judge.

Instead of throwing the unions out on the theory that management decides team composition, or basing a decision on federal law that was clear enough, Judge Nickerson accepted the unions into the litigation and referred them to the special master to hear their arguments on the values that would be lost if the city reduced the role of social workers in the initial evaluations.

The social workers made their case during a three-day hearing. There was a new special master, however, as Marvin Frankel had resigned after four years as special master to concentrate on his private law practice. Judge Nickerson in 1983 appointed as the new special master Magistrate John L. Caden. Caden had served five years as an assistant U.S. attorney, after which he had been appointed as a magistrate in the Brooklyn federal court. As a magistrate, he supervised discovery and handled other factual and legal matters on assignment from the judges.

Ducking the main question of social workers' right to complain at all, Magistrate Caden decided that they were more abundant and therefore easier to hire than other categories of experts. On the theory that the city might be unable to meet its hiring plan without social workers, he recommended that the city increase its hiring plan by adding ninety social workers. The city appealed to Judge Nickerson without success.[53] The social workers, without a single statute or regulation backing them, had used the controlling group process to lock in their share of the special education pie.

In affirming the decision on social workers, Judge Nickerson opened a door on an even larger issue: the quality of the evaluations actually completed. Amici, breaking ranks with plaintiffs, faulted the quality of evaluations. Judging the quality of tens of thousands of evaluations would be far tougher than evaluating timeliness. Judge Nickerson refused to take up this daunting task but strongly intimated that he might well be forced to do so unless the board performed better.

Judge Nickerson's threat was enough to reestablish another period of negotiation within the controlling group. The board of education had its own reasons for wanting to negotiate: it had tired of the Gross Program and wanted to replace it. But a new program could not be implemented without Judge Nickerson's approval, and that would not be forthcoming without the consent of the attorneys for plaintiffs and amici.

In July 1988, after more than a year of negotiations, the controlling group came forth with another blockbuster court order.[54] As before, there were few boundaries as to what might be included. The board agreed to hire more professionals until its staff totaled 960 educational evaluators, 960 school psychologists, 572 social workers, and, a new category, 58 monitors to gather special education data. Anticipating shortages of qualified applicants, New York City agreed in another new wrinkle to create a $52 million annual college scholarship program to encourage students to become special education specialists. All of these items were contained in a detailed sixty-eight-page order that, among other provisions, also dealt with office supplies, bilingual teachers and specialists, student medical examinations, participation of parents in placement decisions, and the development of an Architectural Barrier Removal Program.

These specific agreements did not exhaust the controlling group's desires, so the stipulation listed an additional sixteen issues for future negotiations. Among such matters were items clearly within the board's bailiwick, such as coverage by substitute teachers and paraprofessionals and interdistrict transfers caused by decentralization of instructional services. Plaintiffs and amici, consistent with their theory that anything however vaguely related to special education might be included in the decree, demanded that they be added. The board of education disagreed, but compromised. It agreed that plaintiffs and amici could in the future take any of the to-be-included-later list to mediation and review by Judge Nickerson.

After ten years of work, the controlling group had so many stipulations, letter agreements, orders, and informal bargains that no one fully knew what had been agreed to. To sort things out, the controlling group agreed to inventory the agreements and consolidate them into a single judgment. This never happened.

New Disagreements

Negotiations leading to the 1989 stipulation had been completed during the term of Chancellor Richard Green, who had succeeded Nathan Quinones in March 1988. Chancellor Green stated at his first board meeting that he was "terribly dismayed" to learn of the city's noncompliance and made as his first appointment to a senior position the top spot at the Division of Special Education.[55] Unfortunately, he died suddenly a year later in May 1989. His deputy,

Bernard Mecklowitz, was thrust into the job, agreeing to serve only until the end of the year. The board of education, led by board president Robert F. Wagner, Jr., a former deputy to Mayor Koch, conducted a national search for a new chancellor. In late 1989 the board settled on one of the most prominent school superintendents in the country, Joseph A. Fernandez, who had achieved great success as head of the school system in Dade County, Florida.

Taking office on January 1, 1990, Fernandez became the sixth chancellor to deal with the *Jose P.* decree. He wanted a reevaluation of the board's obligations. Within months, relationships within the controlling group again fell apart. Each side filed motions before Judge Nickerson. Plaintiffs and amici asked that the city be held in contempt, while Chancellor Fernandez and the city asked for a six-month moratorium on controlling group meetings. Fernandez complained that the meetings and consultations had risen to such detail and multiplicity that he and his staff could not focus on the task of compliance. Fernandez told the court that he was committed to bringing the city into compliance but needed time to develop his own plan.

Judge Nickerson would have none of this. He chastised the new chancellor for finding the prior agreements "irksome," and with sarcasm stated that this was "not the first time that promises of a bright future for the education of handicapped children have been made to this court." He added that he was "heartened by [Fernandez's] expression of commitment" and that he "look[ed] forward to the submission of a comprehensive plan" promised by Fernandez. "Up to now," Judge Nickerson wrote, "progress towards compliance has resulted chiefly from the persistent efforts of the attorneys for plaintiffs." He denied the city's motion for time to realign its plans and referred the matter again to the special master for contempt hearings.[56]

During Chancellor Fernandez's tenure the number of special

education students continued to climb, but evaluation and placement deadlines remained elusive and costs continued to rise. In 1991 he reorganized the special education bureaucracy, but without achieving any greater success than his predecessors. When Fernandez resigned in 1993, 134,000 children were in special education. The city then found yet another nationally known school official to take over the school system. Ramon C. Cortines became chancellor in September 1993 just as the city entered another period of financial belt-tightening.

Mayor Rudolph W. Giuliani took office shortly thereafter on January 1, 1994, to find a worsening crisis in city finances. Forced to cut the budgets of city agencies, Mayor Giuliani demanded that the board of education cut nonteaching expenses. The board elected as part of its cuts to reduce the number of special education monitors, which had ballooned to seventy-three as a result of another *Jose P.* stipulation signed in 1992, and to broaden the monitors' duties to general education as well as special education programs. Plaintiffs and amici objected, so the board asked Judge Nickerson to modify the stipulation governing monitors. Judge Nickerson referred the motion to the special master, Magistrate Caden.

In a long, legalistic opinion Magistrate Caden refused to allow the city to reduce the number of monitors. He wrote that consent decrees were really contracts that were to be strictly enforced. The contract written by the controlling group, he ruled, was clear and without ambiguity, and the city was stuck with its bargain regardless of the new circumstances. The board would have to find cuts elsewhere. As for the budget, Magistrate Caden treated it as irrelevant, mentioning it only in a footnote where he recounted that the city's attorney admitted that the budget had motivated the request for the modification.[57] Judge Nickerson affirmed the decision.[58]

If the lesson had not been clear enough before, it was clear now that the controlling group could protect favored programs from elected officials by writing them into a *Jose P.* stipulation.

The Decree Expands to New Issues

In 1990 Congress passed the Americans with Disabilities Act (ADA), which required public facilities to be accessible to the disabled. The *Jose P.* decree had included accessibility requirements in 1979, but the ADA went much further. Rather than litigate issues raised by the new statute and regulations, the controlling group quietly added them to their menu for negotiations. When city attorneys questioned such an enlargement, attorneys for plaintiffs and amici threatened to bring a new lawsuit under the ADA and ask Judge Nickerson to consolidate it with *Jose P.* That ended the debate, and the controlling group under the Education for All Handicapped Children Act of 1975 also became the controlling group under the ADA without ever having raised the issue in court.

One of plaintiffs' attorneys told us, with irony but accuracy, that this arrangement actually favored the city. The *Jose P.* attorneys, he observed, were more reasonable to deal with on accessibility than the more radical disability rights and veterans groups who might otherwise have sued the city and taken over the issue.

New Studies

In April 1994 Chancellor Cortines shook up special education by shifting hundreds of officials from the central office in Brooklyn to the school districts. He said that there were as many as five layers of people providing "alleged services." Echoing his predecessors, Cortines said that "special education should not be a catchall for every problem in our schools, but in many cases that is what it has become." The *New York Times* gave front page and extended coverage to Cortines's comments and to the criticisms of special education. Joseph P. Viteritti, now a research professor of public administration at New York University's Robert F. Wagner Graduate School of Public Service, voiced doubt that Cortines's efforts would succeed. "Special education," he warned, "has spawned the most entrenched bureaucracy in the central school administration," and that bureaucracy was cemented in by federal laws and the *Jose P.* decree.[59]

In December 1994 Cortines asked the NYU Institute for Education and Social Policy to advise on how to reorganize and better integrate special education into the city's general education. The institute assembled a large team of specialists, including the deans of the NYU School of Education and the Wagner Graduate School of Public Policy, as well as Jay Gottlieb, now professor of special education at NYU, who had conducted the major study for the Beattie Commission ten years earlier. In October 1995 the NYU team filed its report. The team, like its predecessor, found that special education did not serve the students well despite absorbing 25 percent of the city's public school budget. Only 15 percent of the students classified as learning disabled actually met the standard criteria of learning disability. The cost of evaluating, transporting, tracking, reevaluating, mainstreaming, and decertifying students who may not be disabled was siphoning off resources from a resource-starved public education system. The report recommended that the board integrate special education more with the school's primary mission, reduce the number of evaluations, dissolve separate evaluation teams assigned to each school, reassign the former evaluation team members to assist regular classroom teachers, and assign children presenting more serious handicaps to district committees for evaluations rather than to school committees.[60] None of this could be done under existing court orders.

No End in Sight

Cortines had little time to adopt the NYU or any other recommendations. Mayor Giuliani forced his resignation in October 1995. After another bruising search, the board in December 1995 appointed another nationally known educator as chancellor, Rudy Crew.

Since 1995 the controlling group has settled into a routine of continuing negotiations. Members review issues, study results, identify problems, and adjust protocols. One subcommittee of the controlling group deals with accessibility, another with staffing, others with monitoring bilingual education issues and more. The meetings are closed to the public, and no formal minutes are kept. It is an insider's game of sharing information and working out agreements that are sometimes but not always memorialized in writing.

Judge Nickerson became all but invisible. He made only one substantive ruling between 1990 and 2000—a brief decision in 1995 confirming Magistrate Caden's recommendation refusing to allow the city to reduce the number of special education monitors. His primary activity was signing orders every few months, approving fee applications by plaintiffs' attorneys for attending meetings, reviewing data and statistics, and drafting more stipulations and agreements. For example, for the six-month period January through June 1999, the twentieth year of the *Jose P.* saga, the city paid a total of $246,338 to plaintiffs' attorneys.[61] During this period no court litigation of any kind occurred. The time spent by plaintiffs' attorneys had been devoted entirely to meetings and other activities associated with the work of the controlling group.

The coziness of the controlling group produced an extraordinary consent order in 2000. In November 1999 Chancellor Crew, responding to a demand to end social promotion, promulgated tougher promotion guidelines. Under the new guidelines, each school principal would make promotional decisions for all children and do so under standards designed to end social promotion and to make principals more responsible for performance in special education classes. Plaintiffs' attorneys, however, did not want principals to decide promotions for children in special education; they wanted those promotion decisions to be made by each child's Individualized Education Program (IEP) team.[62] On December 30, 1999, they asked Judge Nickerson to overturn the new guidelines.

The city opposed. In its memorandum the city pointed out that promotion policy was not directly mentioned anywhere in the *Jose P.* consent decree or anywhere else related to the lawsuit. It might equally have argued that no child had actually been hurt by the new policy. Without a child being hurt by the policy, the complaining attorneys had no client to represent; they were acting on their own in favor of a policy they preferred over Chancellor Crew's.

Judge Nickerson referred the dispute to a new special master, Magistrate Judge Steven M. Gold, who had been appointed on the death in 2000 of Magistrate Caden. After Magistrate Gold unsuccessfully tried to mediate the dispute, the controlling group hammered out a fourteen-page consent decree that allowed the board to go ahead with its new policy as long as school principals kept IEP teams and parents informed.[63] If the board wanted to change the guidelines at a later date, all it had to do was give plaintiffs forty-five days' notice.[64]

This was an unusual consent order even by *Jose P.*'s standards. The parties agreed that the order was not part of the *Jose P.* consent order even though it was signed and "so ordered" by Judge Nickerson and could be enforced by him.[65] Federal judges, however, are not allowed to volunteer their powers. If the stipulation were not part of the *Jose P.* consent order needed to correct federal violations, then what was it?

For all the litigation and effort that surrounded it, the order appears to be no more than a free-floating bargain that the controlling group for various reasons wanted Judge Nickerson to bless.

The city achieved a highly prized goal; it insulated the board's new policy from further court challenges by children in need of special education. Plaintiffs' attorneys, who represent the entire class of children in need of special education, agreed to waive any further challenge to the chancellor's rules. As a result, no one could later challenge the rules as written, but rather only as applied to particular children. Plaintiffs' attorneys also conceded that changes in the guidelines could later be made with forty-five days' notice to them, a departure from the main *Jose P.* decree, which could be changed only with the plaintiffs' actual consent or a positive court ruling.

Plaintiffs' attorneys also got something important. During the course of the negotiations, they were able to review and edit all aspects of the board's promotion guidelines, rules, protocols, operational manuals, and draft notices. And they got fees for this work. For the period July 1, 1999, through June 30, 2000, during which this matter was the only court activity, although not the only activity of the controlling group, plaintiffs received $328,950 in fees.[66]

Jose P.: An Evaluation

Jose P. never finished high school and returned to Puerto Rico.[67] The city still misses deadlines, the number of children in special education hovers at 168,000, and costs climb. Harold Levy, a new chancellor, was appointed in 2000. The controlling group continues to meet. There is no end in sight.

The most notable fact after more than twenty years of court supervision is the size of the special education program. For the 1999–2000 school year, out of a school system of 1.1 million children, 168,000 received special education—three times the number when

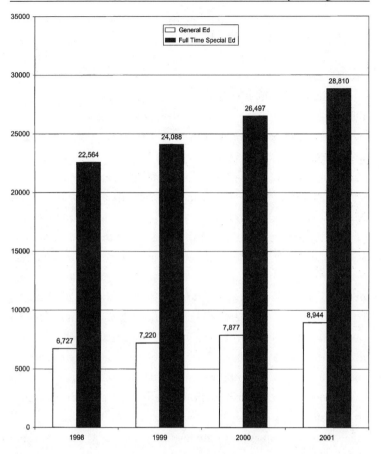

Figure 3.2. New York City per-pupil spending for general education and special education programs (fiscal years 1998–2001). *Source:* New York City Board of Education.

Jose P. was filed. Public school costs for these services reached $2.7 billion, 25 percent of the entire public school budget. The board spends in excess of $26,000 (Figure 3.2) per student in special education, nearly three times more than the resources devoted to students in regular education.[68]

Altogether, thirty-five thousand teachers, evaluators, aids, providers of related services, speech therapists, and others worked solely in special education for the board of education during 1999–2000. Cumulatively, 26 percent of all board employees are devoted to special education.[69]

The city scheduled 143,626 evaluations in 1999–2000 and completed 131,803—still not enough to meet the thirty- and sixty-day deadlines. Only 60 percent of the evaluations required to be completed within thirty days met that deadline.[70]

Plaintiffs' lawyers say that things would have been far worse without *Jose P.* "We've established these kids as a priority," says Michael Rebell.[71] He looks at the number of students and resources and, without denying the many problems with New York City's special education programs, says that far fewer students would have been served or would have been more poorly served had there been no *Jose P.* litigation. Rebell has written extensively on *Jose P.* and on education litigation generally. He defended the lawsuit at its ten-year point as accomplishing the priority that Congress intended for children with disabilities. It was Congress, he reasoned, that established the issue as a priority and offered the federal courts as a forum for managing reform. Discrimination against children with disabilities in education was, in Rebell's view, of a structural nature for which trial courts were an appropriate forum. In 1990 he wrote: "Through the [trial] judge's personal knowledge of local conditions and the remedial processes that the court can directly monitor, a trial court is able to implement effectively the general principles established in statutes or appellate decisions. In other words, structural discrimination is an 'open' doctrine whose broad parameters can be established at the level of principle or overarching public policy [by Congress], but whose substance can be determined only by a grassroots-level implementation process."[72] For Rebell, *Jose P.* represents a success because, as he sees it, change came faster than would otherwise have occurred.

John Gray, Rebell's co-counsel, reached a similar conclusion but unabashedly characterizes the process as political, root and branch. In an interview in 1999 with the authors, Gray said that "everyone knows that getting a law passed is a political process. What they don't know is that implementing a law is also a political process. There are bureaucrats who have no political power, but have the information that will convince the court to act. It is a collaborative process, an odd coalition. Informers on the inside, attorneys on the outside." But he also has a limited view of what the court can accomplish: "Courts are effective in getting enough money into the system, in getting planning, staff, and data. But courts are not so good on quality of the program like achieving the least restrictive environment."[73]

Critics of *Jose P.* view it far more harshly. Leonard Hellenbrand, a former budget director for the New York City board of education, saw *Jose P.* as undermining general education. "Kids who don't have court orders in their hands are dead meat," he says.[74] Charles I. Schonhaut, a former director of special education and later dean of education at Long Island University, agreed with Hellenbrand: "What you had was a road that was falling apart, and right alongside, they were building a superhighway called special education, which provided no end of money."[75] Other board officials who worked under the decree conceded that *Jose P.* caused a restructuring of special education but complained that the scope of the judgment and the minutiae of detailed procedures it required sometimes shifted the focus from what's best for students to numerical compliance with fixed time lines.[76]

In 1999 we asked former Chancellor Macchiarola, now the president of St. Francis College in Brooklyn, why he did not simply provide sufficient resources in the beginning to hit the thirty- and sixty-day deadlines and in that way get out from under the court decree. His reply: it made no educational sense. We were educators, he said, and were focused on the kids and not the process. "Educators couldn't define a handicapping condition, couldn't tell me who was and who was not learning disabled. The court only cared about getting the children placed, but I refused to send the kids into programs where there was no curriculum. It was like the death camps."[77]

The law itself, especially as applied, had its own flaws. Special education turned out not to be special. Evolving definitions of learning disability and emotional disturbance overwhelmed the natural bell curve of the classroom. Slow learners of all kinds could be classified as qualified for special education, and they were. Nationally, 59.2 percent of the 5.5 million students in special education are there because of learning disabilities or emotional disturbance.[78] In New York City the learning disabled and emotionally disturbed categories account for more than 62 percent of students placed in special education.[79] New York City's public schools were not the only place where these special education definitions have been gamed. In some upper-income public schools nearly one-fifth of the children have been classified as learning disabled—not to get them out of the classroom, but to garner such valuable perquisites as extra time to take tests or even tuition to private schools at public expense. Seventeen percent of all the school children in Greenwich, Connecticut, were in special education in 1997.[80] At the Dalton School, a highly selective upper-class private school in Manhattan, 36 percent of its five-year-olds at one point were categorized as "at risk" for learning disabilities.[81]

Jose P. failed to produce sound special education because it was premised on a basic misunderstanding of institutional change. The court set about to reform a single program in a vast educational structure—a fool's errand because special education could not be reformed without reforming the entire system. The upshot was a huge, gold-plated, dysfunctional cog in a rusty educational machine. The issue of preventive services and the recommendation of the Beattie Commission and all of the subsequent studies are telling. What was needed was to overhaul the *system,* only a part of which was special education. The New York City board of education could not stop the gaming of special education unless it also stopped gaming in other areas such as seniority, union perks, principal rights, custodian authority, and inadequate programs of all kinds, from athletics to grammar. What the court order did was cause the board to focus effort on one area of institutional performance without altering the culture of which it was a part. That, and the very rigidity of the *Jose P.* decree and the process it required, made it more difficult for new mayors, new chancellors, or new boards of education to improve the entire system.

Judge Nickerson believed that the controlling group led by a special master could solve his "polycentric" problem. He consciously copied that term from an earlier federal court opinion concerning racial discrimination written by his judicial colleague Judge Jack B. Weinstein. Judge Weinstein had written that solutions in his own "polycentric" case would "involve a multitude of choices affecting allocation of educational, housing and other resources, and each choice will affect other choices. Such many-centered problems call for informal consultations and weighing of complex alternatives using a managerial decision-making process. . . . A skilled master, with expertise in government housing laws and in educational administration to coordinate the efforts of the parties, is crucial if a just and workable remedy is to be devised."[82]

This formula for complex social engineering proved to be unworkable. Achieving idealistic, affirmative goals is a matter of neither logic nor expertise. Neither Michael Rebell nor John Gray made that mistake even for a moment. They knew they were in a political arena and acted accordingly. It was Judge Nickerson who either did not know this or more likely saw his role more as a political catalyst.[83] In either case, he had strayed far from his judicial mandate, and the results hardly justify the substitution of a controlling group for democratically elected officials and their appointees.

All of this leaves the rationale of plaintiffs' attorneys as the only plausible justification for the more than twenty years of court supervision. Their claim is that things could be worse and that they surely would be without the court order. There is no way to prove or disprove this claim because it compares what has occurred with what might have been—a hypothetical standard, the results of which vary with the views of the observer. From the viewpoint of plaintiffs' attorneys, however, it allows them to take credit for whatever good happened while still damning the board of education for never reaching an idealized performance. New York City's special education programs, however, were growing substantially before the lawsuit. There is no reason to assume that New York City would have ignored strong demands for special education arising from parents, educators, and political leaders. These pressures would have forced the board to enhance programs irrespective of federal law, although not likely in the same direction as compelled by Judge Nickerson's remedial decree.

We can reach some conclusions on this record.

First, under the judicial regime, no governmental official or institution has taken responsibility for what happened. Certainly not Judge Nickerson. In entering the original 1979 decree, he relied on the acquiescence of the board of education rather than make an independent determination that the decree's requirements were good. Since then, he never once evaluated the results of his imposition. What he did do was maintain the power of the controlling group. In the few instances in which disputes within the controlling group reached him, he bottomed his decision not on any finding that the decree helped the public, but rather on a near mechanical reference to the words of the 1979 decree.

The board of education disclaimed responsibility for the consequences of court supervision from its initial refusal to consent to the Gross Program. Only once did the board make a concerted effort to

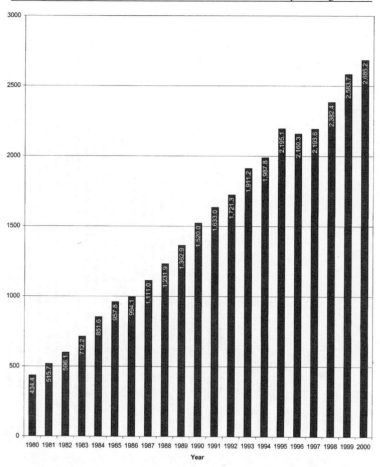

Figure 3.3. New York City special education budget (in millions), 1980–2000.
Source: New York City Board of Education.

get out from under the decree, but found that the more it tried to get free, the tighter it was bound. Conciliation and compromise proved more promising. Board officials alternately used and attacked the *Jose P.* process, but overall stayed with it. Mollifying the controlling group kept the court off its back.

The federal Department of Education has been a conspicuously

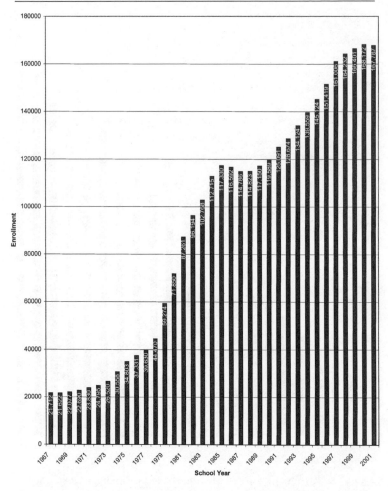

Figure 3.4. New York City special education enrollment, 1967–2001. *Source:* New York City Board of Education.

absent participant from the beginning. It first appeared on the legal scene in the eighteenth year of the case but only to point out racial disparities in the assignment of students to special education—a situation that had been documented for years by board of education data and independent studies and was at most a symptom of more fundamental problems.[84]

And what about Congress? Congress originally justified its entry into the field of special education in 1975 by promising to pay 40 percent of the states' costs. It reneged. Its contribution peaked at 12.2 percent in 1980 and has declined since.[85] Congress now appropriates at most 7 percent of all costs nationwide.[86] Much less reaches individual states like New York. In 2000, New York City received $70 million in federal special education funds against costs of $2.6 billion—less than 3 percent of its costs.[87] Congress continues to call the tune, but the states and localities pay the piper.

The *Jose P.* litigation raises profound doubts about continuing to rely on federal courts to supervise state and local governments. Unsatisfactory results of this proportion—$2.6 billion of New York City money spent annually, more than 168,000 New York City children involved—deserve attention (Figures 3.3 and 3.4). This attention should not be to fix blame on the individuals in charge of the case. They are superbly trained, well intentioned, and widely recognized as outstandingly successful judges and lawyers. Nor should that attention be fixed on questioning the worthy objective of special education. Rather, the failure of such competent people in pursuit of such a needed objective should compel attention on whether we should continue to rely so readily on courts to manage the complex institutions of state and local governments.

The *Jose P.* order and its process can conceivably continue forever. The court has never said what the board must do to terminate supervision.[88] When in February 1999 we asked John Gray, Jose P.'s attorney who filed the complaint in 1979, whether there was an end game, he replied that his more immediate problem was how to handle the case should Judge Nickerson retire. The judge was then eighty years old. On January 2, 2002, after a long and honorable career, Judge Nickerson died at age eighty-three. *Jose P.,* now twenty-four years old, lives on.

CHAPTER 4

Something New Is Going On In Court

It is not new that state and local officials find themselves as defendants in federal court. Federal judges from the earliest days of the United States entertained cases against state and local governments. The lawsuits, however, were mainly limited to whether the government had taken property, interfered with contracts, or violated some other property-based right. This limited judicial control of government met the needs of most citizens in an era of smaller government. Today, a greatly enlarged government provides education, welfare, housing, health care, and much more. When citizens first complained to courts about how government carried out these activities, judges were far less receptive than they had been to cases protecting property. They sometimes dismissed such cases on the basis that the plaintiff demanded a "benefit," not a "right," or that the controversy should be left to the political process.

"The New Property"

Judges found it increasingly indefensible to keep the courthouse door shut to claims for governmental "benefits." The most telling attack came from Charles A. Reich, a young professor at the Yale Law School, in a 1964 article titled "The New Property."[1] These supposed benefits, which he dubbed "the new property," were as important to the modern citizen as land had been when farming was the core of the economy. Reich wrote that government "draws in revenue and power, and pours forth wealth: money, benefits, services, contracts, franchises, and licenses."[2] By protecting the old property but not the new, argued Reich, courts held government to the rule of law only when the complaints came from landowners and businesses. There was no justice for the family improperly cut off from welfare, the veteran improperly denied benefits, or the truck driver improperly denied the license needed to work.

Reich made an impression on the Supreme Court. It ruled in 1970 that the Constitution's requirement of due process of law (which forbids the taking of life, liberty, or property without procedures to check error, such as notice and a hearing) protects a person's eligibility for welfare.[3] The legislature could repeal welfare if it wished, but no recipient could otherwise be cut off without notice and a hearing. The new property would receive the same procedural rights that protected the old property.

The new property might be welfare or other entitlements rather than real estate or cash in the bank, but the job of the court remained the same: to stop violations of plaintiffs' rights. That job remained the same whether the city shut off a recipient's welfare benefits without a hearing or trespassed on a landowner's backyard without permission. In either case, the court's job normally was simple and could be done quickly: tell the city to cut it out.[4]

In contrast, in cases of democracy by decree such as *Jose P.,* what courts did was neither simple nor quick. Something else was going on that drew judges into policy choices traditionally left to mayors, governors, and state and local legislators.

From Rights to Aspirations

In cases against state and local governments, courts drifted from enforcing rights to overseeing the pursuit of aspirations. Rights are like the "good fences" that "make good neighbors." They specify the duties we owe each other, as in forbidding the city from trespassing or cutting off a recipient's welfare without a hearing. Sometimes, of course, a court faces difficult questions about how to define rights, such as where to locate the boundary between squabbling neighbors. But once the respective rights of the parties are determined, the court's job is to give each party its due. The court's job is most definitely *not* to order the defendant to try to do more for the plaintiff, such as "be a better neighbor." That is an aspiration not a right, and aspirations traditionally were not enforceable in court.[5] We "honor" rights, and in the general case, completely; we "pursue" aspirations and, in the general case, attain them only partially because they are idealistic.

The shift to overseeing the pursuit of aspirations came not from any one, openly announced decision but from a combination of impulses, many of them quite laudable. One was the drive to end segregation. In *Brown v. Board of Education* the Supreme Court recognized a traditional kind of right that had been denied by an egregious failure in the political process of the Jim Crow states. The Supreme Court interpreted the equal protection clause of the Constitution as a clearly defined right—a right against government discriminating on the basis of race, not a right to have government *try* to produce equal outcomes for the various races.[6] Government did not have to produce schools in which blacks and whites attended in equal proportions or in which blacks and whites got the same grades on exams, as long as any disparities were not a product of racial discrimination by the defendant.

Once the lower federal courts set out to implement *Brown v. Board of Education*, however, their remedial authority foundered on the defendants' strategy of "massive resistance." Federal judges could not rely on state and local officials to obey orders to stop violating the law, but rather had to give those officials minute instructions on how to walk on the path of legality.

What that instruction should include was plain enough in concept. Each school district would have to dismantle its dual school system divided on race lines and stop assigning pupils on the basis of their race. Each school district would also have to repair the consequences of its past discrimination. It would have to provide remedial education to the victims of past discrimination, while taking into account in assigning pupils to schools how past school segregation had influenced residential patterns.[7] The objective, according to the Supreme Court, was to achieve "the greatest possible degree of actual desegregation."[8]

How these concepts translated into remedies was often difficult to discern in concrete cases. No one could tell exactly what the housing patterns or test results would have been if school districts had never discriminated. The greatest possible degree of actual desegregation was a strangely utopian objective for a court of law. How can the courts hope to eliminate all the vestiges of the terrible institution of Jim Crow when they are inextricably intermeshed with the vestiges of the even more terrible institution of slavery? Consider that Western civilization has yet to eliminate all the vestiges of the feudalism that was officially terminated centuries ago.

Courts had more pressing concerns than pondering such imponderables. Faced with defiant officials and mobs, courts understandably pressed hard in the opposite direction. With defendants apt to use any opportunity to cheat, it was also natural for courts to make their orders crisp and therefore easily enforceable.

Courts slipped into attempts to maximize racial balance rather than to remedy past discrimination.[9] In some cases, they targeted the gap in test results between the races.[10] If plaintiffs were thereby getting more than their constitutional due from the courts, there was a certain rough justice to it because many federal judges in the South had previously given them much less.

The point is that federal judges began to acquire the habit of making policy to pursue aspirational goals.

In the 1960s, prisoners put themselves forward as additional victims of egregious failures in state and local political processes and so in need of special judicial solicitude. These cases also invoked a constitutional right—the right against cruel and unusual punishment found in the Eighth Amendment. As in the school desegregation cases, the courts used the occasion of a violation of a right to make policy in pursuit of aspirational goals. Lower courts set out not just to stop unconstitutional punishment and conditions, but also to turn prisons into more humane, ethical institutions that more successfully rehabilitated their inmates.[11]

The judicial slide from enforcing rights to making policy in pursuit of aspirational goals is again understandable. The judges had reason to suspect that the elected branches of state and local governments would fail to act honorably. The first of the prison cases in which federal judges granted broad relief to inmates arose in the South. Defendants were segregationists and ran prisons in much the same way antebellum slave owners ran plantations, but without the slave owners' concern for preserving the value of their flesh-and-blood assets. Judges found it particularly hard to ignore the prisoners' claims because judges themselves played a part in keeping people in prison. Judges began to use their decrees, ostensibly designed to cure violations of a right, as a legal hook to advance policies that would make prisons better. Plaintiffs were still required in contested cases to prove that defendants had breached some duty, or threatened to do so, before reaching the remedies stage of the litigation in which the new concept of remedies applied.[12] To the extent that the Supreme Court spoke to the subject, it insisted upon the traditional concept of enforcing rights.[13] But in crafting remedies, courts not only cured violations of rights, but also imposed a better public policy as they saw it.

We call these aspirational goals *soft rights* because they are enforced only to the extent that the controlling group or the judge thinks it makes sense to do so in view of society's competing priorities. In contrast, courts ordinarily enforce traditional rights to the hilt. A right is, after all, a right. Soft rights, on the other hand, cannot ordinarily be fully achieved. The court must inevitably decide how far it will push government to pursue a soft right, and that decision will necessarily balance the soft right against government's competing priorities. A central concern of this book is whether these decisions about priorities should be made by the controlling group or by officials accountable at the ballot box.

Congress Creates Soft Rights to Be Pursued in Court

What the courts had done retail, Congress in the 1970s began to do wholesale. The obligations made enforceable against state and local governments were aspirational. The statutes were complex and bristled with obligations and processes of great specificity, but these specifics did not make the goals of the statutes any less aspirational. The specifics served the aspirational goals. Even with lists of requirements, due dates, and timetables, no one could realistically expect, for example, that curb ramps would be constructed at every intersection by 1995, that all children in need of special education would get a fine education, or that the air would be made fully healthy by the end of the 1970s as the Clean Air Act of 1970 mandated.

The new statutes smuggled controversial aspirations into legislative language enacted as necessary to protect widely supported moral rights. In enacting a statutory right for children with disabilities to receive an appropriate education, Congress emphasized the image of deaf, blind, and wheelchair-bound children kept out of the school building or, even more pathetically, simply denied any education. We can all agree that such neglect is morally wrong. It was that widely shared public sense that moved many states to provide education for such starkly disabled children before Congress created the federal right to special education. The right that Congress wrote into the fine print of the act, however, went far beyond the image that lent poignancy to the campaign to create the right. The right in fine print included not only starkly disabled children, but also children who suffer from vaguely defined learning disabilities and emotional disturbances who now make up the bulk of the children assigned to special education. Moreover, these children would be entitled not just to some compensatory help, but rather to special education that would have a whole string of attributes enumerated in the statute. The aspiration was, of course, admirable, but how far society should go to turn it into reality has proved highly controversial.

Each of the statutes that created soft rights had consequences manyfold more important than a single, broad lower court decree because each statute typically created many kinds of obligations and applied to states and localities throughout the country. The legal lexicon does not have a standard name for what we have called soft rights. One scholarly article called them "aspirational commands."[14] Michael Rebell called them "priorities."[15] Whatever the name, they exist and are different from the rights that courts traditionally enforced. The question is how courts should respond to violations of soft rights by state and local governments.

The Difficulty of Enforcing Soft Rights

Traditional common-law rights, such as the right against trespass, are typically negative. They tell government what it can not do. Soft rights, such as the right to healthy air, are typically positive. They tell government what it must do. Not only are common-law rights mostly negative, but so are the civil rights in the Constitution: government officials may *not* impede the free exercise of religion or censor speech. The right against racial discrimination in the equal protection clause is also negative. The Supreme Court has repeatedly read it to forbid government to discriminate on the basis of race without a compelling justification, but not to require government to achieve racial balance or equalize outcomes according to race.[16] Constitutional rights are aimed at sins of commission, not sins of omission.

Courts have long understood that it is hard for them to enforce positive duties. Private contracts regularly call for positive acts such as delivering goods or performing services. If the contract is broken, courts shy away from ordering the positive act to be done in order to avoid the difficulty of supervising compliance with a positive duty. Courts will usually award money damages unless the buyer can show that money is not an adequate substitute for actual performance. Even then, courts are reluctant to order performance of contracts for personal services, partly because they pose special difficulties in judging the adequacy of compliance.[17] Soft rights that courts enforce in decrees, in contrast, often call for performance whose adequacy is difficult to judge.

Government officials frequently do not know how to obey a court order enforcing soft rights, and it is possible that no one knows. Officials can often comply with traditional rights by just not doing what is forbidden. In contrast, the school board in New York City struggled for two decades to achieve the aspirational goal of a free appropriate education for all children with disabilities. And no wonder. The school board, and many others across the country, also regularly failed to provide an appropriate education for students with no disabilities. People have theories about how to provide special education; some are worth trying, and some will work to an

Table 4.1. The parade of defendants and elected officials responsible for complying with federal law and the *Jose P.* decree

In July 1979 the *Jose P.* and *United Cerebral Palsy* plaintiffs sued the state commissioner of education, the chancellor the New York City public school system, the president of the New York City Board of Education, the six members of the board of education, and the top state and city bureaucrats responsible for special education. All the defendants were appointed officials or departments responsible to either the government or the mayor. The officials initially sued have long since left office. Under court rules, when an official initially sued leaves office, that person's successor is automatically substituted as a defendant and must comply with all previously entered court orders just as if he or she had been initially sued. Is it possible that all, or any, of these officials opposed meeting the educational needs of children with disabilities?

Governors
    Hugh Carey (1979–83)
    Mario Cuomo (1983–95)
    George Pataki (1995–)

Mayors
    Edward I. Koch (1979–89)
    David Dinkins (1990–93)
    Rudolph Giuliani (1994–2001)
    Michael R. Bloomberg (2002–)

New York State Education Commissioners
    Gordon M. Ambach (1979–87)
    Thomas Sobol (1987–95)
    Richard P. Mills (1995–)

New York City School Chancellors
    Frank J. Macchiarola (1979–83)
    Anthony Alvarado (1984)
    Nathan Quinones (1984–88)
    Richard Green (1988–89)
    Bernard Mecklowitz (1989)
    Joseph A. Fernandez (1990–93)
    Ramon C. Cortines (1993–95)
    Rudy F. Crew (1995–2000)
    Harold Levy (2000–)

Table 4.1. continued

Presidents of the New York City Board of Education
   Stephen R. Aiello (1979–80)
   Joseph G. Barkan (1980–83)
   James F. Regan (1983–86)
   Robert F. Wagner, Jr. (1986–90)
   Gwendolyn C. Baker (1990–91)
   H. Carl McCall (1991–93)
   Carol A. Gresser (1993–96)
   William C. Thompson (1996–2001)
   Ninfa Segarra (2001–)

Approximately thirty other defendants served as members of the New York City Board of Education or as directors of the state or the city's special education program.

---

extent. Nonetheless, no one can say for sure whether any combination of them will fully achieve the aspirational goals.

Individual officials often lack the power to fulfill the aspirational goals of a soft right. If a state law, for example, commands an official to take private land for a particular municipal purpose, once that law has been declared unconstitutional and the official enjoined, the official is fully capable of obeying the law without anyone else's help. All it takes is to do nothing. In contrast, to comply with aspirational goals, officials need funding, legislation, and significant cooperation from other agencies and the public. Federal law might command local officials to provide an appropriate education to disabled children as defined by federal standards, but delivering that education requires appropriations, cooperation by various unions, and the willingness of school personnel to alter educational practices and cultural beliefs.

Soft rights are difficult to enforce because judges have trouble laying their hands on those ultimately subject to the duty (Table 4.1). Courts in enforcing traditional rights impose burdens on identifiable people before the court, but with soft rights, judges try to impose duties on society generally. There are defendants against whom orders can be directed, but governors, mayors, and commissioners generally appear only "in their official capacity." They are named only because they temporarily hold positions at the sufferance of society and therefore have temporary authority to act on society's behalf. On leaving office, they shed the title and the responsibility like a ceremonial robe. The duty is in essence on society, not on the defendants. The real defendants might as well be identified as *All the People of the City and State,* just the reverse of a criminal case in which the people are the plaintiff, as in *People v. John Doe.* The victim seeks compliance by society, but society is a slippery fellow for a judge to grab.

Courts must allow leeway in enforcing soft rights. With a traditional right, such as the right against trespass, the defendant either does or does not have a right to be on the land and, if not, must get off. Courts, however, must be tentative in enforcing soft rights precisely because they are aspirational. No court would tell New York City to put ramps on all its curbs by the statutory deadline. Although the language of the goals may be absolute, the reality of enforcement cannot be. Both judges and plaintiffs' attorneys understand that public acquiescence in court control is fragile and can be undermined by pushing things too far. For curb ramps the measure of what the local government must do turns out not to be everything necessary to comply, but something less. How much less is a policy judgment.

Courts cannot come down hard on defendants when they fail to achieve the goals of soft rights. With traditional rights the defendant knows how to comply and the court can readily judge compliance. It will issue highly specific orders with stern warnings that failure to comply will be punished as contempt of court. Failures to achieve soft rights, however, are often not a matter of lack of will by the named defendants personally, but instead reflect that they do not know how to comply, that they cannot secure the necessary cooperation of others, or that society at whose pleasure they serve resists living up to the soft right once it learns the real cost of compliance and upon whom these costs fall.

How Enforcement of Soft Rights Led Courts into Managing Policy

By failing to take adequate account of the peculiar difficulty of pursuing aspirations, courts disrupted the traditional division of power between themselves and the elected branches of government. Enforcing traditional rights did not put courts in a policy-making role. When faced with violations of traditional rights, the courts ordered state and local governments to stop acting unlawfully. Courts could then bow out, leaving it up to defendant officials to craft new policies that did not violate the rights in question. Courts went beyond such orders to manage performance by state and local defendants only in those extremely rare cases in which officials were unwilling to comply or unable to because of bankruptcy. Even in such cases, courts have traditionally leaned over backwards to leave the policy choices with the state and local defendants.[18]

With democracy by decree, this rare exception covering the outlaw or bankrupt official has swallowed the general rule that courts should leave ordinary governmental policy making to the elected branches of state and local governments. In cases involving aspirational goals, courts routinely sign highly specific orders against state and local defendants, with or without their consent, which answer policy questions that elected officials traditionally answered.

Judicial enforcement has gone from being a declaration of rights to a managerial process. As a result, the courts have found themselves up to their necks in budgetary, personnel, regulatory, and programmatic choices of the kind previously made only by elected state and local officials and their appointees. Federal courts were making public policy at its core, not the margin. There had been policy implications in the enforcement of traditional rights against state and local governments, but nothing like that which came with the managerial style that federal courts now adopted.[19]

Take the federal Medicare and Medicaid programs. If a state "chooses to participate" by accepting the federal money Congress offers, it becomes obligated to meet all conditions attached to the federal money. Every state, of course, chooses to participate, with the result that federal law effectively preempts all fifty state health programs, which in turn makes federal judges the final arbiters of state medical assistance programs.

A federal court, for example, in 1994 ruled that California failed to meet federal conditions when only eighteen of its fifty-eight counties provided methadone maintenance treatment for drug abusers. The judge ordered California to extend the programs to all counties.[20] In 1999 a federal judge ordered Florida to raise its cash allotment for adults needing a wheelchair. The judge ruled that the state's limit of $582 was unlawful under Medicaid because the allotment covered only standard wheelchairs, not motorized ones.[21] In 2000, a district court judge ruled that Texas violated the federal Early Periodic Screening, Diagnosis and Treatment Act, an amendment to the Medicaid program, by not meeting outreach goals or providing required medical and dental checkups, among other obligations. This Texas federal decree now oversees a health program covering 1.5 million Texas children.[22] The Early Periodic Screening, Diagnosis and Treatment Act has also resulted in lawsuits or decrees in Michigan, New York, Oregon, and Tennessee.[23]

Lawsuits have been filed in every state under the Individuals with Disabilities Education Act,[24] the same statute that supports the *Jose P.* special education decree in New York City. Court decrees can end up supervising the education programs of an entire school district or a state. Federal courts, for example, recently ordered Connecticut to provide special education evaluations for children housed at juvenile detention facilities, appointed a special master to hear complaints whenever the District of Columbia failed to provide timely hearings for children seeking special education, and stopped New York City from applying its suspension policy to children assigned to special education who were attending summer school.[25]

The Americans with Disabilities Act of 1990 compelled state and local governments to make public programs and facilities accessible.[26] As a result, in excess of one hundred new lawsuits per year are brought against state and local governments.[27] Relatively simple cases involve such issues as installing curb ramps; providing access to courthouses, schools, public auditoriums, and government buildings; and accommodating people with disabilities for public activities such as voting and attending athletic events in a public stadium. Other lawsuits have forced states under judicial scrutiny to rethink the management of complex social programs. Fifteen states, for example, have either been sued or are currently under federal court decree over the choice between institutionalization or community care for people with mental disabilities. Relying on a Supreme Court interpretation of the ADA, the lawsuits claim that a decision not to move a person into a community care facility when it is medically possible to do so discriminates against people with disabilities.[28] States with court orders or lawsuits include Arizona, California, Florida, Hawaii, Indiana, Louisiana, Massachusetts, Michigan, Mississippi, New York, Ohio, Pennsylvania, Washington, and West Virginia.[29] Similar lawsuits in Louisiana and Michigan on behalf of people with disabilities housed in nursing homes demand that they be moved to community-based care facilities.[30]

Many federal judges did not have to be asked twice to intervene in state and local policy making. Judges were no longer tolerant, or at least no longer as tolerant, of decisions reached by political compromise. Judges were no longer impressed, or at least no longer as impressed, with defendants who had been elected or the experts on their staffs. Rather, activist judges wanted to do the right thing, which meant the rational thing, and if expertise were required, they would rely on plaintiffs' and defendants' attorneys and their experts or hire their own experts and work it out with them. Professor Donald Horowitz captured the new judicial mind-set in a nutshell: "Here is a credo at once rational and skeptical, intolerant of flexibility, discretion, and expertise in the [elected branches of government] but exceedingly trustful of all three when employed in the service of the court. Indeed, central to what is fast becoming the received wisdom is the need for expertise in shaping and enforcing remedies, for judicial discretion in framing and monitoring novel remedial devices, and for flexibility in adapting the machinery of the courts for the job. The old virtues have found a new home."[31]

Courts slipped into managing public policy. Here the nomenclature is telling. Lawsuits that had originally been known as *public interest cases* to enforce specific rights have become known by a new name, *institutional reform cases*. Managing reform of institutions is different from enforcing compliance with traditional rights. Courts have blended the enforcement of soft rights with the management of institutional change and, in the process, have become managers and power brokers rather than judges.[32]

CHAPTER 5

How Court Management Works

For today's young attorneys, the change in what courts do was already embedded in the law when they were schooled. For older attorneys, the change was gradual and happened in areas of the law remote from where most of them practiced. We, however, lived through the change.

We went to law school when most of the curriculum was based on the old way of doing things but found ourselves practicing the new kind of law in the mid-1970s at the Natural Resources Defense Council (NRDC). The cases we had read in law school in the 1960s involved Smith suing Jones for breaking a contract, causing an accident, or trespassing on property. Smith wanted damages or his property back. The cases we brought in the mid-1970s were far different. We had no single individual, no Smith, for a client. The plaintiff was usually a large, loosely organized group known by an acronym—for example, NRDC—for the membership of that organization. We, rather than our putative clients, decided what relief to seek from the court, and that usually was not damages or the return of some property but a decree requiring government to adopt new policies, such as renovating the subway system in New York City or reducing pollution in Puerto Rico.

We knew instinctively that the law we were practicing was somehow different from the law we had studied in school, but we had no systematic understanding of the difference until, in 1976, Professor

Figure 5.1. Professor Abram Chayes. His 1976 article in the *Harvard Law Review* remains the most widely cited explanation and defense of court supervision of state and local governments. Photograph by Richard Chase.

Abram Chayes (Figure 5.1) of the Harvard Law School published his article "The Role of the Judge in Public Law Litigation."[1] Our practice left us little time to read law review articles, but we made time to read this one because someone was finally explaining to us what we were doing. We were not alone in this. Chayes's article was so perceptive that virtually everyone who subsequently wrote on the new role of courts started with his description.

Chayes contrasted the old way of doing things, which he called "private law litigation," with the new way, which he called "public law litigation." Private law litigation was the contract, accident, and property cases we had learned in school. Public law litigation was the law we now practiced. For Chayes, what distinguished the two was not the identity of the parties, but the nature of the dispute. Public law litigation was no longer about the enforcement of private rights (for example, whether a given doctor or hospital must pay damages for alleged malpractice in a case brought by a particular patient), but the reform of public policy (for example, what the level of medical care should be in a prison). He concluded that public law litigation prompted five key changes in the way courts work:

- *Private law litigation is normally a contest between two people, but public law litigation, being about public policy, necessarily deals with a host of interested individuals and groups.* For example, a case about special education concerns not only nominal plaintiffs and defendants (a child with disabilities and the school board), but also all the other students with or without disabilities as well as teachers, social workers, and taxpayers. Such "polycentric" cases cannot, like a private law dispute about who owns the property, be decided on a winner-takes-all basis.
- *Private law litigation usually focuses on what happened in the past, but public law litigation focuses on what should happen in the future.* This is so because the remedy seeks to shape the future of public policy, not to compensate for past violations. In *Jose P.*, the board of education readily admitted that it had failed to place children by the deadline; the fight was over what should happen in the future.
- *Private law litigation is a self-contained episode, but public law litigation is an ongoing saga.* Private law cases usually end with the entry of judgment, either dismissing the case or transferring money or property from defendant to plaintiff. In public law cases, the entry of judgment is just the beginning of the court's prolonged control of government.
- *Private law litigation bases the remedy on the nature of the right violated, but public law litigation bases the remedy on considerations of public policy.* In private law litigation, according to Chayes, "the plaintiff will get compensation measured by the harm caused by the defendant's breach of duty—in contract by giving the plaintiff the money he would have had absent the breach; in tort by paying the value of the damage caused."[2] In a public law case such as *Jose P.*, the remedy is based on what experts believe ought to be done rather than the rights in statutes and constitutions.
- *Private law litigation "is party-initiated and party-controlled" (emphasis in original), but public law litigation is structured and*

controlled by the judge.[3] Judges let private parties run private law cases because everyone affected by the outcome is likely to be in court. Judges, according to Chayes, manage public law cases because the public at large is affected.

Taken together, the changes Chayes described largely swept away the functional distinctions between the work of courts and that of legislatures, governors, and mayors. Chayes, of course, noticed that judges had reversed their usual reluctance to make public policy. That was the point of his article. But he generally approved of the change. In his view, judges would often be better than elected officials at resolving policy disputes and would produce better outcomes.

Chayes's conclusion that good results justify arguably antidemocratic means is totally understandable. We agreed with him at the time. Most of the legal community did, too. *Brown v. Board of Education* and the constitutional cases that followed were widely supported. Most law professors, law students, and lawyers did not criticize the judicial role that produced such satisfactory results. *Brown* itself presented the most favorable circumstances for court intervention imaginable—a racist rejection of the ideal of equality tolerated by a log-jammed Congress.

Chayes, however, did not fully credit the magnitude of the change that was under way. He was writing at a time when lower courts were covert in providing positive, aspirational remedies for negative constitutional rights, and the new statutes that Congress had created had not yet worked their way through the judicial process sufficiently to manifest the special difficulties courts would encounter directing the pursuit of aspirations. These difficulties were not alien to Chayes's description of public law litigation. Indeed, they were suffused with it and helped to explain the five characteristics that he identified. But he neither brought these difficulties into sharp focus nor noticed their full effect on how courts did their work.

With the advantage of the quarter century since Chayes wrote, we augment his description as follows.

STATE AND LOCAL GOVERNMENTS ARE
THE TARGETS OF CHOICE

Although Chayes wrote that the targets of public law litigation included private businesses and the federal government as well as state and local governments, it is now clear that state and local governments are the targets of choice. Even when the federal government is sued in public interest litigation, state and local governments are often the ultimate targets because many of the suits seek to force a federal agency to impose stricter duties on state and local officials.[4] With reforming society as the ultimate goal, government tends to make a better defendant because government, unlike private firms, has the power to regulate, tax, and spend public funds. Moreover, private firms will fight more vigorously than state and local governments to defend themselves. So will the federal government. It can afford larger, more highly paid legal staffs, and courts show more deference to federal agencies than they show to their state and local counterparts.

THE JUDGE IS A PASSIVE SUPERVISOR;
THE MAIN ACTOR IS THE CONTROLLING GROUP

The central actor in Chayes's "The Role of the Judge in Public Law Litigation" is the eponymous judge managing public policy through the decree—judicial activism in enlarging rights followed by judicial activism in imposing a remedy. This description proved inaccurate.

Judges found delight but also fear in their new public policy role. The delight came from the opportunity to do good. The fear came from the responsibility that would fall on judges if they themselves undertook to make controversial policy choices that necessarily would arise in working out a remedy. Chayes minimized the change throughout his presentation. For example, he wrote "right and remedy are interdependent."[5] That was a strikingly bland way of saying that judges were no longer sailors steering according to the law, but admirals charting the course.

Chayes further minimized the new powers judges assumed by likening those powers to the courts' traditional job of fact finding. He, of course, recognized the difference between work-a-day fact finding such as involved in deciding whether Smith actually signed the contract and the more complex fact finding that judges do in patent or antitrust cases. As difficult as some of these cases might be, they bear little resemblance to resolving public policy disputes. Experts, least of all social scientists, cannot provide authoritative answers to policy questions such as how quickly to proceed with building curb ramps, how much of the burden of cleaning up the air should be allocated to a particular pollution source, or what portion of the school budget should be devoted to children with learning disabilities. Whoever makes such political choices cannot hide behind facts, law, or expertise.

Success in making policy choices requires sensitivity to a wide spectrum of information. Adjudication is ill-suited to assembling and processing such information because judges lack the necessary experience and court procedures are too narrowly focused and backward looking.[6]

Lacking the time, capacity, and political legitimacy needed to assume such responsibility, judges generally sought to shift it to the parties by getting them to consent to a decree. That, in turn, has led to the establishment of what we have termed the controlling group— a bureaucracy consisting of attorneys for the parties, the functionaries and experts they bring into the negotiating room, and various court-appointed officials such as special masters. Although Chayes wrote about litigated cases, the decrees in most cases proved to be settled, not litigated. Chayes thus erred in portraying the judge rather than the controlling group as the central actor in public law litigation.[7]

The leading role of the controlling group undermines Chayes's justification for making public policy in court. He wrote in 1976 that judges, moderated by the inherent conservatism of the judicial community, would base public policy on reasoned and principled decision making. This ideal is rarely achieved. The bulk of the court orders in institutional reform cases result from bargains that, like the legislation they most resemble, are not necessarily logical or principled. When a proposed order is submitted for judicial signature on consent of the parties, judges are freed from having to choose among policies and can remain true to a still powerful judicial culture based on the separation of powers, which expects judges to let elected officials manage government.

Judges are not, however, entirely passive. The judge anoints the controlling group and keeps it going by pressuring the parties and holding the defendants and their successors in office to the bargain. Some of the most dramatic confrontations over enforcement of decrees against state and local governments have involved decrees that were entered by consent.[8] By allowing the judge to say, in effect, "I am only holding you, the defendants, to the bargain that you (or your predecessors) made," consent decrees allow judges to wield real power without appearing to do so. The judges are not so much "active" as "passive-aggressive"—passive in deferring to the policy judgments of the controlling group, active in maintaining its power.[9]

Judge Nickerson in *Jose P.* generally followed this pattern. He was active during the short liability stage when he adjudicated the initial motions. He also established the parameters of the controlling group by incorporating the totality of special education into the case and imposing a special master over the process. After these major decisions, however, Judge Nickerson during the next twenty-three years issued only ten written opinions, each of which resolved a discrete controversy brought to him after the parties had failed to work out an agreement on their own. When it came to the remedy, he was passive as to the substance of public policy and active only in his insistence that the group empowered by his decree should continue to reign.

Judge Nickerson's passive-aggressive role is typical. In a foster care lawsuit begun in Alabama in 1988, plaintiffs alleged that the state failed to meet federal standards in the state's foster care program.[10] When the federal judge refused to dismiss the plaintiffs' complaint, the state avoided further litigation by negotiating a comprehensive consent judgment. The resulting decree, which the court approved in 1992, called for the reform of most aspects of Alabama's foster care program. By the fall of 1993 the state was falling behind milestones to which it had consented, and the parties negotiated a new consent order, which the court signed in October 1993. Plaintiffs went back to court for additional relief in 1994, but a decision was averted when the governor added funds to the program and agreed to additional modifications to the consent order. In 1996 the state asked to be released from the order entirely, but the court refused. Plaintiffs filed another motion for contempt, which was again mooted when the parties in March 1999 agreed to another consent order. In twelve years of litigation, other than the two decisions refusing to let the state out of the litigation, the judge has not made any substantive judicial decisions.

In another child welfare lawsuit a group of plaintiffs in 1977 sued the state of Missouri over management of Kansas City's foster care programs.[11] A highly detailed, process-oriented consent decree was signed in 1983. Compliance lagged. In 1985, when the state sought a modification, plaintiffs moved to hold the defendants in contempt.

The parties settled their motions by another consent decree. Compliance continued to lag and plaintiffs filed another contempt motion in 1990. A trial was held, and the court, finding the defendants to be in contempt, threatened to issue its own remedial decree if the parties did not come up with one themselves. This threat led to extensive discussions, off-the-record meetings among the parties, more negotiations, and a new consent order by which the state allowed a panel of experts to evaluate its child welfare program. The panel issued its report and recommendations in 1994, which led to yet another consent decree, which, this time, included an exit plan. Implementation still proved a problem, so the parties in 1995 created a procedure by which the independent monitor reports every six months to the court on how well the state is doing in achieving compliance with the various items in the exit plan. The state met some requirements, but failed to meet others. Under the revised and extended exit plan, the defendants hoped to be released from court supervision sometime in 2002 or 2003, a quarter century after the initial complaint was filed. Progress stalled, however, when key people retired from the agency, with the result that the release date has shifted to 2003 or beyond. Meanwhile, the parties meet in regular meetings every two months but have had little actual contact with the judge.

The Kansas City foster care case has been studied by two law professors acting as consultants to the Center for the Study of Social Policy, an institute active in child welfare cases, including the one in Kansas. The professors, who approve of lawsuits as a method of reform, concluded in their 1997 report that the value added by the judge in the Kansas City case was to "provide a forum in which the relevant players can negotiate a solution to the underlying problem, and a powerful incentive to do so."[12] The powerful incentive, as with *Jose P.*, was the judge's explicit threat in 1993 to hold the individual defendants personally liable for contempt. The judge has not made a significant substantive decision of his own since his threatening contempt in 1993.

Such cases are the rule and not the exception. The National Center for Youth Law identified in 2000 some fifty-seven child welfare institutional reform lawsuits arising in thirty-six states, with consent decrees in at least thirty-five of the lawsuits. In only a handful of the cases did a judge impose any remedy except on consent of the parties.[13]

STATE AND LOCAL DEFENDANTS CONSENT TO
THE DECREE RATHER THAN FIGHT IT

Institutional reform litigation can be a lifeboat for the official. As early as 1965, plaintiffs' attorneys were writing how cases should be structured to invite officials to take advantage of the lawsuit to pursue professional and programmatic objectives.[14] An analysis in 1997 of the Kansas City foster care settlement found that lawsuits were at their most productive when officials "learn to look for the many opportunities that litigation presents to improve the delivery of public services."[15]

Settlement offers real advantages. Agreeing with plaintiffs' attorneys on a corrective program allows defendant officials to switch from the role of lawbreaker to that of reformer. Officials can protect and expand budgets and programs, trump political bodies, gain protection against even more stringent laws and rules, and avoid the risk that the judge might impose a worse remedy. These powerful motivations make settlement attractive, even when the consequences of the decree are little understood. Confronted by a lawsuit that they cannot escape, and seeing advantages in a consent decree that they help draft, officials almost invariably consent.

THE CONTROLLING GROUP OPERATES
WITHOUT BOUNDARIES

Although the job of courts is to remedy violations of law, the controlling group is free in practice to advance its vision of good public policy.[16] For example, in *Jose P.*, the controlling group at one point thought it good policy to require that social workers play a role in evaluating children with disabilities even though no law required it.

Why do judges enter decrees that go beyond correcting violations of law and usurp the policy-making prerogatives of the elected branches of state and local governments? By signing the decree as presented, the judge minimizes work and responsibility. Adopting the terms consented to by a governor or mayor shields the judge from criticism by the official who is likely to be the most politically potent actor with an interest in the case. Without consent, a mayor or governor might blast the judge for entering even a narrowly tailored decree. Future mayors and governors, of course, cannot speak up at the time, and isolated state or local legislators generally command little attention from the press. From the judge's perspective, signing the controlling group's decree is good politics.

THE CONTROLLING GROUP MAKES UP THE LAW
AS IT GOES ALONG

Statutory law is the plaintiffs' ticket into court but can be ignored once the controlling group goes into action. Obligations that look mandatory and precise in the statute books may be passed over in favor of substitutes that the controlling group thinks are more desirable. The parties horse-trade programs and schedules, milestones and resources. The law as applied, as opposed to the law on the books, is what the controlling group says it is. Congress may be purposefully vague on the means to achieve open-ended goals so that state and local governments can craft programs sensitive to local concerns. But with the controlling group in charge, it, rather than elected officials, does the crafting.

PLAINTIFFS' ATTORNEYS TEND TO ADVANCE THEIR VISION
OF THE PUBLIC INTEREST, OFTEN AT THE EXPENSE OF
SOME OF THEIR CLIENTS

In ordinary private litigation, the client controls the attorney. In democracy by decree, the plaintiff, usually a large class of people, is unable to control the attorney. This should be no problem because all the members of the plaintiff class have been hurt by the same violation of law, and the purpose of the lawsuit is to end that violation. This is, however, only theory. In practice, democracy by decree is not just about ending violations of rights but also about making policy; and, as to policy, there are often sharp conflicts of interest among the plaintiffs and between them and their lawyer. For example, in the early class action to end unconstitutional conditions in a jail in lower Manhattan, plaintiffs' attorneys wanted the city to close the old jail and build a new jail on Rikers Island adjacent to LaGuardia Airport. Many prisoners, however, opposed being relocated because their families would have to make an arduous trip to visit them at the new location.

These clients and their attorneys fought, and the attorneys prevailed. Michele Herman, a former legal aid attorney, documented the dispute in a master's thesis written in 1977 under the supervision of Professor Chayes. She concluded that the prisoners were "not a manageable class, that there were no representative spokesmen for the class, and that class members were totally uninformed of the litigation most of the time. Furthermore, the [legal aid] attorneys for the plaintiffs had no representative group of clients to whom they were accountable. They had, at the very least, the appearance of a conflict with their clients' interests. Additionally, the lawsuit was not initiated in response to the primary concerns of the plaintiff class."[17]

In many other cases as well, plaintiffs' attorneys pursued objectives that clashed with the wishes of many of those in whose name they litigated.[18]

THE CONTROLLING GROUP PREFERS TO WORK INFORMALLY AND PRIVATELY IN ORDER TO PRESERVE CONTROL OF PUBLIC POLICY

Meeting without observers and outside the reach of sunshine laws and administrative procedures, the controlling group prefers privacy and meetings that are not publicly scheduled. The parties claim a privilege of confidentially like that which keeps confidential private parties' negotiations over private lawsuits. But confidentiality in public law cases keeps negotiations over public policy private and thereby preserves the controlling group's proprietary control. Decisions by the controlling group tend to become less formal and more idiosyncratic. Bargains are made on handshakes, exchanged by correspondence, or entered into without any external indication, signaled only by what has been omitted from discussions and court submissions.

De facto secrecy extends to other aspects of the controlling group's activities. In *Jose P.* neither the decree and its detailed plans nor any of the subsequent stipulations and amendments were ever published, even in periodicals on special education litigation. Only the parties and people to whom they had given copies of these operational documents possessed them. Special reports and tabulations of statistics that the decree required the board to prepare in order to measure compliance were regularly sent by the board of education to plaintiffs' attorneys and were not published or evaluated by the court except when plaintiffs' attorneys chose to bring them to the court's attention. Every six months or so plaintiffs' attorneys applied for their fees, which totaled hundreds of thousands of dollars. Documents justifying these fees were not shared with the public. The fee applications are found only in relatively inaccessible court filings.

Plaintiffs' attorneys in our experience, and the *Jose P.* attorneys in particular, have willingly shared documents, but you have to know what you are looking for and ask for it. Copying charges can be high, and record keeping for old cases can often be chancy, even by court clerks. When we asked the clerk of the federal court in Brooklyn for a copy of the *Jose P.* docket, the official master list of all court filings, the clerk could not find the docket for the first fourteen years of the case, from 1979 through 1993. His excuse: in 1993 the court changed its filing system from handwritten dockets to computerized dockets and sent the paper records to a warehouse, which had apparently lost them.

Judges have little incentive to alter these cozy arrangements because a low-visibility controlling group tends to reach agreements that keep hard-to-handle issues off the judge's desk. As one federal judge told us, he had plenty to do as it was without inviting the public in to comment on what the controlling group had in mind. If others want to participate, let them find a way; he was not going to make his job more difficult by bringing them in.

THE CONTROLLING GROUP RULES THROUGH
LONG-TERM PLANS

Consent decrees typically embody long-term plans for the operation of the governmental institution that is the target of the suit. Typical arrangements include detailed specifications of tasks to be performed by particular people or offices, due dates and interim milestones, periodic reporting requirements, and an obligation to meet and iron out problems. The more detailed the instruction, the more powerful will be the controlling group.

PLAINTIFFS' ATTORNEYS HAVE THE DE FACTO POWER TO VETO MODIFICATIONS IN THE LONG-TERM PLAN

Minutely specified plans usually fail to work as hoped because life rarely proceeds as expected, especially in large, political organizations. Court-ordered plans that fail to work, or that appear less desirable when implementation later begins, present grave difficulties for defendants because they are responsible for the service provided to the public, yet they can be charged criminally for contempt of court if they willfully deviate from the decree and its plans. Defendants may try to escape this bind by asking the judge to modify the decree, but they are in for trouble if opposed by plaintiffs.

Under court rules, consent decrees are analogized to private contracts and a deal is a deal. Plaintiffs come to feel that even decrees dictating public policy are in fact contracts that cannot be changed quite apart from whether the violation that gave rise to the lawsuit in the first place has been corrected. Judges resist allowing modifications unless plaintiffs' attorneys consent, even if the term sought to be modified is unnecessary to correct a violation of law. The law of modifications requires more than a showing by the defendants that they have a better and perfectly legal way to serve their constituents. They must show that some "unforeseen circumstance" got in the way of their carrying out the consent decree-*cum*-contract, that they did not assume the risk of the change of circumstances in the original decree, and that the modification does not go beyond that which is necessary to accommodate the changed circumstances.[19] The upshot is that consent decrees are largely insulated from change by elected officials even though the decrees have not been ratified by either the legislature or the voters, and they include commitments that go beyond legal requirements or are irrelevant to them.[20] Because of this tough standard, plaintiffs' attorneys often hold a veto over changes as a practical matter and can use it to barter for further commitments or hold up change for long periods.[21]

Take, for example, *Escalera v. New York Housing Authority*.[22] The litigation began in 1967 with a complaint that the New York City Housing Authority failed to give adequate procedural due process to tenants who were delinquent on rent or broke Housing Authority rules. The problem was real, but the federal judge was not content to declare a violation of due process of law. That probably would have been enough to solve the problem because the tenants and the authority agreed on a new set of procedures before eviction that gave the tenants extra notice and assistance beyond constitutional minima. Instead of terminating the case, the lawyers for the tenants and the authority in 1971 submitted a consent decree to the federal judge that mandated the elaborate new procedures and ceded to the judge perpetual supervisory power over the procedures.

In 1993, twenty-two years later, crack cocaine had emerged as a serious issue. The New York City Housing Authority received urgent requests from tenants to evict those tenants who dealt drugs from their apartments. The authority wanted to invoke the Bawdy House Law, a special procedure available under state law that would allow rapid eviction of proven drug dealers who used their apartments for sales, yet still accorded them due process.[23] Legal aid attorneys, citing the twenty-two-year-old consent decree, objected. They were still attorneys of record and, on behalf of all tenants, argued that the special procedure was illegal because it varied from the more protracted procedure specified in the old decree. It took two years of intensive litigation before the Housing Authority was allowed to use the special procedures.

The courtroom scenes would have been comic if they had not been so tragic. Experts called by both sides battled over whether the advent of crack cocaine was sufficiently new and unexpected to warrant revising the old decree, whether living next door to a drug dealer actually increased the risk of criminal violence, and whether hiring more housing police might be a better solution, that is, "more suitable" than evicting drug dealers. After three days of testimony, Judge Loretta A. Preska issued a fifty-five-page opinion deciding that on balance it was permissible for the New York City Housing Authority to use the lawful, speedy procedures. While this litigation continued, the tenants, the purported beneficiaries of the old decree, lived with the danger and intimidation of drug dealers next door. The snarl of litigation so incensed the organization of elected representatives of all the tenants of the New York City Housing Authority that it hired new lawyers to fight on the side of the Housing Authority and against the lawyers who theoretically were representing them.[24]

HIGHER FEDERAL COURTS RARELY PLAY A ROLE

With most remedial decrees entered on consent, appellate courts get few opportunities to review lower court decisions. Consenting parties cannot appeal. If they later fail to perform and are cited for contempt, courts do not allow them to challenge belatedly the obligations to which they consented. Even if there is no consent, federal district court judges possess wide discretion to mold the remedial decree. The only way an unhappy party might appeal is to claim that the district court judge abused his or her discretion, a standard that is difficult to meet. The result is relatively little appellate review of the terms of remedial decrees, leaving the controlling group and the lower court judge with a virtual free hand.

THERE IS POTENTIALLY NO END

Decrees of twenty and thirty years' duration are common. This is the logical consequence of three forces: (1) statutes with impossibly high aspirations, (2) consent decrees that go well beyond the statutory or constitutional rights they supposedly vindicate, and (3) traditional court rules under which decrees cannot be terminated unless they are complied with, even if the violation of law that gave rise to the lawsuit has ended.[25] The upshot is that termination is often an impossible dream. Even defendants who work in good faith to satisfy the court find that decrees can last for decades.

The judicial process thus settles into a long-term control of public policy traditionally handled by the political branches. Public officials who may not even have been high school graduates when the decrees were negotiated find themselves locked in the grip of ancient plans enforceable in court. The process that *Jose P.* created could continue indefinitely. The court has never said what the New York City Board of Education must do to terminate supervision short of total compliance. Early on, Judge Nickerson rejected good-faith planning coupled with affirmative actions as the basis for ending supervision. Federal law offers no help at setting an end game because the key statute established such high performance goals that the board is likely to fall short of full compliance forever.

The absence of an end game is not as unsettling to the parties as an outsider might think. All of the main participants may have a stake in continuing, not ending, the process.

- *Many judges prefer the role of reformer to other judicial duties such as presiding over civil disputes and sentencing criminals.*
- *Plaintiffs' attorneys prefer to sit at the table as equal participants in policy making.* For this privilege, they are awarded attorneys fees paid out of public funds at high commercial rates rather than the much lower rates at which most of these lawyers or their govern-

mental counterparts are paid. Such streams of income at generous hourly rates are a huge boon, whether the funds go to the
attorneys' retirement account or causes they hold dear. For the
Wilder foster care case discussed in the Introduction, the City of
New York paid Marcia Lowry and other plaintiffs' attorneys $3.9
million in fees.[26] The case was settled in 1986; nevertheless, the
attorneys received the bulk of the payments, more than $2.1 mil-
lion, for work performed between June 1989 and January 1999,
during which their work consisted of monitoring the decree and
litigating whether the city had fully performed. In the later case of
Marisol A. v. Giuliani, filed in 1995 and settled in 1998, the court
ordered the City of New York to pay $5.8 million to Marcia Lowry
and the law firms assisting plaintiffs' attorneys. The trial court
accepted proof from plaintiffs' attorneys that they spent nearly
forty thousand hours in pretrial litigation and preparation for
the trial.[27] Special masters, monitors, and other court-appointed
participants not already on a government payroll get similar fees
at commercial rates along with power over government policy.

- *Mayors and governors are afraid to direct their attorneys to move
  for termination for fear of stimulating plaintiffs to launch a critique
  of their administration—one that could be highly publicized and
  may well induce additional dictates from the judge.* Better to mollify plaintiffs' attorneys than to rock the boat.
- *Lower-level officials from the agency being sued who chafe at ordinary bureaucratic restrictions gain valuable purchase on policy and
  budgets.* Government attorneys get away from the law books and
  get to make some policy themselves as members of the controlling group. Commissioners and other heads of departments keep
  the budgetary advantages that can come from being subject to a
  decree. To retain such advantages, defendants sometimes actively
  resist efforts to terminate the decree. In a 1998 opinion a California appellate court ended a long-standing decree over the objection of the San Francisco Unified School Board, the defendant in
  the case. The school board had a compelling financial incentive
  to depict its school system in the most dismal light, the court
  wrote, and to "admit" it was still in violation of the law.[28] In
  another recent case the Boston Latin School used a decree as a
  cover for its preferred admission policy that favored diversity
  over achievement long after the vestiges of discrimination that

had justified the decree had disappeared.[29] As Professor Deborah Rhode has noted, "defendants have depended on lawsuits to compel what they 'would *like* to do but lack the political courage to accomplish on their own.'"[30]

Even when court supervision ends, the consent decree itself does not necessarily end. As long as the decree has not been terminated, its terms can return to haunt defendants even decades later.[31] Judge Raymond J. Broderick, for example, in 1998 terminated court supervision but not the consent decree in *Pennhurst State School & Hosp. v. Halderman*,[32] one of the earliest (1974) and most cited institutional reform cases. The special master in the case reported that the state and county officials were substantially fulfilling their obligations under the decree and were acting in good faith. Despite this glowing assessment, the special master, along with the plaintiffs, asked the judge to keep the case alive pending another evaluation two years later. Judge Broderick said enough was enough and closed the special master's office but still left the consent decree in place so that it could be revived and enforced in the future.[33]

MEMBERS OF THE PUBLIC HARMED BY THE DECREE ARE OFTEN DENIED A FULL VOICE IN THE LITIGATION

Citizens harmed by decrees often find that they are denied a real voice in the litigation.[34] The named defendants may be governmental officials, but the real cost of complying with the decree falls on members of the public such as children who are *not* in need of special education. Those citizens who are affected have no real voice in litigation because only parties to the case can withhold their consent from a decree or appeal its entry.[35]

For example, Chinese-American parents in San Francisco became upset because a consent decree adopted in a desegregation case put their children at a disadvantage compared with African-American and white children in getting into the better public schools.[36] Although the court had named the Chinese Americans as part of the plaintiff class, they got no help from the attorneys supposedly representing them. The parents then tried to intervene in the case, but the judge denied their request. When they sought to bring their own case against the school board for discriminating against their children on the basis of their race, some thirty different attorneys from civil liberties groups and leading San Francisco law firms refused to represent them. The case was finally taken by a lawyer who specialized in bringing accident and securities cases and a liberal law professor. Once in court, the Chinese-American parents found that their claim for equality was opposed by the San Francisco NAACP, the main plaintiff organization, and by the city school board, the state education department, the court-appointed monitor, the court-appointed advisory committee, and the judge himself. The parents ultimately got relief for their children, but only after two appeals.[37]

People, like the Chinese-American parents, who learn that they may be hurt by a decree often find that the courthouse door is shut in their faces.[38] Interveners threaten the power of the controlling group and make it less likely that controversies can be settled by consent. The antipathy of those already in the case means that trying to intervene can be expensive. Many of those harmed by the decree do not even try. Those that do try often find that their request is denied, typically on the ground that they should have sought admission earlier.

The initial parties and the judge have a legitimate interest in preventing newly admitted parties from reopening previously decided issues. But the lateness of the latecomers is often not their fault. Court rules do not require that formal notice be given to the members of the public who would be hurt by a decree, and frequently they have no reason to know that they will be hurt until the decree is implemented.

The Federal Rules of Civil Procedure that govern intervention in federal court work perversely in institutional reform cases. Intervention is most likely to be granted, if at all, early in the case before liability is determined. But as Professor Chayes correctly pointed out in his article, the liability stage of public law litigation is the least important part of the case. The critical fact finding in public law litigation takes place *after* liability has been decided while the decree is being framed and implemented. Fact finding at that stage is ongoing because, as Chayes also pointed out, the court is engaged in policy making by trial and error. Deborah Rhode later echoed Chayes's analysis by adapting Winston Churchill's famous quote. Entry of a decree signals "not the end, nor even the beginning of the end, but only the end of the beginning of the remedial process."[39] Yet for most potential interveners the door to the courthouse is already locked.

The fault is not that the interveners are too late, too many, too diverse, too conflicting, or too costly. The fault is that judges think that courts are appropriate mechanisms for resolving policy issues with far-flung, long-lasting, ever-changing, widely felt effects. When a group of citizens discovers that a decree is now hurting them, they cannot get into the case without significantly disrupting the proceedings. In contrast, the elected branches are designed to hear complaints from the public at any time.

PLAINTIFFS' ATTORNEYS AND THE TRIAL JUDGE ARE
THE ONLY CONSTANTS—EVERYONE ELSE CHANGES

Defendants—governors, mayors, and commissioners—come and go, but plaintiffs' attorneys and the trial judge stay. In effect, the attorneys and their organizations end up owning the litigation and the issue. No policy can be adopted or advanced without their approval. People would be shocked if the insurance industry owned regulation of insurance companies or drug companies owned regulation of drugs. But single attorneys or small advocacy organizations own environmental, special education, or homeless policies by virtue of their command of the court orders. The Eastern Paralyzed Veterans Association owns the issue of accessibility in many jurisdictions, the Environmental Defense Fund owns DDT, the Children's Defense Fund and Children's Rights, Inc., own foster care, and so on. Even individual attorneys may own issues. Marcia Lowry, working for the Children's Rights Project out of New York City, in 1998 was counsel in thirteen foster care cases in eight states and the District of Columbia.[40]

There is deep irony in this. The modern concept of public interest law developed as a response to the sense that single interests in society should not be allowed to control the direction of public policy for all.[41] Yet through court decrees, these advocate-descendants of the early public interest lawyers have achieved a high level of entrenched control of public issues affecting entire communities.

AGENCIES CHARGED WITH ENFORCING STATUTES
RARELY PLAY A ROLE

Most federal court orders compelling local and state officials to comply with federal programs proceed with a federal judge as the only federal official participating. Congress officially designates a federal agency to manage each federal program, but in practice the hard work of management often gets downstreamed to plaintiffs and federal district court judges who labor without advice from or the presence of the expert federal agency. The federal Department of Education, the designated federal expert on special education, never made a court appearance in *Jose P.*, although *Jose P.* orders drove the special education programs in the largest school district in the country. Federal executive branch officials were not only invisible, they were rendered irrelevant because all the action took place in the private meetings of the local activists and officials of the New York City Board of Education.

As a technical legal matter, this happens because plaintiffs do not ask in their complaint for relief against the federal agency. They seek a remedy only against state and local officials whom they claim have denied plaintiffs their rights under the federal statute. As a result federal agencies stay out of private enforcement actions just as the federal Department of Education has in *Jose P.*

The absence of the federal agency does not bother plaintiffs, defendants, and the federal officials themselves, all of whom are happy that the federal agencies are left out. For plaintiffs, the presence of an expert federal agency would diminish their power. A federal agency wears a mantle of expertise bestowed by Congress. Judges are obligated to give deference to its interpretations and enforcement decisions. If a federal agency tells a judge that the state and local officials are doing an adequate job, are managing the program appropriately, or have prepared an acceptable remedial plan, plaintiffs will be less likely to get the judge to go along with their wishes. Plaintiffs would have to argue against the state and local officials on one side and the federal agency on the other, a two-front war that is difficult to win. A federal agency might also undercut plaintiffs' litigation position by interpreting or amending governing regulations. Active litigation by the federal agency would also mean fewer hours of work and lower fees for plaintiffs' attorneys. The justification for fees, the absence of official enforcement, is compromised with a federal agency on the scene.

Defendants have many of the same reasons for not wanting the federal agency in court. They, too, risk being boxed in by the federal agency and have even less chance of winning against a united plaintiff and federal agency. Even more threatening for state and local officials, an active federal agency could put federal funding at risk, a remedy most feared by defendants as well as by plaintiffs who count on the federal funds to pay for the rights they seek.

Federal officials do not mind being left out either. They are pleased to deliver the dollars to state and local officials but not so pleased to strictly enforce federal rules that are often impractical or imprecise. For federal officials, getting involved in a court action to enforce such rules risks exposing the puffery in the laws they proudly administer. In our air pollution case against New York City, for example, we tried to get the federal Environmental Protection Agency (EPA) to confirm to the district court that the city had failed to implement the Clean Air Act plans. This request caused immense problems for federal officials sitting in the EPA's regional offices across Foley Square from the courthouse. Many of the strategies in the federally approved plan were, even in the EPA's view, too extreme, and the congressional deadline was generally understood to have been unrealistic from the start. Adding to their discomfort, political leaders of the city and state were making it extremely hot for agency officials. Congress was at that time considering amendments to the Clean Air Act, and Washington EPA officials feared that strict enforcement by a regional office could jeopardize congressional support for the law or funding for the agency. Under these circumstances, agency officials did what any bureaucrat would do: they waffled before the court but privately urged us to continue our litigation because we could take the heat that they could not.

Agency behavior like this helps to hide the disconnection between law as written and reality. Compliance gaps and enforcement failures are less easily swept under the rug when the failures are those of the federal agency. When the EPA, for example, tried to tell states such as California that they had to restrict auto driving to meet federal air pollution standards, Congress deleted the requirement and switched instead to tighter controls on auto exhaust. Gaps and failure, however, can be and are swept under the rug when they come up in miscellaneous private enforcement actions around the country. The more that courts and their controlling groups absorb the problems that inhere in federal programs, the less likely that Congress will reconsider the issues.

Writing in 1976, Professor Abram Chayes was troubled by the new judicial role that he described. Nonetheless, he wrote that he "would concentrate not on turning the clock back (or off), but on improving the performance of public law litigation, both by practical attention to the difficulties noted in [his] Article and by a more systematic professional understanding of what is being done."[42] His measured approval of the new judicial role despite its many anti-democratic attributes pivoted on his greater desire for the judge-mandated outcomes that he and many others saw as more just, fair, and rational than the outcomes emanating from the political branches of government. This view still dominates much judicial thinking. Yet democracy by decree is not government by judges. Nor is it a government of laws or a government by the people. It is government by a few of the people—the controlling group. The widening gap between the theoretical rationale and hopes for democracy by decree and the practical results of court management in the field has become too prominent to ignore.

CHAPTER 6

A Good Thing Gone Wrong

Many people are drawn to a system of rights that promises to make government more trustworthy and compassionate. For them, democracy by decree stands for vindication of rights, while government-as-usual stands for the violation of rights. By this reckoning, the necessity of democracy by decree is proved by the very existence of the decree which supposedly reflects a judicial finding that government-as-usual cannot be trusted.

Government should honor rights, yet democracy by decree is a good thing gone wrong: It goes beyond the proper business of courts; it often renders government less capable of responding to the legitimate desires of the public; and it makes politicians less accountable to the public.

The Proper Business of Courts

Courts are justified in forcing government to honor rights because rights are, by definition, that to which their holders are entitled. Rights, to put it simply, trump ordinary policy considerations. Plaintiffs must allege violations of rights to get in the courthouse door, but the decrees ultimately signed frequently have little to do with enforcing rights and much to do with the policy preferences of the controlling group.

The perversion of court enforcement from rights enforcement to policy imposition is the fault not only of the controlling groups that negotiate the decrees and of the judges that enter them, but also of Congress. Congress enacts rights that cannot be fully honored. A traditional right, such as the right against government treating people differently on account of their race, can trump ordinary policy considerations because government can, as a practical matter, comply with that right in the real world. But many rights in modern statutes are aspirations rather than practical possibilities. No one really thinks these soft rights are like traditional rights—not even their beneficiaries.

This insight was driven home to one of us (Sandler), who, as a private attorney, represented JC Decaux, a hugely successful French company that builds and maintains freestanding, coin-operated public toilets located unattended on the sidewalks of more than a dozen European countries. Decaux sought in 1992 to do business in the United States but came up against the federal regulation that requires public facilities to be accessible to wheelchairs. In Europe, the company installed wheelchair-accessible public toilets but found that their large interior could be used for other purposes such as sleeping, crime, drugs, and sex. To maintain civility, Decaux limited access to the larger toilets. For New York, Decaux proposed that one in four toilets be wheelchair accessible, their doors opening with special tokens to be made available free to people in wheelchairs.

The issue came to a head in a formal presentation to Anne M. Emerman, then the city's director of the Office for People with Disabilities, and her advisory council, made up of people with various disabilities. Jean-François Decaux, the English-speaking son of the company's founder, explained the proposal to Emerman, who sat in a wheelchair behind a long conference table in her office in the Tweed Court House behind City Hall. She was flanked by members of an advisory council, some of whom were also in wheelchairs. They angrily rejected Decaux's proposal. The director and her advisory council were adamant: accessibility was a federal right; every toilet had to be accessible; no exceptions would be made.

Just as Decaux was about to leave, in walked another member of the advisory council whose disability was that he grew to be only about three feet high. When the director explained her decision to him, he objected. "I don't care about wheelchair accessibility," he said. "I can't reach the higher toilet seat in wheelchair-accessible toilets. What about that?" This elicited a discussion between Emerman and the newcomer that left Decaux and his team as mere observers. Emerman explained that wheelchair accessibility took precedence over accommodating other disabilities. The man argued back that he, too, had a right to be accommodated. The irony was apparent. First the director invoked federal law making accommodation a universal right, and then she immediately denied that right when confronted by a person with a different disability.

Accessibility for all disabilities at all locations is not a practical possibility. It is an aspiration. Congress may declare accessibility a right, but that does not settle whether all, most, or only some toilet facilities must be accessible and for what type of disability. Any allocation of accessibility would likely be found constitutional under the equal protection clause as long as government tried to draw the line fairly. Accessibility as a right requires policy choices and balancing not usually associated with rights. How, for example, should one provide accessibility to wilderness trails in national parks where accessibility would require motorized vehicles, or in landmarked buildings where preservation of the structure would permit accessibility only through a backdoor entrance? Government programs inevitably draw lines that separate those who benefit from those who do not, and not every problem must be solved at the same time. A statute that calls such choices of degree a "right" creates a soft right.

When Congress turns a policy choice into a soft right, state and local officials can no longer make the choices. Once a judge rules that a right has been violated, the judge has limited power to revise it in a contested case.[1] Courts can withhold injunctive relief if compliance would be impossible or cause great hardship, but not because it would be impractical or unwise.[2] That is a far cry from the freewheeling balancing of priorities characteristic of policy making. But balance is inevitably called for.

Even if judges were allowed to do the balancing, what they have to offer is not what policy making requires. They can offer logical judgment about logical problems, but policy making requires the political resolution of political disputes. That is why judges look to the controlling group to introduce flexibility into the decree and to shoulder responsibility for the compromises.

When Congress calls a policy choice a right, it shifts important policy-making power from elected officials to plaintiffs' attorneys. The controlling group's process is, in its own way, as political as the ordinary political process. The essential difference is that in its negotiations plaintiffs' attorneys hold the trumps. Power has shifted. The controlling group, in the words of Professor Colin Diver, uses "litigation less as a method for authoritative resolution of conflict than as means of reallocating power."[3]

Plaintiffs' attorneys often end up with enormous power. They play a pivotal role in deciding, for example, whether New York City must really spend $9 billion to improve its drinking water system. Large elements of this staggering sum are court mandated under statutes that create a right to clean water yet are less important than water projects that the city is voluntarily pursuing. One of these court orders, for example, compels the city to eliminate sewer pipes that carry both household waste and street runoff. In heavy rainstorms, the combined sewer lines carry flows so large that sewage bypasses treatment plants and is discharged into the surrounding waters. This raises pollution levels but is not a particularly severe problem because the receiving waters around New York City are large and salty and not used for drinking. To eliminate the combined sewer discharges the city plans to construct vast holding tanks to contain the overflow until treatment plant capacity becomes available. The cost to correct this problem is $1.4 billion.

The city would like to spend its limited capital on more pressing water-system projects not mandated by court orders, such as constructing a third tunnel to bring water into the city. Without a new tunnel, the failure of either of the two existing tunnels would jeopardize the supply of pure water for millions of people.

The city would also like to keep water charges within reasonable bounds. The mix of mandated, court-ordered programs and highly necessary but voluntary programs has pushed the costs so high that even the environmentalist attorneys who won the court orders question them. An attorney for the Environmental Defense Fund said that "it's logical to ask whether *we* have to do everything at the same time. Can *we* spread things out? Can *we* delay some of the investments?"[4] The royal "we" is appropriate because he and his colleagues have the power to govern. Without their approval, the court cannot shift money from the combined sewers to constructing a third water tunnel.

Granting plaintiffs' attorneys and other members of the controlling group so much power over government rests upon the premise that rights must be enforced. After all, we think that violating the law is equivalent to social deviance. But with democracy by decree, the violations are so numerous and the decrees so long lasting that violations are no longer necessarily deviations from the norm. The reasons for many, but not all, violations are no less socially legitimate than the desire for the rights in the first place, which is precisely why the judges let the controlling group modify them. The large number of decrees, their frequently superfluous reach, and their long duration call into question the way courts have responded to soft rights.

Hobbling Government

Court intervention saps the power and responsibility of governmental officials by limiting what they can do and by telling them what they must do. Along the way it hobbles government. Consider government by decree from the perspective of Commissioner Nicholas Scoppetta (Figure 6.1), the head of New York City's Administration for Children's Services (ACS) from 1996 to 2001, the agency responsible for forty thousand children in foster care and another four hundred thousand children potentially in need of protective services. He was an attorney in private practice when six-year-old Elisa Izquierdo was beaten to death by her mother in late 1995. Her death made headlines in New York City and stayed there when it came out that the Child Welfare Administration had failed to take the little girl into protective custody despite strong evidence that she was endangered and that this fatal omission was symptomatic of sloppiness within the city's child protective services program.

These revelations prompted Mayor Rudolph W. Giuliani to assume personal responsibility for solving the problem. He removed the child protection program from the New York City Human Resources Administration, put it on its own feet as a separate agency, and directed that its commissioner report directly to him. In January 1996 he appointed Scoppetta as the first commissioner of the ACS.

Scoppetta brought unique qualifications to the job. He had been a foster child himself in New York City in the 1930s, his parents being too poor to feed him. He worked his way through law school as a caseworker for the Children's Aid Society, played a starring role as a federal prosecutor in the real-life drama that later became the book and movie *Prince of the City,* and served with distinction in the 1970s as the city's commissioner of investigation, ferreting out crime and

Figure 6.1. Commissioner Nicholas Scoppetta. As commissioner of the New York City Administration for Children's Services, Scoppetta refused to consent to a decree controlling the city's foster care services.

inefficiency. Then for ten years as a private lawyer he chaired the board of the Children's Aid Society.

Commissioner Scoppetta and the team he assembled developed a detailed plan to reform the new agency. In December 1996, eleven months after taking over the ACS, he and the mayor released a report acknowledging the systemic failures of the agency and outlining a comprehensive reform program. Under the plan, caseworkers charged with protecting children would have smaller caseloads, better training, closer supervision, and state-of-the-art information systems. Each of these improvements went well beyond the marginal. For example, the ACS hired 1,425 new caseworkers who met heightened eligibility standards and reduced the number of children assigned to each caseworker from twenty-seven to twelve.[5]

In December 1995, just before Scoppetta's appointment, Marcia Lowry, the same lawyer who had handled the *Wilder* litigation discussed in the Introduction, filed a federal lawsuit, *Marisol A. v. Giuliani,* claiming that the city systematically violated constitutional and statutory duties to protect children from abuse. She had won judicial takeovers of child welfare agencies in Washington, D.C., and elsewhere and wanted the same done in New York City to accomplish what the *Wilder* case had failed to do over the prior twenty-two years.

Although the advocates including Lowry had previously wanted a court to appoint Scoppetta as a receiver in charge of New York's child services program and he was now in fact in charge of the program and had launched ambitious, expensive reforms, they pressed ahead with the litigation.[6]

Defendants in such a case would normally consent to a decree that imposed a detailed, long-term plan on the disputed governmental program. That is the course of least resistance. That is what was done in *Jose P.* Reaching an agreement in *Marisol* would have been easy. Plaintiffs would likely have consented to a decree that ordered the city to carry out Scoppetta's reforms because they provided the plaintiffs' attorneys with just about everything they could want except power. A consent decree would have given them power.

Commissioner Scoppetta adamantly refused to cede control, not because he lacked commitment to the same goals as plaintiffs' attorneys, but because he believed that ceding control would betray that commitment. He concluded that a decree would lock the city into a set of initiatives that were the best anyone could design but some of which would inevitably fail or even prove counterproductive.[7]

The control that plaintiffs' attorneys wanted would make them co-commissioners in fact. With a dual command structure, one in the city's offices and one in the plaintiffs' offices, clashes of ego and differences in constituencies would inevitably produce friction and conflict. Negotiations to revise the decree would end up encrusting it, as had happened in *Jose P.*, with new and revised bargains, compromises, and promises that might have little to do with the underlying law. Beyond that, every change in direction would take time because of the need for consultation, study, and negotiations. Running a large governmental institution requires constant brokering among the mayor's office, the controller's office, the city council, and the various agencies in charge of budget, personnel, and purchasing as well as various outside interests, such as unions and private foster care agencies. Reaching understandings with each of these other actors and making them dovetail is difficult enough without having to ask permission from side-saddle commissioners every step along the way.

Scoppetta had learned this lesson the hard way. A part of the *Wilder* decree dating from ten years earlier required that evaluations of foster care homes be completed within thirty days of the child's placement with the foster family and that they be done a certain way. During his examination of the agency's procedures, Scoppetta learned that sufficient information on whether a child should be left with the family could be assembled in three days. That would reduce risks to the children. To change the process, however, Scoppetta ran up against the old decree and its mandatory thirty-day process. Plaintiffs' attorneys, who controlled that decree, were skeptical, took a show-me attitude, and invoked litigation rights. It took Scoppetta ten months of painful and sometimes bitter negotiations to persuade plaintiffs' attorneys to approve the change. Meanwhile, the old system remained in place. An official with lesser commitment to protecting children might have given up. The new, shorter time frame opened Scoppetta to blame, while the old system gave him cover and protection. It took personal leadership to seek change in an institution where blame avoidance is too often job number one.

Democracy by decree hinders conscientious commissioners in other ways. Doing a good job for the public requires not only making good plans but motivating people to achieve common goals. Issuing commands is not enough. Agency personnel must feel that they can depend on the commissioner to reward good work and back up good-faith efforts that may go awry, as some inevitably do. Agency personnel are less able to trust a commissioner who must mollify outsiders with veto power. Scoppetta refused to share responsibility with plaintiffs' attorneys partly because he wanted to retain the ability to lead the agency's personnel.

Judges generally cannot provide the necessary leadership. Judges have plenty of power to punish, but none to reward. Democracy by decree works fine in pointing out what went wrong, but it works badly in putting things right.

Democracy by decree also inevitably leads to an emphasis on the quantifiable dimensions of the defendant's mission and deemphasizes the rest. In *Jose P.*, plaintiffs and defendants both proclaimed quality of education to be their main interest, but the litigation inevitably drove them to focus on the things that could be measured: the length of time taken to evaluate children and the size of the staff. Democracy by decree aggravates the unfortunate tendency of bureaucracies to focus on counting things rather than helping people.[8]

Democracy by decree aggravates another unfortunate tendency of bureaucracies: to give the highest pay and most prestige to those who write the instructions for others down the chain of command, or who check on compliance and prepare reports to go back up the chain of command. Yet it is those on the lower reaches of the chain of command who actually deliver the services that people need.

For Scoppetta, even getting advice from outside experts to help reform the agency was constrained by the pending litigation. He feared frank disclosure of the agency's problems to outside experts in order to get their advice because plaintiffs' attorneys could subpoena the same experts and force them to use Scoppetta's candor against him. Commissioner Scoppetta, with a mandate to reform his agency and contemplating a possible court takeover of his ACS, put it succinctly at a March 1999 seminar at New York Law School: "Litigation is not a way to reform a government institution."

By steadfastly maintaining this position, Scoppetta in late 1998 successfully negotiated a consent order that left full control of the remedy in his and the agency's hands as long as the agency in good faith advanced its own remedial plan. As Judge Robert Ward wrote in approving the arrangement, it was doubtful that any order prepared by the court would improve on the remedial plan that the agency had developed on its own. In another innovation, the parties and court agreed that even the inactive supervision of the court included in the decree would terminate after two years if the agency continued to demonstrate good faith for that period—a result that the agency achieved.[9]

That court decrees interfere with the operation of government is, of course, not the whole story. When government officials resist compliance with the law, the court ordinarily must impose the law on them, even if that takes a detailed decree. Overcoming intransigence and compelling compliance is what judges routinely do in private law litigation.[10] In public law litigation, however, defendants fail for many reasons besides intransigence. Governor Michael O. Leavitt of Utah in 1994 signed a foster care and child protective services consent decree of the kind that Commissioner Scoppetta rejected but regretted it two years later. He said that "the litigation has become a hindrance to our ability to fix the system, a diversion. It's the single part of my job that I find most difficult. We are dealing with social trends we don't control."[11]

Large public institutions have multiple, conflicting objectives. Power is widely diffused. Congressional mandates may be unrealistic. Quick action is difficult because of the necessity of going through legislation, rule making, competitive bidding, and civil service requirements, each of which is mandated to meet an objective other than efficiency. Perhaps most difficult of all, it is hard to reach the lower-level staff members who actually implement policy. When courts react to routine failure as if it were intransigence, they may succeed in focusing the attention of top leadership on the problem in court but at the cost of taking attention away from other problems, thus making government less responsive to the overall needs of the public.

Commentators may not agree on whether court decrees successfully change institutions, but they must still notice that court decrees regularly fail to achieve all of their promise and many do not come close. They cannot ignore that many decrees have yet to achieve their hopeful objectives despite having reached their twentieth or thirtieth year. Nor can they ignore the multitude of contempt proceedings plaintiffs repeatedly bring, nor the bulging files of modifications and amendments attached to decrees issued long ago. These realities are usually discussed as implementation problems, not as fundamental factors that throw into the question the entire enterprise of judicial management of governmental institutions. As one scholar has noted, the advocates of judicial control of institutional change treat problems of implementation as merely ones of effort, "like an orchestral conductor insisting that he can extract a splendid performance from his ensemble merely by flourishing a larger baton."[12]

Professor Gerald Rosenberg's *Hollow Hope*, attacking the claim that courts have brought about social change, argued that courts rarely matter.[13] Reviewers who challenge Rosenberg's thesis do not discount his position entirely. As one reviewer wrote, political and social forces outside the courtrooms are "infrequently studied and grossly underestimated. . . . Combined with inherent limits on the judiciary's power to manage reform, these nonjudicial forces suggest that social reform through litigation is a gamble. But these constraints speak to caution, not to the abandonment of court-initiated reform."[14] John J. DiIulio, Jr., in his study of failures and successes of prison decrees, noted that the successes were accounted for by small incremental advances and compromises rather than full-scale assaults.[15] His point is that the more judges act like legislatures rather than judges, the more likely they are to succeed. This advice, however valid, conflicts with the rights-based rationale for judicial intervention, which by definition calls for reform that is neither incremental nor compromisable and is geared solely to fixing the illegality.

The illegality is, of course, the legal hook that endows the controlling group with power. The long-term plans it writes into the decrees typically go well beyond fixing the illegality. Yet it usually turns out that successful reform is much more complicated than thought when the plans were originally spun, which is why the court and its controlling group remain in power.

Even the enthusiasts for democracy by decree have grown to doubt its efficacy and begun to search for new ways to achieve their goals for society. Our colleague Nadine Strossen, president of the American Civil Liberties Union, informs us that leading public advocacy organizations have shifted resources from litigation to lobbying, public education, political organizing, and other avenues of reform.[16] The most elaborate proposal has come from, ironically, the lead attorney in *Jose P.,* Michael Rebell.[17] For him, new techniques are necessary because the challenges faced in court go beyond the dimensions of the law. He uses as an example the conflict between the requirement of the federal special education statute to mainstream children with disabilities in regular classes whenever possible and the desire of many parents, teachers, and administrators to put them in special classes. Noting that some courts have been willing to, in effect, rewrite the law at the behest of the controlling group, Rebell proposes a way for more reluctant courts to take that leap.[18] He calls for courts to set up community meetings that would include students, parents, teachers, and administrators as well as representatives of civic, religious, and business institutions. The meetings would be led by what Rebell calls a "community dialogue organizer," in all probability either the plaintiffs' attorney or someone in sympathy with that attorney. The organizer would set the agenda for the group, which would then ratify decisions, monitor implementation, and evaluate results. The court in Rebell's model would be in the background, always ready to keep the process going and give orders. Such a process would, for Rebell, be better "than negotiations between the attorneys for defined class representatives and a school board."[19]

Rebell calls his proposal the "community engagement dialogic model." Every state and city already has a model for giving everyone in the community a voice in a dialogue led by organizers. These models are established by state constitutions and city charters, which put elected officials in charge of leading the dialogue. Rebell's proposal amounts to replacing these constitutions and charters with an amorphous process structured by plaintiffs' attorneys and the rest of the controlling group. Rebell's proposal makes manifest what was implicit all along in government by decree—rejection of democratically accountable government.

Democratically accountable government is rejected partly out of a belief in expertise. Experts obviously have much to offer in solving policy problems, and the controlling groups do make use of them. Yet we do not have to choose between giving up the help of experts and giving up on democracy. Elected officials also make use of experts. Their actions are not, of course, always completely dictated by the experts, but neither are the controlling groups' actions because expertise takes one only so far in deciding how to run a school system or other governmental institution. Expertise does not provide any right answers to the questions of priority that governments inevitably face. The choice is not between expertise and democracy, but whether those with the policy-making power should be wielded by the lawyers in the controlling group or by the politicians elected by the people. The lawyers in the controlling group want the power and the politicians often do not mind shedding the difficult responsibilities that go with it.

Another basis for rejecting democratically accountable government is disappointment with the results it produces. Advocates disparage Congress for failure to follow up on its grand ideals, disparage state and local legislatures for failing to fund them adequately, disparage agencies of state and local governments for failing to achieve those ideals, and disparage federal agencies for failing to enforce those ideals with sufficient zeal. To these advocates, every political actor is at fault but themselves. With democracy by decree they are free to blame everyone else and never have to acknowledge that their expectations are out of line with the world we live in.

Undermining Democratic Accountability

Democracy by decree undermines accountability of government to the voters. Democratic accountability is, in our constitutional scheme, not an unalloyed good. The framers of the U.S. Constitution recognized that a democratically accountable government may reflect bigotry or be inattentive to the people's needs or rights that they should have. For that reason, the Constitution includes rights and authorizes Congress to enact statutes necessary to ensure that state and local governments honor them. These are rights, not aspirational goals dressed up as rights.[20]

As long as rights are honored, everything else, including how the rights are honored, is a question of policy to be left to elected officials. The Constitution and its state and local counterparts set up the ground rules for how policy should be made. These ground rules are designed with careful attention to the potential faults of people and those they elect. The guiding principles are division of power and accountability.

Division of power is required because of distrust of both the people and those whom the people elect. Power is divided, first of all, between those who are empowered to govern and those who are governed. Those who are governed retain the power to vote the elected out of office. The power of those who govern is further divided many ways—between the federal government and the states, and within each level of government among the legislature, the executive, and the courts. Inherent in the whole scheme is that elected officials should bear the responsibility for the key policy choices and must retain the power to change policy.

Although this system is far from perfect, democracy by decree makes it worse. It does not substitute the dispassionate rule of judges for the rule of politicians. Decisions by controlling groups are politics in a different form. By hiding ordinary politics behind the robes of judges, democracy by decree makes government much less accountable and therefore less responsive. Judicial reason does not supplant politics. Instead, the courts become political. As Professor Donald Horowitz foresaw in his early study of courts and social policy, "the danger is that courts, in developing a capacity to improve on the work of other institutions, may become altogether too much like them."[21]

Accountability depends on the ability of elected officials to change policy in response to elections and society's changing needs. Under democracy by decree, past policy victories get cemented into decrees that frustrate necessary and healthy reconsideration of policies. Power is actually exercised by the controlling group.

The problem begins with Congress. As the Supreme Court wrote in the 1997 case overturning a portion of the Brady Handgun Violence Prevention Act: "By forcing state governments to absorb the financial burden of implementing a federal regulatory program, Members of Congress can take credit for 'solving' problems without having to ask their constituents to pay for the solutions with higher federal taxes. And even when the States are not forced to absorb the costs of implementing a federal program, they are still put in the position of taking the blame for its burdensomeness and for its defects."[22] Having shifted the blame for costs and disappointments to federal judges and state and local officials, the national legislators feel no need to consider the consequences of their past handiwork. Their response to the impossibility of its curb ramp mandate was, in essence, "What, me worry?" Even if legislators did worry, it would be hard for them to moderate their past commitments because they had put them in terms of rights.

It is said in defense of judicial management that courts can change a decree, but court limitations and rules make it difficult for a decree to be terminated or modified unless the plaintiffs consent. In *Jose P.,* for example, even though the New York City Board of Education objected to the entry of the decree on the basis that it wanted to retain the option to revise the Gross Program, and even though the special master indicated in approving the proposed decree that the program could be changed in light of experience, the board found that it was stuck with the terms as entered unless the plaintiffs consented. As Professor Horowitz puts it, "courts suffer from an unusual poverty of resources to minimize the incidence of unintended consequences in advance and especially to detect and correct them once they occur."[23]

Plaintiffs' attorneys do not see themselves as the cause of such problems because they sincerely think of themselves as having good intentions. Plaintiffs' attorneys are, of course, not alone in identifying the goodness of their intentions with the good of humankind.

The framers of the Constitution thought this mistake inherent in all human nature, including their own, and certainly a characteristic shared by the zealous as well as the greedy.[24] It was with such self-understanding that the framers designed a form of government to temper the dangers of such conceits.

The controlling group lacks the safeguards that the framers built into the political process. Our representative democracy is founded on "one person, one vote." Democracy by decree is founded on "one plaintiffs' attorney, one veto."

Another constitutional safeguard is that legislative policy judgments be made in the open. The controlling group prefers to make public policy behind closed doors.

Still another safeguard is that any department of government that wants more money or power must get the explicit approval of a general legislature. It is the inevitable tendency of people in charge of particular governmental programs to attach inflated importance to their own doings. By forcing all project directors and special interests to compete for funds and authority in one legislative process, egos and interests would tend to thwart each other.[25] In contrast, democracy by decree gives the controlling group preemptive power over how much money and power to put at its own disposal.

The controlling group of course also includes representatives of the defendants, but usually neither elected officials nor those directly appointed by them. Plaintiffs' and defendants' representatives, although opponents in the courtroom, have a mutual interest in building up the budget and power of the government agency that is the target of the lawsuit. Officials of state or local agencies often have more in common with plaintiffs than they do with the voters or even their own mayors, governors, budget offices, or local legislatures. As Judge Morris Lasker once told a high New York City prison official whose testimony was undercutting the city's defense, "Sometimes I really wonder . . . whether the defendants themselves shouldn't be represented by separate counsel, about whether there is a conflict of interest between the Commissioner of Corrections, for example, and the Mayor of the City, and I don't know in this particular line of questioning who you represent."[26]

The participants in the controlling group use the court to shield from scrutiny deals that serve their own interests through the constitutionally mandated mechanisms for holding government accountable to the broad public interest. The victims of this collusion are the subsequently elected officials, who find their options restricted, and the public, who cannot hold officials accountable for decisions locked into decrees.

There is a real irony here. Public law litigation began with broad-based rights such as equal protection and due process. The congressional rights agenda, however, created group rights, not general rights. When these groups enlist judges willing to manage public policy through controlling groups, they effectively take over their categorical program and remove it from general governmental control. Court rules that ensure all citizens equal protection become special pleading when invoked by groups against society.

Professor Jeremy Rabkin, in his book analyzing the analogous topic of judicial control of federal agencies, wrote that the "more government is accountable to private litigants, then, the less it can be accountable to anyone else. . . . [L]imiting the choices of government officials limits their responsibility, for they cannot be responsible for choices they are not allowed to make." Rabkin concludes that "courts can only insulate policies in pieces, and then not for the benefit of the general public but for the satisfaction of particular interest or advocacy groups." These groups then "invoke legalistic rationales to protect their preferred polices from reconsideration or adjustment over time."[27]

There is still another problem with democracy by decree: voters lose the ability to communicate with government. Democracy by decree shifts power from the village council, city hall, and statehouse to bureaucracies in Washington and the courtroom. When elected officials at the state and local levels make decisions, the power of special interests is offset in part by the ease with which voters can approach their representatives and the credibility of the threat that a small group of angry voters can make a real difference at the next election. It is much harder for voters to approach federal bureaucrats and judges, neither of whom are elected. Influencing federal bureaucrats requires a lobbying/litigating operation in Washington. Influencing judges requires intervening in a lawsuit. Court rules exclude many concerned interests from meaningful participation. Normally, only official litigants get to speak. Always, only official litigants get to make motions, offer evidence, and appeal.

Citizens with a palpable interest in the outcome of the court's policy making often cannot intervene. Some, like children not classified as having disabilities, do not qualify under the rules of court procedure. Even if they do, they may lack the funds to hire a lawyer. Many federal statutes compensate successful citizen litigants for their attorneys' fees, but compensation is available only to citizens who intervene on the side of plaintiffs, not the government.

Democracy by decree, in the end, privileges those groups and interests that have the tight organizations and sophistication needed to get Congress to pass a federal statute that creates rights, and then to follow up with litigation leading to a decree enforcing that right. The great mass of less organized and sophisticated interests and the public at large get no seats at this judicially managed, invitation-only table of government. Democracy by decree, which is justified by opening up government to those who have been disenfranchised, ends up disenfranchising others—the very sorts of people that the public interest bar claims to represent.

Voters lose their ability to communicate with government for another reason: democracy by decree shifts attention from the concerns of local voters to the preoccupations of technocrats. The technocrats engage in a prolonged process to specify comprehensive, universally applicable solutions to policy problems. The process typically begins with a detailed federal statute, then yet more detailed regulations from a federal agency, and then state-by-state plans of action. All of this is planning and thus only foreplay to action to solve the problem. When the federal or state requirements come to be violated, enforcement proceedings begin. Litigation proceeds at its own slow pace until still more elaborate and sometimes different requirements are imposed in a judicial decree. Only with the issuance of the decree do the state and local officials truly get their final marching orders, and they are stated in technobabble at many removes from what prompted voters' concerns in the first place.

In *Jose P.,* for example, concrete concerns for special education got turned into a contest between education experts and lawyers over whether bureaucrats had violated a certain regulation or missed a particular milestone. Practical issues disappeared into legal technicalities and bureaucratic outputs: deadlines hit, psychologists hired, evaluations performed, placements made. These bureaucratic measures were at best surrogates for the educational quality that the public wanted, but they were all that the courts could measure.

Who can the people hold accountable for *Jose P.*? The series of chancellors who tried to meet federal standards and failed? Congress, which set the standards in the first place but left all of the hard choices to the states, and then reneged on the money? The judge and special masters who said they were following Congress's lead but delegated the remedy to the controlling group? It "makes it that much easier," in Professor Peter Schuck's words, "for everyone—legislators, bureaucrats, judges, lawyers, and litigants—to disclaim [responsibility]. The buck stops nowhere. . . ."[28]

Parents of all children, with disabilities and without, demand quality education. Their greatest strength in getting what they want lies in holding officials accountable in elections. Democracy by decree undermines that strength by diffusing accountability and fragmenting operational control.

In *Jose P.* the social and political support that prompted Congress to act in the first place came from the desire of citizens to do the right thing by children with disabilities. That desire was and is there and would have been felt by members of a local school board even if Congress and the courts had not gotten into the act. What did change when Congress imposed its mandate was who got the credit and who got the power.

What also changed was that we lost the opportunity to get a better understanding of our own desires. We understandably but naively favor rights and benefits and disfavor costs and inconveniences. Democracy by decree hides our own ambivalence from ourselves. Our contrary desires are represented by two separate camps: plaintiffs with rights and defendant-officials with duties. We do not recognize these opposing parties in the lawsuit as components of ourselves.

Policy conflicts, once shifted from matters of pragmatic accommodation to matters of high principle, become irreconcilable. The parties in their role as the controlling group can, in drafting a decree, agree on pragmatic measures to be taken in the near term, but these are almost never enough to lift the legal and moral cloud that hangs over state and local governments. The decree must always call for further steps to vindicate the high principle. Because the principle is usually so high as to be unattainable, the decree and the complications it spawns stretch out into the indefinite future. Each case becomes a legal bramble.

Plaintiffs and their lawyers can have it no other way. What turns otherwise ordinary citizens into powerhouses in federal court with special claims on government and an entitlement to attorneys' fees is the asserted ownership of high principle. It is sacred and golden and must be defended. Peace becomes impossible.

Americans learned once before that peace is what we lose when we cease relying on democratic processes to reconcile our conflicting desires and turn instead to courts acting on supposed high principle. When in the 1930s a conservative Supreme Court tried to thwart the liberal New Deal, the result was a crisis. It was that crisis that moved Justice Robert Jackson to write in 1941 that "the vice of judicial supremacy . . . has been its progressive closing of the avenues to peaceful and democratic conciliation of our social and economic conflicts."[29] Sixty-two years later, democracy by decree as invoked by liberal reformers has the identical effect of closing the avenues to peaceful and democratic conciliation of our social and economic conflicts.

CHAPTER 7

Why the Wrong Thing Continues

Court enforcement against state and local governments would have remained a good thing and not gone wrong if district court judges had stuck to their proper role. That role, according to the Supreme Court, limits district courts to protecting the rights of injured plaintiffs and respecting the policy-making prerogatives of elected officials. These traditional restraints have had little purchase on many of the lower court judges when they are presented with actual cases. There, in the district courthouses, a strikingly different culture has evolved. It accepts an expansive responsibility for managing social change and is squarely at odds with the norms enunciated by the Supreme Court.

The Split Between Supreme Court Principles and Lower Court Practice

The principles laid down by the Supreme Court have two overriding objectives. First, courts should limit their decrees to their one and only legitimate purpose—a demonstrated necessity to protect plaintiffs from illegal injury. And second, even when a decree is necessary, courts must strike a balance between protecting plaintiffs and allowing governments to function. There exists, however, a great divide between these principles and the practices of lower courts:

- *The Supreme Court holds that decrees are solely for remedying violations of rights.*[1] Nonetheless lower courts regularly enter decrees that advance policy agendas extraneous to the protection of violated rights and impose requirements far beyond the rights in question. In *Jose P.,* for example, Judge Nickerson was not content to remedy the only violation admitted in the case—the failure to screen and place special education students by the state-imposed deadlines. Instead, he signed decrees directed at rights that had not been shown to be violated and to achieve policies that were not rights at all but simply the policy creations of the controlling group. Judges in prison condition cases typically went beyond correcting constitutional violations to impose their own ideas of good prison policy, and judges in school desegregation cases frequently sought to end not only government-imposed segregation but also the effects of individual choice not traceable to government action.[2]

- *The Supreme Court holds that decrees are solely for protecting plaintiffs.*[3] Nonetheless lower courts regularly enter decrees to protect not only plaintiffs, but everybody. In *Jose P.,* a case originally brought in the name of those denied special education, the court extended relief beyond special education to protect rights violated under another statute, the Americans with Disabilities Act. Similarly, in prison cases brought by individual prisoners, judges often expanded remedies to all the prisoners.[4]

- *The Supreme Court has long held that decrees are for protecting only those plaintiffs faced with imminent injury.*[5] Nonetheless, lower courts frequently issue decrees to protect all potential plaintiffs without regard to whether they are threatened. In one such case reaching the Supreme Court the trial judge issued a detailed decree in favor of thousands of prisoners when, upon closer examination, the Supreme Court found that only two prisoners had suffered actual injury. The Supreme Court, in reversing this broad injunction, held that the court's only legitimate role was to provide relief to those threatened with actual injury.[6] The lower courts have largely ignored this holding except in prison cases.[7]

- *The Supreme Court has held repeatedly that lower courts should give priority to letting state and local governments function.*[8] As it stated in *Milliken v. Bradley,* federal courts "must take into account the interests of state and local authorities in managing their own affairs. . . ."[9] Although this principle is a staple of law school learning, it nonetheless gets scant attention in the lower courts.[10] In *Jose P.,* Judge Nickerson generally overlooked this principle. In prison cases, many judges have systematically brushed aside state and local control.[11]

- *The Supreme Court has maintained that in framing relief lower courts should give due deference to the policy judgments of state and local officials on how to obey the law.*[12] As the Supreme Court stated: "it is not the role of courts, but that of the political branches, to shape the institutions of government in such fashion as to comply with the laws and the Constitution."[13] Nonetheless, in *Jose P.,* when confronted with policy disagreements between the plaintiffs and the defendants about how best to vindicate plaintiffs' rights, the court frequently sided with the plaintiffs' policy preferences rather than defer to the defendants. Similarly, in prison cases, lower federal courts often call the shots rather than defer to the elected branches of state and local governments.[14]

- *The Supreme Court has said that lower courts should avoid imposing decrees that require technically complex and evolving policy choices, especially in the absence of judicially discoverable and manageable standards.*[15] Nonetheless lower courts regularly enter decrees that require ongoing surveillance of matters that are highly subjective or technical.

Professor Donald Zeigler, a colleague of ours at New York Law School who had once been a legal aid lawyer battling governments in institutional reform cases, commented on reading an early draft of this chapter that "maybe the disconnect has more to do with the difference between sitting in Washington writing lofty opinions and actually getting immersed in the facts of a real case. Prisons are hellholes." He continued: "I don't think you begin to understand the level of bad faith that states and cities exhibited in the prison cases of the 1970s and 1980s. The judges were not hasty and liberal, but also came from Republican and conservative law firms. And shouldn't the mayors and governors have been more careful about what they consented to in the first place?"

Our colleague's appeal has emotional punch because it plays directly to the district court norm of problem solving and the view that judges and public interest attorneys are the best and most powerful commanders to lead social change. Yet his arguments still beg the question of why district courts do not follow the espoused norms of the Supreme Court. The answer lies in the culture of the lower courts and the lack of a structure strong enough to bridge the gap between the espoused values of the Supreme Court and the actions of the lower courts.

Loose Appellate Supervision

Federal judges are prone to the human failing of thinking that they know better. Taught to believe in rationality as the way to solve policy problems, they tend to look down their noses at the work-a-day politicians who habituate city hall and the state capitol. According to Judge Ralph Winter, many judges "feel hostility to a pluralist, party dominated political process" and believe in a need for "rationality in public policy."[16] Plaintiffs' attorneys come to court as the tribunes of such rationality. Compounding the tilt in favor of supplanting ordinary government at the behest of plaintiffs' attorneys, the federal judge is apt to be presented with moving scenes of great harms to plaintiffs and obvious failings by defendants. For the judge, the understandably felt urgency to solve the problem is apt to distract attention from the abstract concern of letting government function.

On appeal, it is hard for appellate courts to discover whether a district judge has stuck to enforcing rights or unnecessarily wandered into policy making. The Supreme Court has yet to put in place an effective mechanism for enforcing its own rules. Drafting decrees is a notoriously detailed business. Doing it right calls for many close calls of judgment that leave plenty of room for covert policy making. The idea of putting plaintiffs in their rightful position is clear in concept, but its application in practice is subject to manipulation. The traditional idea allows the remedial decree to repair tomorrow the consequences of yesterday's violations, a concept that gives the court wide discretion in the typical institutional reform case. For example, where prisoners have suffered past unconstitutional prison conditions, judges may order offsetting benefits in the future to compensate for the irreversible harm done in the past.[17] No clear criterion controls the court's choice of the kind of benefit, its extent, or its duration so that the concept of repairing past damages can be used to justify a wide variety of judicial policy choices on how to run the institution of local government that is before the court.

If the judge believes that the defendant is likely to evade the decree, the court is allowed to give plaintiffs more than their rightful position. The rationale of preventing evasion justifies intrusive decrees that specify, for example, the water temperature in prison showers, the brand of soap to be used on prison floors, the frequency with which prison windows are washed, and other minutiae.[18] The theory is not that the Constitution speaks in such detail but that the court needs to make the decree sufficiently specific to be readily enforceable against recalcitrant defendants. Because the court gets to make the judgment calls about the risk of covert violation and the terms of the prophylactic measures required, the court has wide scope to use the decree not only to protect rights, but also, illegitimately, to impose policy.

State and local defendants who object find it hard to get help from appellate courts under current court doctrines. Plaintiffs' attorneys will defend the decree as merely enforcing their clients' rights. To overturn the decree, defendants would have to show that the trial judge's entry of the decree was an abuse of discretion.[19] This tough standard is especially difficult to meet when the trial judge's action was the product of so many judgment calls.

Judge Sonia Sotomayor, who is now an appellate federal court judge but who before sat on the federal court in Manhattan, recently contrasted the difference between how a district court judge and an appellate court judge think. A lower court judge knows that less than 20 percent of the cases are appealed, that the facts found will be accepted unless clearly wrong, and that what is done in the case will affect only those parties and does not become a precedent binding other cases. A lower court judge is more likely to do "justice," solve problems, and look to outcomes. An appellate court judge, however, knows that the higher court's decisions bind all the lower courts in the circuit. That puts a greater burden on the appellate judges to be careful about what they do and say.[20]

Consent

When a remedial decree is entered on consent, the lack of appellate supervision is total. Parties cannot appeal a decree to which they consented. Even if defendant officials change their minds or new ones come into office, they cannot later appeal because appeal is allowed only for a short period immediately after entry of the decree (Figure 7.1).[21] If defendants wait until they want the decree modified or terminated, or until they are brought up on charges of contempt for violating it, the appellate court generally says that they are too late.[22]

It is perfectly rational for mayors and governors to consent to decrees that go further than needed to enforce the laws. They get rid of a political problem for the moment and often postpone the most onerous part of compliance to a time when they hope to have gone on to higher office, or at least gotten themselves reelected. What is rational from the perspective of the consenting officials is often

"There are times when I feel that I may have filed my appeal a bit late."

Figure 7.1. New York City Mayor Abraham D. Beame's misfortunes as portrayed by Paul Rigby in the *New York Post* in 1977. In a case we brought, the federal court had just ordered the mayor to ban parking in the Manhattan business districts to comply with federal clean air requirements. The cartoonist is making the point that Mayor Beame did not file a timely appeal when the federal requirements were first put in place. In fact, the only time to appeal occurred four years earlier in 1973 when John V. Lindsay was mayor. Mayor Beame never had an opportunity to appeal his predecessor's decision.

irrational from the perspective of their constituents and successors in office who must bear the costs and face the problems of compliance.[23]

Defending lawsuits carries risks beyond losing and embarrassment. Plaintiffs can invoke expansive discovery under federal court rules. They might inspect facilities normally closed to the public, take depositions under oath from elected and appointed officials, and obtain confidential official documents. Discovery risks unpredictable legal and political consequences, and rarely proves elected officials to be saints. Settlement allows officials to gain control over what will be disclosed and how.

Litigation is also risky because a judicial finding of violation in a federally funded program can result in funds being cut off. A cutoff, however unlikely, would have fiscal and political consequences so grave that even a small risk of it makes most state and local politicians blanche.

Officials who do not settle also risk being deprived of the powers of their office. Judges have taken the extraordinary step of appointing monitors to recommend or dictate remedies and, in rare cases, receivers who literally take over governmental programs altogether.[24] Settlement, in contrast to litigation, has real positives. By agreeing with public interest attorneys, defendant officials transform themselves from lawbreakers into reformers.[25] They escape having to defend the mistakes of the past and switch to announcing reforms for the future. Pennsylvania's secretary of education explained to Congress why his state consented to a decree covering special education rather than defend the state's laws and policies: "[We] took a look at the facts," he said, "and concluded that indeed it was not possible to say that in fact we were providing appropriate education. Governor [Milton] Shapp then asked me and the Attorney General to work with [plaintiffs and the court] in developing an appropriate Consent Decree."[26] Note that he did not say that the state's laws were unconstitutional or unlawful, just that the educational outcomes were not to their liking. Their quick settlement prevented the court from adjudicating whether any state laws were actually unconstitutional.

Settlement is especially tempting when elected officials can blame the past administration or put off more onerous remedies to the next administration or at least until after the next election. In 1989, for example, New York City mayoral candidate David N. Dinkins sought gay and lesbian support in New York City in part by promising to provide domestic partners of city employees with the same health benefits that spouses of employees receive. After his election he found that he could not deliver on the promise because the city council refused to authorize costly benefits for the large number of primarily heterosexual domestic partners who would also qualify under the proposed law. Fed up with the legislative logjam, the Lesbian and Gay Teachers Association filed a lawsuit claiming that the city was required to provide such benefits under various human rights laws and constitutional provisions. The city under Mayor Dinkins vigorously disputed the claim, but before the courts decided who was right, and just a few days before the 1993 mayoral election in which he was a candidate for reelection, Dinkins consented to a state court order purporting to bind the city in perpetuity to providing benefits to domestic partners and their children despite the lack of approval from the city council. He lost the election anyway, but the duty to comply continued into the next administration.

Government officials, who always operate under fiscal and political constraints, "frequently win by losing," as Professor Margo Schlanger put it.[27] When an expense finds its way into a court order, it leaps to the top of the budget priorities and must be funded. Budgeteers reluctantly honor court-ordered programs as uncuttable. Program costs shift from optional to mandatory expenditures. Being subject to a decree may even bring added funding, as the *New York Times* noted in discussing foster care class activities.[28] For an agency head, these possibilities offer seductive opportunities to insulate programs from ordinary budget processes. Plaintiffs' counsel are equally complicit in this, being even more outspoken in seeking to insulate programs.

Negotiations also open up the possibility for removing or modifying unrealistic or noxious federal requirements and substituting more favorable ones. Often this involves deadlines long since past, as with curb ramps. But the possibility is not limited to dates: any obligation is fair game.

Plaintiffs' counsel, of course, have many reasons of their own to settle, and they develop their litigation strategy around tactics that will keep the defendants moving as quickly as possible in a direction leading to a favorable settlement. An early consent decree brings quick relief, less work, certain victory, and fees.

Judges also want settlement, and they pressure defendants to consent. Otherwise, the judges must squarely shoulder responsibility for difficult and touchy policy choices. Better to approve a decree that the parties drafted. The judge thus gains protection from editorials and articles excoriating the decree and avoids reversal by appellate judges. Justice Antonin Scalia in 1996 berated a lower court judge for imposing an "inordinately—indeed, wildly—intrusive" prison reform decree on the nonconsenting State of Arizona and for failing to "give adequate consideration to the views of state prison authorities."[29] The same provisions, had the state consented, would have been unappealable and binding. As one federal judge wrote exonerating himself when signing an especially far-reaching consent decree, the decree was "not drawn up by a remote federal court, rather it was prepared in large part by the most talented local experts in the [state], the defendants themselves."[30]

The consent of the defendants is no guarantee that the decree benefits the public. Politicians are regularly tempted to sacrifice the long-term public interest for their own short-run private political gain. One device popular in the nineteenth century was to use the public's credit to borrow large sums of money for projects that would bring immediate political benefits. The debt would, of course, have to be repaid, but that would come later when the politician who benefited no longer needed the public's support. After many mayors and governors impoverished their governments through such time-shifting tricks, state constitutions and city charters were loaded with provisions designed to make it harder for politicians to impose ill-conceived long-term debt on their constituents.[31] The absence of similar limitations on consent decrees opens the door for political manipulation by officials acting in concert with plaintiffs.

The Supreme Court, of course, shrinks from baldly asserting

that a trial judge may enter any decree to which a defendant consents. To make consent decrees look like the proper work of courts, the high Court says that the trial judge must look to see whether the case is within the trial court's subject matter jurisdiction and whether the decree furthers the objectives of the lawsuit and relates to the general scope of the pleadings.[32] These are exceptionally loose standards. The judge must also find that the decree is fair, reasonable, and in the public interest. To say that a trial judge must do "nothing" before entering a consent decree would, according to Professor Owen Fiss, "be a bit of an exaggeration, but not much."[33]

Because courts do little to vet consent decrees, their justification for signing them is that the defendants have consented.[34] The consent of a private party concerning private matters may well be enough to justify an unnecessarily broad decree because private parties are generally entitled to dispose of their own rights as they wish. But this logic does not carry over to cases against government and government officials.

Government lawyers, mayors, or governors are not entitled to give away the right of the people to a democratically accountable, constitutional government. It is the people, after all, who must bear the costs of the decree and live with its consequences. Individuals duly elected or appointed as representatives of the general public are authorized to act for their constituents for a limited period of time and only by acting in ways sanctioned by the state constitution or local charter.[35] The annals of democracy by decree are full of cases in which defendants consented to a decree in order to avoid responsibility for politically difficult choices or to evade constitutional requirements for legislative action.[36]

The principle that drives representative democracy is that voters should have the power to pressure incumbents to change policy or replace them with successors who will. For that reason our federal and state constitutions and city charters do not let legislators and chief executives contract away their own power or that of their successors in office to change policy.[37] Neither the national Constitution nor the state constitutions allow one legislative session to bind the next, by either law or budgetary appropriation.[38] Public policy must always be up for grabs. Democracy by decree, however, acts as if officials can give particular interest groups impregnable entitlements that are immune from ongoing reconsideration.

There are exceptions to the general rule that government may not contract away the power to change policy, but they are narrow. For example, government may not grant property and then take it back again. Government may enter into contracts to purchase goods or services, but this power to contract is confined to business rather than governmental matters. Although this distinction leads to hard cases, any way of drawing the distinction yields the unmistakable conclusion that a "contract" designed to reform a governmental institution clearly falls on the wrong side of the line.

Even the exception for business contracts fails to justify the ongoing enforcement of overly broad remedial consent decrees over the objection of governmental defendants. Most governments require that contracting officials insert in contracts a clause allowing the government to cancel for "convenience," without giving a reason.[39] The contractor is entitled to damages for expenses incurred, but not anticipated profits, and is explicitly barred from getting an order to enforce the contract.[40]

Here we must acknowledge that the Supreme Court itself has muddied the water. It ratified a consent decree in a voting rights case on the consent of the state attorney general who under the state constitution lacked authority to act. In *Lawyer v. Department of Justice*, the state attorney general consented to a judicial redistricting of the Florida legislature, and the court approved the decree although the state constitution explicitly gave authority for approving new districts only to the state legislature.[41] Mr. Lawyer (that was his

name) objected that this was done without the trial court determin-
ing that the old apportionment was illegal. The Supreme Court
upheld the consent decree in a five-to-four decision.[42] For the court
majority, the democratically accountable way of doing things was
simply an inconvenience to be swept out of the way on the premise
that the defendant had consented.

Hurdles to Modification or Termination

The Supreme Court's own rules for modifying and terminating decrees lock government into overbroad decrees with little hope for
revision or escape. A consent decree is like a maze: it is easy to enter,
but hard to exit.

Courts have good reason to make it hard for private parties to
revise decrees against themselves, whether the decrees have been
imposed after litigation or entered into by consent. Judges understandably wish to avoid reopening old issues or upsetting the bargains on which the parties relied. For such reasons the Supreme
Court announced in a 1932 case against private defendants that a
defendant wishing to get a decree modified had to show not only
changed circumstances, but also that the changed circumstances
caused it a "grievous wrong."[43] Except in unusual circumstances, a
private business that has consented to an overbroad decree is stuck
with the deal.

The Supreme Court revisited this issue in its 1992 decision in
Rufo v. Inmates of Suffolk County and made it slightly easier for
governmental defendants to get a decree modified, but not enough.
In 1979, Suffolk County, Massachusetts (which includes Boston),
consented to a decree requiring that it replace an old, inadequate jail
with a new one in which every prisoner would have his own cell.
Eleven years later, with its prison population soaring, the county
asked that the court modify the decree to allow two prisoners in

a cell because the Supreme Court had since ruled that double bunking is constitutional. With these facts before it, the court held that the county could not double bunk prisoners because it had made a bargain years earlier and the harm that it now caused was not grievous.[44]

On review the Supreme Court recognized that this grievous harm test made no sense in cases against governmental defendants. It modified the rule to allow a party in an institutional reform case to secure a modification if it could demonstrate both an "unforeseen" significant change in circumstances and that the proposed modification was suitably tailored to the changed circumstances.[45] The Court believed that any less rigid rule would dissuade plaintiffs from negotiating settlements.

The Court did not go far enough. If the decree was broader than needed to put plaintiffs in their rightful position, the courts have no legitimate basis for holding subsequent officeholders to the old decree. The unspoken but illegitimate premise of the Supreme Court's test is that officials have contracted away the power of their successors to change government policy.[46] This cannot be right. Consent decrees generally are not intended to create contractual obligations apart from the court order.[47] The Court should adopt a standard for modifying court orders against government officials that is sensitive to the limits on their ability to contract away the rights of their constituents.

The impracticality of the Supreme Court's decision in *Rufo* has become evident in subsequent lower court proceedings that have tried to follow the rule. Parties now argue in lengthy hearings over what circumstances long-out-of-office officials foresaw or contemplated when they consented years or decades earlier, and whether the proposed change, even though lawful, is "suitably tailored" and not "overly tailored." Such litigation distracts from the main work of courts, which is to enforce rights, and from the main work of elected officials, which is to change government policy in light of experience and the changing wishes of voters.

It took, for example, four years and three trips to the appellate courts before Massachusetts could complete modifications of a twenty-year-old consent decree involving incarcerated sexual offenders, even where the justification for the decree had entirely evaporated. In 1972 civilly committed inmates held at a mental health treatment center sued Massachusetts, claiming violation of their constitutional rights. The inmates had been classified as sexually dangerous people and were legally under the care of the state's Department of Mental Health, but the prison in which the treatment center was housed was managed by another state agency, the Massachusetts Department of Corrections. The plaintiffs alleged that they were injured when corrections personnel made decisions that should have been made by mental health officials. A consent decree, signed in 1974, ordered that the treatment center be managed by the Department of Mental Health and, in addition, prohibited the use of isolation as a punishment.

In 1994, twenty years later, the Massachusetts legislature ended dual management at the prison by placing it solely under the Department of Corrections. The state asked for modifications of the decree to reflect changes in state law and treatment procedures, but the attorneys for the inmates refused to consent and, by invoking the *Rufo* case, held up modifications for four years.

The district judge initially ruled that the change of law was not significant enough to warrant a modification. A federal court of appeals in 1995 reversed. It wrote that the Constitution was "indifferent" as to whether corrections personnel or mental health personnel ran the treatment program as long as whoever ran it did not violate the Constitution.[48] But because the district court had not ruled on the second prong of the *Rufo* test, that is, whether the modification was suitably tailored, the case went back to the district court for more litigation.

In its second attempt, the district court approved the modification and in addition eliminated the flat prohibition against the use of isolation as a punishment. This time, plaintiffs appealed. Again, the court of appeals vacated.[49] Its 1997 opinion ruled that the district court had not sufficiently developed a record to show why the provisions on isolation should also be modified.

In its third attempt to get it right, the district court oversaw a battle of experts on how the mental health treatment center ought to be operated. Massachusetts, to overcome plaintiffs' refusal to consent, produced a comprehensive treatment plan based on a report by a Governor's Special Advisory Panel on Forensic Mental Health and affidavits from experts from other states on treatment, including testimony by one expert that no state as a matter of practice any longer barred isolation as punishment. The hearing also included a personal visit by the judge to the treatment facility. In opposition, plaintiffs' attorneys submitted testimony by their own experts that the treatment facility should be managed without isolation. In the end, the district judge ruled in favor of the state. Again, plaintiffs appealed.

By this time the appellate judges were tired of the lengthy litigation over modifying the decree. "While we cannot expect 'closure' of tensions and problems," the appellate court wrote in its 1998 opinion, "we may hope for problems of smaller dimension capable of systematic resolution without the necessity of heroic effort."[50] The court further stated that the "monolithic acceptance of the mental health approach that existed a quarter of a century ago has yielded to the acknowledgment that there is no royal road to treatment and cure. Behavioral control programs including defined offenses and sanctions are now featured in institutions operated by corrections personnel."[51] Yet for four years plaintiffs' attorneys had frustrated the operation of a state statute and the application of contemporary treatment standards without, it should be noted, there being any judicial acknowledgment of a current violation of law occurring at the treatment facility. Meanwhile, state officials were compelled to use "heroic efforts" in order to escape policy decisions made two decades earlier.[52]

The Supreme Court's test under *Rufo* is perversely at odds with the frankly managerial spirit with which trial court judges approach the administration of decrees against state and local governments. The judges see their role as managerial and feel themselves free to engage in experimentation.[53] Yet when state and local officials wish to make a midcourse correction, judges stop talking management and start enforcing the contract written into the decree.

The Supreme Court also makes it hard to get a decree terminated. The burden is on the government to prove a negative—that the decree is no longer necessary to protect plaintiffs' rights.[54] Proving a negative is notoriously difficult. Proving this particular negative is especially difficult because, no matter how well officials run a prison, police department, or other governmental institution, they simply cannot guarantee that all of its employees will stick to rules designed to safeguard plaintiffs' rights.

A defendant must also show that it has complied substantially with all the terms of the existing decree. With decrees typically requiring more than was needed to protect plaintiffs' rights, the decrees can last long after the actual threat to plaintiffs' rights has vanished.

When the defendant is a state or local government, more is at stake than the judicial interest in the finality of court decrees. Judges should also consider the public interest in democratic accountability.[55] The public's constitutional right to a democratically accountable government is fundamental to liberty.[56] This does not mean that judges should free officials from constitutional or statutory duties, but it does mean that judges should seek to avoid depriving elected officials of the flexibility needed to govern.

Respect for Rights *and* Democratic Accountability

Professor Zeigler's argument in favor of decrees quoted above is ultimately based on political expediency rather than principle. For plaintiffs' attorneys it may be expedient to have a powerful seat at the table of government through control of the decree.[57] We do not object to those who seek to push society in their preferred direction, but we wish also to protect our democratically accountable form of government. The use of the courts for expedient ends without restrictions that preserve their legitimate role reflects contempt for democratic accountability and depreciates the legitimacy of the courts. Courts should instead strike a balance that equally respects democratically accountable government and plaintiffs' rights.

The Supreme Court struggled to achieve such a balance in a heart-wrenching case brought by parents of the four Kent State University students killed in 1971 protesting the Vietnam War. The parents claimed that decisions by the governor of Ohio and the head of the Ohio National Guard unconstitutionally deprived their children of their lives. Despite the legal and emotional weight of this claim, the Supreme Court refused to let the case go forward. Writing for the Court, Chief Justice Warren Burger concluded that governmental officials were immune to damages unless the violations were intentional or reckless. This conclusion rested ultimately on the Court's concern for letting government function rather than dry doctrine. Public officials, the Court reasoned, have to act and make decisions in order to faithfully perform their duties. It is one thing for an official to make a decision on the spot, and quite another for a jury to reflect on the wisdom of that decision long afterward from the detached perspective of the courtroom. If such second-guessing were routinely permitted, officials acting in the best of faith would be afraid to exercise their best judgment. "The concept of immunity," the Chief Justice wrote, "assumes [that officials may err] and goes on to assume that it is better to risk some error and possible injury from such error than not to decide or act at all."[58] By limiting damages to violations that are intentional or reckless, the Court struck a balance between enforcing rights and allowing government to function.

In a more recent case involving the firing of an outspoken nurse by a public hospital allegedly in violation of her First Amendment rights, the Supreme Court in 1994 wrote that government, when it acts as an employer, stands on special footing because the government must be able to function. Justice O'Connor for the majority balanced the nurse's First Amendment right to free speech with the need for a government to control the expressions of its employees:

> The extra power the government has [to regulate employee speech] comes from the nature of the government's mission as employer. Government agencies are charged by law with doing particular tasks. Agencies hire employees to help do those tasks as effectively and efficiently as possible. When someone who is paid a salary so that she will contribute to an agency's effective operation begins to do or say things that detract from the agency's effective operation, the government employer must have some power to restrain her. The reason the governor may . . . fire [a governmental employee] is not that this dismissal would somehow be narrowly tailored to a compelling governmental interest. It is that the governor and the governor's staff have a job to do, and the governor justifiably feels that a quieter subordinate would allow them to do this job more effectively.
>
> The key to First Amendment analysis of government employment decisions, then is this: The government's interest in achieving its goals as effectively and efficiently as possible is elevated from a relatively subordinate interest when it acts as sovereign to a significant one when it acts as employer. The

government cannot restrict the speech of the public at large just in the name of efficiency. But where the government is employing someone for the very purpose of effectively achieving its goals, such restrictions may well be appropriate.[59]

In both the Kent State and employee free speech cases, the Court sought to strike a balance between protecting rights and allowing government to function. Whether the balances struck were precisely the right ones, the important point is that in striking a balance the Court placed great importance on allowing government to function even in the face of the right not to be deprived of life without due process, or the right to free speech.

In contrast to these damage cases, federal courts in modern decree cases often place far less importance on allowing government to function. Courts routinely impose detailed, long-lasting decrees without carefully examining whether they are really necessary for protecting rights, even when the rights at stake are aspirational and substantial uncertainty exists as to the methods for achieving them.

It is the decree cases and not the damages cases that are out of line. With damages, the threat is that officials will fear to govern. With decrees, the threat is worse: officials will be kept from governing. Chief Justice Frederick Vinson made just this point in *Larson v. Domestic and Foreign Commerce Corporation:* "[I]t is one thing to provide a method by which a citizen may be compensated for a wrong done to him by the Government. It is a far different matter to permit a court to exercise its compulsive powers to restrain the Government from acting, or to compel it to act. There are the strongest reasons of public policy for the rule that such relief cannot be had against the sovereign. The Government as representative of the community as a whole, cannot be stopped in its tracks by any plaintiff who presents a disputed question of property or contract right."[60]

The Chief Justice in 1949 was writing about a negative injunction restraining government from taking an illegal action. The threat in modern institutional reform cases is more severe because the court not only stops illegal action, but also chooses between legal policy options.

The list of reasons why district court decrees depart from Supreme Court principles does not include a seemingly obvious explanation—that judges are too "liberal." Decrees have been handed down by judges of all political persuasions. The problem is not liberal judges but temptations felt by all the participants in democracy by decree to use court orders for improper purposes, and the lack of institutional constraints to stop them. To strike a proper balance between protecting rights and allowing government to function, we need new principles to help federal courts resist the temptations that lead them to go too far in governing our states and localities by decree. The principles must be new to deal with the new realities of democracy by decree, but they can rest comfortably on traditional doctrines that limit courts to protecting rights and require them to respect the need for democratically accountable governments to choose between the many legally available policy options.

CHAPTER 8

Road to Reform

Change is possible, as Congress showed in the Prison Litigation Reform Act of 1995.[1] Reacting to a popular outcry over expansive federal court orders controlling prisons, Congress announced new rules for decrees in prison condition cases. The new rules drew judges back within traditional judicial boundaries without removing their authority to remedy violations of federal law. Federal judges should have imposed similar limitations on themselves, but they did not do so. Congress acted in the prison cases not so much to support state and local officials, to whom Congress normally accords little respect, but rather to reprimand federal judges for issuing orders that jeopardized public safety.

The story began in 1982 when ten prisoners in Philadelphia's Holmesburg prison filed a federal court suit charging Mayor Wilson Goode and seventeen other city and state officials with violating their federal constitutional rights. After preliminary skirmishing, Mayor Goode began negotiations with plaintiffs. Prosecutors on the staff of District Attorney Ronald D. Castille got wind of the negotiations in 1986. To their surprise, Mayor Goode was about to agree to procedures that would limit the number of prisoners that could be kept in Philadelphia's jails. This set off sirens in the district attorney's office. The prosecutors knew that a forced reduction in the prison population would result in bail jumping to avoid trial. The district attorney, a separately elected state official, had not been named in the federal lawsuit.

Reducing the number of prisoners had an irresistible political logic for Mayor Goode. He could solve his immediate legal predica-ment over the inadequate conditions in the jails not by fixing the prisons, but by changing the rules of criminal procedure that fell to the district attorney to enforce. It was a classic shift. The political heat for costly remedies such as paying damage awards to prisoners whose rights had been violated or improving conditions by expand-ing staff and building better facilities would have fallen on Mayor Goode. Changing the rules by which the district attorney operated, however, got the mayor off the hook at little cost. The only problem was that prisoners who would have been detained before trial would now be on the street, but that was the problem for the district attorney and state judges to solve.

District Attorney Castille, fearing the worst, put one of his as-sistants, thirty-one-year-old Sarah Vandenbraak Hart, on the case (Figure 8.1). Hart's first thought was to ask the federal judge to allow the district attorney to intervene in the lawsuit so that he could put before the court evidence that the consent decree would increase the number of no-shows at trials and result in more crime. Also, with the district attorney as an intervener, the district attorney's consent might be needed before the judge could sign the order. But there were few precedents for intervention in institutional reform cases by those not actually coerced by a proposed consent decree worked out by plaintiffs and defendants.

Working over a hot August weekend, Hart drafted papers that asked the federal judge, Norma L. Shapiro, to admit the district attorney as a party to the litigation. Judge Shapiro, with the consent decree all but fully negotiated, received Hart's papers with the en-thusiasm of a tenant receiving an eviction notice. She rejected every legal and factual argument Hart made and ruled that Philadelphia's

Figure 8.1. Sarah Vandenbraak Hart. As a young assistant district attorney in Philadelphia she tried to stop a federal judge from approving a consent decree imposing a cap on the number of prisoners that could be housed in the city's jails.

elected district attorney had no legal interest in a decree that affected his prosecution of state crimes in state court. All Judge Shapiro would allow was for the district attorney to file his objections. Finding the objections unpersuasive, Judge Shapiro on December 30, 1986, endorsed the agreement made by Mayor Goode and imposed a cap on the prison population that Mayor Goode had added to the package.[2]

Attempts to reverse Judge Shapiro's denial of the district attorney's intervention occupied Hart for the next two and one-half years as federal courts quibbled over the legal niceties of standing, intervention, and judicial discretion.[3] Even after the Pennsylvania state legislature passed a law that gave district attorneys a statutory interest in incarceration of prisoners, the federal court still refused to allow the intervention, ruling that only a federally recognized interest would unlock the door of the federal courthouse for the district attorney.[4] Looking back on this period, Hart says that it seemed that the federal judges were more concerned with settling the case than considering its effect on the public.

That effect was worse than Hart or the district attorney had predicted. It was a blood-chilling crime wave. The number of fugitives nearly tripled from 18,000 to almost 50,000. In an eighteen-month period from January 1, 1993, through June 30, 1994, Philadelphia police rearrested 9,732 defendants released because of the consent decree. These defendants were charged with 79 murders, 959 robberies, 2,215 drug-dealing crimes, 701 burglaries, 2,748 thefts, 90 rapes, 14 kidnappings, 1,113 assaults, 264 gun-law violations, and 127 drunk-driving incidents. Criminals moved their operations to Philadelphia to take advantage of the certain release that would follow an arrest. One drug dealer asked an undercover narcotics officer to move a drug transaction across the street to locate it on the Philadelphia side so that he could take advantage of the consent decree if they got caught in the act. Another drug dealer was so certain of his quick release under the consent decree that, when asked by his prebail interviewer where he could be reached, he gave as his address Cali, Colombia.[5]

The crime wave was not the only concern. Drug addicts who might have been placed in drug treatment centers were released to the street where they received no treatment and often became more enmeshed in drugs. Judges who in the past had conditioned bail on faithful attendance of a drug treatment program found that they could not make good on the threat. Many released prisoners who would have benefited from treatment were repeatedly arrested and released. For Hart, the youths and young adults sent on this treadmill of crime and drugs were victims of the cap no less than the victims of the crimes they committed.

The disastrous effect on public safety in Philadelphia became major news when a car thief and fugitive, who had been released twice under the cap, shot and killed a twenty-one-year-old rookie cop who had stopped the fugitive for stealing yet another car. The cop's father, himself a veteran Philadelphia detective, ultimately told the story of his son's murder to a sympathetic Congress as an example of the dangers federal courts were imposing on communities.

With Philadelphia's media trumpeting the news, the public quickly understood that the crime wave had something to do with the prison cap the federal court had imposed. Hart took the story of the Philadelphia prison cap and its public safety consequences on the road. Working first with the National District Attorneys Association and then with the National Association of Attorneys General, Hart lobbied congressional staff members to support legislation that would get views of district attorneys heard in federal courts and end prison caps enforced by federal judges. She found support from John J. DiIulio, Jr., then a professor at Princeton University and a fellow at the Brookings Institute who had studied prison reform cases.[6] Hart, who had always seen herself as a liberal, found herself delivering the major address at the December 1994 Edwin Meese Luncheon at the Heritage Foundation in Washington.

On January 1, 1992, Edward G. Rendell succeeded Wilson Goode as mayor of Philadelphia. Under the federal rules of civil procedure, Mayor Rendell automatically took the place of Mayor Goode as the main defendant in the litigation. Rendell knew all about the prison cap. He had been Philadelphia's district attorney earlier in his career and had testified in support of Hart's initial 1986 motion to intervene in the federal case. Now, as the incoming mayor, he could directly participate in the litigation. Between election day and inauguration

Hart helped draft motion papers for Rendell asking Judge Shapiro to modify the decree. Rendell filed the papers with the federal court as one of his first official acts after taking the oath of office. The motion cited the crime wave and argued that the decree forced officials to violate state law and that a newly elected mayor could not be bound by the consent and policies of the prior mayor. These arguments had no effect on Judge Shapiro, who forcefully backed the prior agreements by finding the city in contempt of court and fining it more than $100,000.[7] Litigation continued up and down the federal courts until finally, on August 17, 1995, Judge Shapiro formally rejected Mayor Rendell's motion to end the cap and modify the decree.[8] By then, however, Hart's campaign for federal legislation was about to pay off.

The November 1994 elections had put the Republicans in control of Congress. DiIulio, one of the analysts to whom the new Republican leadership looked for advice, urged the House leadership to pass Hart's proposed legislation. Others in Congress began to climb on the bandwagon, particularly Senator Spencer Abraham of Michigan, whose state also labored under a highly intrusive prison consent order.

The logic of Hart's proposed legislation was so compelling that even the Clinton administration's Department of Justice testified grudgingly in favor of it.[9] Pushed along by broad support from the House leadership, by Senator Abraham in the Senate, and by the White House, Hart's proposal to limit decrees in prison condition cases was added to the Prison Litigation Reform Act of 1995. Included in the act, along with Hart's proposal, were more controversial and questionable provisions limiting the ability of prisoners to sue. All of these items were attached to the omnibus appropriation legislation that finally ended the congressional deadlock and governmental shutdown of 1996. Hart celebrated her fortieth birthday in Philadelphia watching C-SPAN as the House of Representatives voted in favor of her legislation. On April 26, 1996, President Bill Clinton signed into law the omnibus bill containing the Prison Litigation Reform Act. Nine years after Judge Shapiro had denied Hart's motion to allow the district attorney to intervene, Hart prevailed by persuading Congress to change the rules for all prison condition litigation.

The Prison Litigation Reform Act's new rules for prison condition decrees limit federal judges to their proper constitutional role, yet still allow ample authority for them to protect the rights of prisoners. In particular, the act forbids federal judges from issuing orders on prison conditions that are unnecessary to stop violations of federal law, even if a defendant consents to the entry of the decree. The act underscores this limitation by requiring the judge to keep the decree narrowly drawn, use the least intrusive means necessary to correct the federal violation, and give substantial weight to any adverse effect on public safety or the operation of the state's criminal justice system.[10]

To ensure that named defendants like Mayor Goode do not sell out other elected officials or pad their own political nest by agreeing to a prisoner release order, Congress granted to all elected officials with relevant criminal justice responsibility, including legislators who vote on prison budgets, the right to intervene in any federal court prison litigation that imposed a prison population cap or release order. No longer may a federal judge bar elected officials from participating in prison cap litigation.[11]

The act also calls for prompt termination of a decree unless it is still needed to prevent violations of federal law. Once a decree has been operating for two years, the defendants may move for its termination and the judge must grant the motion unless the judge makes written findings, based on a record, that the decree is still needed to prevent future violations of federal law.[12] Those who seek to keep old prison decrees alive must now prove that the decree is still needed.

Forcing plaintiffs to prove the need to continue a prison decree beyond two years is a major change. Under the old rules, plaintiffs had the burden to prove that a decree was necessary in the first place, but once it was entered, the burden to escape shifted to defendants, and they rarely were able to carry that burden, which left prisons under the long-term control of the courts. The Prison Litigation Reform Act takes the opposite tack by leaving the burden on the plaintiffs throughout, first to get the decree installed and then to maintain it. The act in effect opts for local democracy to prevent future problems, rather than perpetual, direct control by federal courts.

To discourage routine appointment of monitors, special masters, and other court functionaries, the act requires judges to justify such an appointment by a finding that the remedial stage of the litigation will be unusually complex. The person appointed must be independent.[13] The act further limits the hourly rates that can be charged and requires the funds to come from the federal court budget, not from the state and local governments.

The Prison Litigation Reform Act is a personal triumph for Hart, but not for the courts. Many federal judges resist the new limitations that put an end to their long-term role as prison managers. Some ruled that the act was unconstitutional, only to be reversed by higher courts.[14] Others constructed uncertain legal theories to sustain past bargains. Some judges even argued that when federal court judges could not enforce the old decree, the underlying bargain might still be enforced as a contract in state court. This theory, too, was rejected.[15]

The act caused earth tremors as plaintiffs, judges, and even defendant prison officials who had long ago grown accustomed to managing prisons through court decrees found themselves unable to justify the old decrees. They simply could not show significant current, ongoing violations of federal law, and so the old decrees were terminated.

With the debate in Congress making Judge Shapiro's Philadelphia prison decree exhibit number one of what had gone wrong, Judge Shapiro on November 30, 1995, removed the population cap portion of the decree but continued other provisions until, finally, in 2000 she terminated the case.

Sarah Hart has remained in public service. After leaving the district attorney's office, she became chief counsel to Pennsylvania's Department of Corrections, where she advises corrections officials and assists other states in terminating consent decrees. Her sustained efforts opposing prison orders have not made her unmindful of the potential for stupidity, violence, and brutality in prisons. In reflecting on the Prison Litigation Reform Act, she recalled in conversation with the authors that "when we were drafting the bill we fully understood that the courts must not lose their authority to step in when needed. I had in mind a prison warden who failed to deal with a TB epidemic. Judges must be able to act quickly in such cases. It was these sorts of thoughts that compelled us to seek a balance in the statute."

The Supreme Court in *Miller v. French,* decided on June 19, 2000, approved the core concept behind the Prison Litigation Reform Act—that Congress can change the rules governing the prospective application of decrees to protect prisoners' constitutional rights, even in instances in which the decrees had been issued years or even decades before. The old decree, the Supreme Court wrote, is not the last word on judicial involvement because the decree is subject to the court's continuing supervisory jurisdiction and therefore may be altered pursuant to subsequent changes in the law.[16]

The Prison Litigation Reform Act applies only to prisons, yet its concept is applicable to other federal court intrusions into state and local governmental matters. Were judges to apply its standards in other institutional reform cases, they would go far toward restoring federal courts to their proper role. It would be best for judges to impose the needed restraint on themselves. Should the judges leave the job of putting the courthouse in order to Congress, it may go too far in limiting flexibility, a claim that is now made against the Prison Litigation Reform Act. If judges do not control themselves, then Congress should nonetheless expand the limitations of the Prison Litigation Reform Act to cover all institutional reform cases or categories of cases.[17]

CHAPTER 9

New Principles

New principles for remedial decrees against state and local government must protect rights, keep the courthouse door open to those injured, and preserve local democracy. The goals may seem to be at odds, yet can be reconciled, as illustrated by the consent decree entered in *Marisol A. v. Giuliani*, the foster care litigation discussed in Chapter 6.[1] It left New York City in charge of its own program without *any* judicially imposed mandates on how it protects children as long as the city worked in "good faith" to improve its program. Plaintiffs agreed to a decree in which the major term called for the appointment of a panel of outside experts, jointly chosen by the city and plaintiffs, to monitor the course of the city's efforts. The court could impose systemic requirements only if the panel later found that the city was not acting in "good faith." At the end of two years, even this narrow decree terminated. The *Marisol* decree reversed the usual practice that permits court supervision to continue indefinitely until the defendant affirmatively proves that it has brought itself into compliance with all of its obligations—a burden that local governments rarely meet. The city did not, however, escape responsibility to individual children. The court retained authority to issue injunctions to protect individual children and award damages should individual children be injured.

Why did the plaintiffs settle? The city, unlike most state and local defendants, refused to settle and demanded a trial on the merits that was projected to take six months. Plaintiffs were facing daunting costs. The city's reform program looked impressive to experts whom the plaintiffs trusted. The first written report of the panel of outside experts called the city's program "a thoughtful, coherent, broad and appropriately ambitious vision and framework to guide the design and implementation of the numerous organizational, system, policy and practice changes that will be required to dramatically improve the city's child welfare system."[2] Commissioner Nicholas Scoppetta's personal background and commitment added further credibility to the city's program and its claim to be acting in good faith. The court could add little to New York City's efforts at reform.

Even where plaintiffs do not consent, judges should consider *Marisol* as a model for resolving many cases against state and local governments. The purpose of an injunction is to avert threatened harm, not to regulate or punish the violator. The Supreme Court made that clear in *Hecht Co. v. Bowles,* a case to enforce World War II price control regulations that the government imposed on businesses.[3] The Hecht Company, a prominent Washington, D.C., department store, had violated the price regulations hundreds of times. Hecht's violations were seen as deadly serious. Congress considered price controls an essential part of the effort to avoid defeat in a war that, in 1942, was all too possible to lose. If a prominent establishment in the heart of Washington, D.C., could get away with multiple violations, that would be an open invitation to price gougers everywhere. The Office of Price Administration demanded that the court impose a prohibitory injunction, but the store resisted. To be branded a price-gouging outlaw in wartime Washington would be a considerable embarrassment. The store persuaded the lower court that the violations were not intentional, concerned only a tiny portion of the items it sold, and resulted from mistakes while trying to apply a complex, novel regulatory scheme to a huge inventory. Also, much like New York City in the *Marisol* case, the store initiated its own reform from within to make itself a model of compliance. On this record the Supreme Court accepted the conclusion of the district court that the management of the department store was already doing everything in its power to prevent future violations.

Neither the district court nor the Supreme Court was predicting zero violations in the future. To the contrary, the Supreme Court expected that some future violations were inevitable, given the difficulty of applying a complicated regulatory scheme to a large inventory. The Court suggested that an injunction would add nothing to the store's own efforts to avoid violations.[4] The district court could retain jurisdiction of the case so that if the store slid backwards, an injunction could be imposed after all. As in *Marisol,* the Supreme Court wanted the district court's authority held in reserve and not to be actively exerted unless needed.

The judge's role in *Hecht* was thus not much different from the judge's actual role in *Jose P.*—to oversee from a distance. The way that *Jose P.* differed from *Hecht* was that the controlling group rather than the defendants was in charge.

Marisol is, of course, only an illustration. Judges need principles to guide them in dealing with the diversity of cases that come before them. None of the new principles we propose attacks the core concept that judges should enforce constitutional rights. Nor do our proposals cut back on modern interpretations of constitutional rights that broaden their scope. Whether such interpretations are appropriate is a question we do not address. For rights announced in statutes, we are willing to be more aggressive. Even here, however, we do not rely on courts to limit the power of Congress to create statutory rights enforceable against state and local governments.[5] Our point is that courts should not enforce such rights in the same way that they enforce constitutional rights or statutory rights in whose formulation the legislature has taken full responsibility for the policy choices.

In formulating our proposals, we have heeded the advice that Judge Harry Edwards of the federal appellate court in Washington gave to law professors who want their scholarship to be relevant in the wider world: give "due weight to doctrine."[6] Our proposals invoke long-standing doctrines, discussed in Chapter 7, through which judges have traditionally limited themselves in enforcing rights and respected the need to let democratically accountable governments function. The Supreme Court in the main articulates these doctrines, but they are not reflected in the practices of the lower courts, as we have shown.

Restating doctrine will not be enough. The threat to local democracy is greater because Congress today has more power to tell state and local governments what to do and has parlayed that power by sharing it with federal agencies. The modern mechanisms for mass-producing statutory rights designed to yield open-and-shut cases against state and local defendants and for enforcing those rights through organizations dedicated to that purpose have created a force with which state and local governments cannot cope.

Judges, for their part, have not figured out how to hold state and local governments to the rule of law without making lawyers the rulers of state and local governments. The cases that arrive in court present judges with real people in need as plaintiffs whose attorneys can point to legal justification for some judicial action. It is not enough to tell such judges, "Just say 'No.' " Judges need a way to do the judicial job, yet resist the understandable impulse to go forth and do more "good" than the judicial job warrants.

The equitable principles we would have the courts invoke have four objectives:

1. *Judges should stick to the judicial job of protecting plaintiffs from illegal injury.*[7] This is an old concept that marks the traditional limits on judicial authority in issuing decrees. We propose applying it to cases against state and local governments so that consent by defendants would no longer be deemed sufficient to allow the court to exceed that limit. Moreover, we propose new means to keep courts to their proper role.

2. *In enforcing rights, judges should to the greatest extent practicable leave policy making to the elected policy makers.* This concept is also old. What would be new is applying it consistently in cases against state and local governments. We again suggest new ways for courts to keep to their proper role.

3. *In those rare cases in which it is absolutely necessary for judges to involve the court in policy making to enforce rights, judges should subject themselves to checks and balances appropriate to judicial administration of state and local governments.* The traditional constraint on judges is to avoid conflicts of interest and ex parte contact, but these constraints are not enough when courts function as ongoing administrators of government policy. We suggest new constraints rooted in traditional values.

4. *Judges should include an "end game" in every decree against state and local governments.* With decrees against state and local governments now lasting for decades, judges should be obligated at the outset to articulate an explicit and realistic strategy for ending their rule.

Such abstract objectives are helpful, but how they apply in practice is what really counts. The balance of this chapter explains how judges should apply them in framing the decree, managing the decree, and ending the decree (Table 9.1).

Framing the Decree

Institutional reform litigation gets off on the wrong foot from the beginning when a judge fails to set limits. Without clear boundaries, decrees expand like accordions. From the outset the judge should

Table 9.1. The new principles for framing, managing, and ending decrees.

Framing the Decree
- As the initial step in the remedial process, trial court judges should adopt findings of fact on the injury done to the plaintiffs.
- A decree, including a consent decree, should be entered only if it goes no further than necessary to protect plaintiffs from illegal injury.
  - A decree should protect only the plaintiffs before the court, not others who may be injured but who are not party to the litigation.
  - There should be no decree at all unless plaintiffs show a significant threat of illegal injury.
  - A decree to repair harm done by violations in the past should be entered only if plaintiffs prove that its provisions are necessary to correct past illegal injury.
- To the greatest extent practicable, judges should leave policy making to elected policy makers.
  - Judges should temper their concern for protecting individual rights with concern for the public's right to democratically accountable state and local governments.
  - Judges should abstain from dictating the means to vindicate rights when defendants show that they will work in good faith to meet their legal obligations.
  - Whenever feasible, judges should oversee change through the defendants rather than special masters, other judicial functionaries, or the controlling group.
- Appellate courts should take positive steps to ensure that remedial decrees are no broader than needed to protect plaintiffs' rights.

Managing the Decree
- Decrees should be modified whenever defendants have a good reason to change how they will honor plaintiffs' rights.
- The remedial obligations in consent decrees, but not the underlying judgment of liability, should be construed to last only as long as the consenting chief executive remains in office.
- The controlling group should be subject to checks and balances.
- The judge should compel continual updating of the decree to ensure that a single, consolidated document is always available.
- To ensure judicial impartiality, decrees lasting longer than eight years should be reassigned to a new judge, and any trial for contempt should be assigned to a separate judge.

Ending the Decree
- A decree should be promptly terminated when the threat to plaintiffs' rights ceases.
- Judges should at the outset announce an "end game" for terminating the decree.

play an active role in limiting the decree and preparing the way for later termination. This means more work and responsibility for judges, but this is the right sort of judicial activism because it minimizes the extent to which the controlling group can use the court's power to control public policy.

AS THE INITIAL STEP IN THE REMEDIAL PROCESS, TRIAL COURT JUDGES SHOULD ADOPT FINDINGS OF FACTS ON THE INJURY DONE TO THE PLAINTIFFS

Injuries to plaintiffs establish the outer limits of the court's legitimate power, yet many judges fail to specify with particularity just what violations have been proved or admitted. In this the judges are being led by the parties. Defendants, to avoid condemnation, prefer not to admit violations or allow them to be proved. Plaintiffs, to avoid limiting their power over public policy, also do not want to specify the injuries that need correcting. *Jose P.* illustrates how a controlling group parlayed a narrow violation concerning deadlines for evaluation and placement into power to deal with the full sweep of special education policy. In obscuring the injuries that the court may appropriately remedy, plaintiffs and defendants, even when well intentioned, are opportunistic and undermine the legitimacy of the court.

Judges should insist on identifying the specific violations and the injuries flowing from them before the decree is framed. This "bill of wrongs" would give trial judges a ready check on the ambitions of the controlling group. It would also give appellate courts a way to test whether the trial judge has stuck to the judicial job of remedying illegal injuries. When trial judges fail to identify the wrongs to be remedied, they and the controlling group are free to reinvent the purpose of the decree—and they do.[8]

Formal adoption of a bill of wrongs would be an innovation in the crafting of remedial decrees but would mimic practices in parallel contexts. Motions for summary judgment usually must be accompanied by a list of disputed and agreed-upon facts, and appellate courts regularly insist on a list of issues before hearing an appeal.

The bill of wrongs could be worked out in large part by the parties.[9] The judge would retain ultimate responsibility to ensure that the decree was grounded in real, not counterfeit, wrongs. Because it would be adopted before the decree and its remedies were written, it would be harder for the controlling group to conspire to enlarge the court's power beyond its proper bounds. Should the defendants later move to modify or terminate the decree, the findings would serve to cut off post hoc rationalizations used to justify its continuance.[10]

A DECREE, INCLUDING A CONSENT DECREE, SHOULD BE ENTERED ONLY IF IT GOES NO FURTHER THAN NECESSARY TO PROTECT PLAINTIFFS FROM ILLEGAL INJURY

Judges may use decrees only to restore plaintiffs to their rightful positions, not to punish defendants or improve public policy.[11] Judges should limit their remedial decrees to prohibiting defendants from violating plaintiffs' rights in the future if future violations are threatened and ordering defendants to repair the consequences of past violations, if practicable. The bill of wrongs will keep the district court judge focused on this basic limit on the judicial task. The limit has important corollaries.

A decree should protect only the plaintiffs before the court, not others who may be injured but who are not party to the litigation. If, for example, a prison warden unconstitutionally denied Spanish-speaking prisoners access to law books in Spanish, it would be inappropriate for the court to expand a remedial order to cover such general prison library matters as time of operation or to detail how the prison library should make materials available to Chinese-speaking prisoners. Restraint of this sort does not, however, bless violations against others. Once a court has defined the law to be obeyed, officials know their duty. If they fail to do it, say, by not correcting other unconstitutional prison library procedures or by not providing materials that Chinese prisoners need, the victims of these violations can bring a new suit or perhaps intervene in the old one and get the decree modified to protect themselves.

Judges, like other people, can easily see that the problem before them is part of a related problem and many want to fix both at the same time. Plaintiffs encourage this, as, often, do defendants, who may welcome the court's remedial order as an opportunity to take care of other concerns. Yet such unwarranted expansion of the remedial decree deprives officials, and their successors, of flexibility on how to meet their legal obligations and transforms the court's limited remedial process into a process for the general management of governmental programs.

Limiting remedial decrees to protecting only plaintiffs will require courts to scrutinize carefully the classes they are asked to certify. Judges do not always do so, with the result that the court and controlling group are left free to protect just about everybody because just about everybody has been made a plaintiff. For example, in *Jose P.* the class certified was children awaiting entry into special education, but the decree was extended to cover those already admitted.

There should be no decree at all unless plaintiffs show a significant threat of illegal injury. Judges wrongly trench on local democratic accountability when they unnecessarily tell an elected official how to comply with the law. Dictating choices about the operation of public institutions, use of public funds, or imposition of regulations or taxes is justified only by proof of significant threats of illegal injury.[12] It is the burden of plaintiffs to prove the likelihood of a significant threat. Without such proof, the court lacks a mandate to direct agency performance.

While acknowledging this principle, courts regularly enter decrees on consent without proof that such a threat really exists. Plaintiffs might, for example, prove that a city violated a federal law on the distribution of food stamps. The court then has two options: (1) enter a judgment *and* a decree controlling the distribution of food stamps or (2) issue a judgment declaring the prior process unlawful without also entering a court order in the form of a decree. The second alternative, called a *declaratory judgment,* intrudes less on the power of the city's elected officials, defining the city's legal obligations without telling it how to meet them. The court would be justified in entering a decree telling the city how to meet its obligations only if the city would likely continue to violate the law even after the entry of a declaratory judgment. This is the plaintiffs' burden to prove. The court is not justified in entering a decree governing future conduct, even on consent, if the plaintiffs cannot meet that burden.

A decree to repair harm done by violations in the past should be entered only if plaintiffs prove that its provisions are necessary to correct past illegal injury. An example of a decree to repair harm already done would be an order against a school board to provide additional special education programs now for students who were in the past illegally denied timely special education.

Both plaintiffs' attorneys and defendants' attorneys have strong incentives to consent to bogus reparative provisions, as was shown in a civil rights lawsuit against Birmingham, Alabama. The plaintiffs claimed that Birmingham had discriminated against African Americans in hiring and promoting city employees. The case was settled by a consent decree that gave preferences to African Americans in future hiring and promotions. Past discrimination was to be repaired by hiring and promotional preferences in the future. White fire-fighters protested that the preferences disadvantaged them and were not needed to remedy past wrongs. The lower courts refused to listen to their complaints. The white firefighters then filed their own lawsuit alleging that Birmingham used the remedial decree to discriminate against them on the basis of race. When the lower courts finally looked at the evidence, they discovered that future racial preferences were largely unjustified in the first place.[13]

Why would city officials consent to a future hiring plan that was not needed? They consented partly because they did not want to pay money damages. City officials made a trade with plaintiffs' attorneys: no money damages for actual harm done in the past in return for racial preferences in the future. The cost of the remedy fell on future city officials and whites who later applied for city jobs and promotions. The trade was also good for plaintiffs' attorneys. It gave them ongoing power over city policy and a justification to spend time supervising the city's compliance.[14]

The injustice in the Birmingham case came to light only because it violated the constitutional rights of other citizens. In the typical case, bogus reparative provisions harm other citizens but do not violate the kind of rights that they can enforce in court. In *Jose P.,* for example, students with no need for special education could not challenge the policies embedded in the *Jose P.* decree even though those policies shifted money and attention away from their education. These students had no right to a specific amount of money that had to be spent on their education.

To protect the innocent, judges must carefully vet the justification for proposed reparative provisions before entering a decree by requiring plaintiffs to show that the harm to be repaired was in fact caused by defendants' illegal action and that the decree provisions are narrowly targeted to repair those injuries.[15]

TO THE GREATEST EXTENT PRACTICABLE, JUDGES SHOULD
LEAVE POLICY MAKING TO ELECTED POLICY MAKERS

Judges who stick to enforcing rights will still encounter occasions in which they have good reason to consider taking hold of policy. Elected officials do not always obey simple, prohibitory injunctions, or judges may end up confronting questions that Congress ducked, the chief of which is whether compliance is feasible. The upshot is that judges who start off trying to achieve broad, generally approved goals of society, such as clean air and better education for children, end up embroiled in policy choices that should be left to politically accountable officials.

Traditional principles of equity jurisprudence anticipate this problem. They counsel judges to avoid assuming legislative powers over state and local governments. Yet as we have argued in this book, lower courts, in their impatience to vindicate rights and their willingness to say "yes" to proposed consent decrees, have forgotten these traditional principles, which require judges to take a less single-minded concept of their duty.

Judges should temper their concern for protecting individual rights with concern for the public's right to democratically accountable state and local governments. A judge does no damage to democratic accountability by issuing a decree that prohibits violation of a constitutional right. Whether to obey the Constitution is not a policy choice in the first place. When the "right" at stake is really a policy aspiration and the order makes policy choices about how to vindicate the right, courts can do great harm to local democracy. Judges should weigh that harm against the objective of putting plaintiffs in their rightful position. The result may be a decree that does not fully restore plaintiffs to their rightful position or, in some cases, no decree at all.[16]

How the weighing comes out depends on the circumstances of

the case. Courts should readily issue a decree to cure a constitutional violation that can be secured without substantial intrusion on state and local policy prerogatives. On the other hand, when faced with a state or locality in violation of an open-ended, impractical statutory mandate such as the impossible curb ramp deadline, the court should enter a judgment of violation but consider issuing no affirmative decree. The effect would be to remand the controversy to the political branches of government, which is exactly where it belongs. If the body that promulgated the impossible requirement—be it the legislature or an agency—wants courts to do more, it will have to make the necessary hard choices. In the case of the curb ramps, the Department of Justice could, if it wants court enforcement, promulgate a new rule in which it makes the judgment about the real deadline for cities to build the ramps.

Judges have, in effect, remanded cases to Congress. Congress sometimes has stuck to its mandates, sometimes not. An example of sending an issue back to Congress occurred when federal judge Abraham D. Sofaer was asked to enforce against New York City a congressional ban on ocean dumping of sewage sludge, a decision that forced extremely high land-based disposal costs on East Coast cities and could produce adverse environmental results of its own. Judge Sofaer ruled that the legislation was unclear as to whether the ban was absolute or required a balancing of costs, and refused to order it. That decision indirectly referred the matter back to Congress to state more clearly what it meant. Congress then made explicit its desire for an absolute ban, which the court then enforced.[17]

Judges should abstain from dictating the means to vindicate rights when defendants show that they will work in good faith to meet their legal obligations. Proof that the defendant violated the law in the past does not automatically lay the foundation for a detailed injunction.[18] The court must be convinced that a detailed injunction, and not just a declaratory judgment, is required to remedy the violation.

Even where the court is justified in entering a decree, the decree should be shaped to maximize the control left to defendants where they will work in good faith toward meeting their legal obligations. Lower courts often reflexively go straight to the mat by issuing a detailed decree, even when the state or locality has shown no hints of massive resistance to plaintiffs' rights and without regard to whether the defendants would work in good faith to end the violation. The reason is partly due to precedents developed in response to massive resistance to school desegregation. Also, plaintiffs' attorneys have developed litigation strategies to get courts to think of intrusive decrees as the default position. Complaints are drafted to facilitate motions for preliminary relief so that the court ends up imposing requirements before defendants have a chance to appraise their own failings and consider whether to adopt a reform program from within. Such strategies result in a preliminary injunction, on consent, containing planning milestones as the initial steps leading to a more detailed court order.

Not every institutional reform case has a basis in equity for trusting defendants' good faith, but many do. Good faith is a notoriously subjective concept, but trial court judges can nonetheless give it operational meaning. One test is for the governor or mayor to make a personal, political commitment to cure the violations. The commitment should be put in terms such that failure will cause the governor or mayor significant political embarrassment. Mayor Giuliani made such a commitment in taking on personal responsibility for the protection of children in New York City. Governors and mayors did just the opposite in the early school desegregation cases.

Few public interest cases actually see top political leaders participating. A lawsuit challenging prison management will typically be answered by the chief warden, corrections commissioner, and other appointed officials, but not the chief executive who appointed them, even when the chief executive is named in the caption of the lawsuit. When it comes time to settle the case, the consent decree will be signed by a lawyer, not the top official. This lets key officials off the hook politically and tends to separate commitment from leadership. Commitments will more likely be met if publicly and personally made by the CEOs of government rather than by their surrogates.

Sign-off by the top-level elected official has the added advantage of checking that the political leadership actually embraces the promises made. It is not only the public that sometimes gets sandbagged by consent decrees. Elected officials can also be surprised by costly and unpopular promises, as happened in a recent Illinois case. In 1999 the governor of Illinois, on learning of a proposed foster care consent decree, directed the state's lawyers to take back their consent to the proposed decree, which the judge had not yet signed. The governor had not been informed of settlement negotiations and after considering the decree, preferred to litigate. The district court entered the decree anyway, only to be reversed by the court of appeals.[19]

Other considerations relevant to whether defendants display good faith are the existence of a plan of attack to cure the violations and a willingness to allow outside observers into otherwise closed institutions.

Defendants need sufficient time to build a record of good faith. In *Marisol,* New York City had two years to build such a record, but only because the city vowed to fight the case rather than capitulate. A court should be willing to give defendants who have made the necessary political commitment adequate time to develop their own plan and demonstrate their ability to carry it out. Plaintiffs' attorneys in *Marisol* would have undoubtedly raged against delay if the court had overtly stayed its hand for two years. Two years is a long time in the face of the terrible facts that often accompany institutional reform litigation. Yet it often takes at least that long for a large governmental agency to change leadership, develop a plan, and begin to demonstrate its capacity to implement it. This is work that must be done anyway, even if a decree is imposed. It took the controlling group in *Jose P.* two years to complete its planning, even under the court order.

Judges should be more willing to credit the defendants with good faith if there are other means to keep defendants in line, such as robust individual remedies in state courts, attention by the press likely to spot failures by defendants, or active oversight by legislative bodies or external auditors.[20]

Allowing agencies time and discretion to work out how they can bring themselves into compliance is not as novel as it sounds. This is precisely what federal judges regularly do when the federal government, rather than a state or local government, is violating the law. When a federal agency violates the law, courts nullify the illegal action but often let the agency decide how to bring itself into compliance. In this way the federal courts avoid usurping the policy prerogatives of the federal agencies.

Judge Gerhardt Gesell, a federal district judge in Washington, D.C., made the point most clearly in a case in which, ironically, a state had sued the federal Environmental Protection Agency for missing a statutory deadline for issuing rules to limit pollution.[21] Speaking extemporaneously from the bench, Judge Gesell said, "These are matters of national policy, political priorities; and I would urge upon the parties with everything at my command that they consider the appropriateness of continuing to rely on courts to accomplish objectives which can only be effectively accomplished in a democracy by resort to the polls, resort to the political processes which the Constitution preserves."[22] The decree Judge Gesell actually issued ordered the EPA to do its statutory duty, left the key policy choices to the agency, and was structured to thrust the ultimate responsibility back on Congress. Judge Gesell was no conservative, nor did he fail to appreciate the health concerns at stake in pollution control. To the contrary, he was moved by concern for the appropriate division of responsibility between federal judges and their counterparts in the legislative and executive branches.

Federal courts owe as much respect to state and local agencies that are willing to try to obey the law, but often do not give it. Giving defendants a chance to clean their own house is not without risk, but so is trying to change a complex institution through court administration. Besides, negotiating and litigating a decree add delays and distractions of their own. Reform from within is worth the chance when it seems likely to the judge that it will work well over the long haul.

Whenever feasible, judges should oversee change through the defendants rather than special masters, other judicial functionaries, or the controlling group. Judges should, to the extent possible, structure remedial decrees so that officials of the defendant institution themselves, rather than a court-created bureaucracy, design and manage the changes needed to comply with the law. Appointment of powerful monitors and special masters, as well as imposition of externally controlled plans, shifts power away from the agency's elected and appointed leadership. External force can induce motivation for change, but cannot lead change. Change led by the organization's leaders has a better chance to become integral to the institution's culture and operations.

The reasons why judges opt for imposing outside authority over a public agency are easy to understand. Frequent elections operate like hostile takeovers of governmental institutions. The comings and goings of top appointed officials can make agency managers timid and leave policies in flux. Judges seek continuity by appointing people responsible to them rather than relying solely on the parade of elected and appointed officials. Judge Nickerson's experience in *Jose P.*, where nine different chancellors labored to meet the court-ordered obligations, is not atypical. In the case of Kansas City's schools discussed in the Introduction, twenty superintendents have tried to comply with the court order during the past thirty years.

Monitors and special masters also solve one of the judge's and the plaintiffs' major problems—getting and absorbing information. Monitors and special masters take otherwise messy facts and neatly package them for the plaintiffs and the judge. These judicially appointed officials, often selected because of their expertise, acquire local expertise on the job so that their opinions carry great weight. In relying on them rather than on governmental officials heading the agencies, the judge avoids responsibility for the policy consequences of decisions. Given these advantages, many judges in cases involving prisons, mental hospitals, schools, and homeless shelters appoint as monitors outside experts, who are often aided by expensive staffs and offices, as part of the court-ordered remedies.

The regular changeover of democratically elected leadership is inefficient, but the possibility of such change is a virtue of our system. It is the very reason we embrace elections scheduled every two or four years. Court orders that overturn a system based on regular elections for efficiency reasons should be the last option, not the first.

Relying on monitors and special masters has a more subtle disadvantage. Experts are likely to apply the expert's standard to ferret out failures and problems, whereas the court is called upon to apply a good-faith standard to decide when to terminate supervision. Once an agency demonstrates good faith by showing that it is adequately managing its responsibilities and that such violations of law that do occur are not the result of systemic illegalities, court supervision ought to end irrespective of the existence of continuing violations. Unless monitors and special masters are carefully instructed by the court, the expert's ability to find and report problems will get in the way of the court's duty to return the agency back to the management of elected officials.

Monitors and special masters can also produce unintended side effects. Documenting imperfection in governmental social programs is no hard task. Monitors hired to find fault will surely find it, but managers have to manage and that requires positive leadership, which the outside observer cannot supply. Unbalanced reports from monitors may whipsaw agency officials away from their own reform plans, demoralize staff, and create an atmosphere of blame rather than the cooperation needed for change.

Judges, for these reasons, ought to rely on existing institutions whenever possible. Many states have, for example, boards of corrections that possess statutory powers to visit prisons and report on conditions. Accrediting commissions oversee hospitals; state education officials supervise local boards of education; legislative committees oversee all governmental institutions. Rather than creating its own monitors and masters or relying on the controlling group, the court could direct or request official oversight institutions to supply the information by reporting to the court. This would breathe new life into some institutions that may have grown moribund and help institutionalize change within the constitutionally created governmental institutions.

Decrees that cement detailed obligations into an institution's practices similarly undermine leadership. Even modest changes in the detailed obligations become difficult, and regular administrative and governmental procedures wither. Many plan obligations could just as well be spelled out in formal agency regulations. Agency regulations are publicly adopted under provisions assuring public comment and notice and can be modified and refined over time through the same open process without having to bargain privately with public interest lawyers. Any aggrieved person may challenge a new regulation or enforce its terms without having to rely on the controlling group.

Kaspar v. Board of Election Commissioners[23] illustrates the proper reluctance of a federal court to appoint outsiders to do what defendants should do. The case was brought by officials of the Republican Party who alleged that board of election commissioners in Chicago sanctioned massive voter fraud by, for example, allowing Democratic Party officials to cast votes in the names of dead citizens. The board agreed to a consent decree that called for the appointment of "United States District Court Observers." The observers were to weed illegal voters from the election rolls—a job that under state election law was supposed to be done by canvassers hired directly by the board of election commissioners. The court refused to approve the decree. Judge Frank Easterbrook, writing for the appellate court, pointed out that state institutions were capable of dealing with the illegal voting and that the "Board's willingness to transfer its responsibilities to the federal court does not oblige the court to accept."[24]

APPELLATE COURTS SHOULD TAKE POSITIVE STEPS TO ENSURE THAT REMEDIAL DECREES ARE NO BROADER THAN NEEDED TO PROTECT PLAINTIFFS' RIGHTS

Appellate courts should not defer to the reasoning of the trial court judge when state and local defendants appeal the scope of the decree.[25] For the appellate court the issue is whether the trial court judge has gone further than necessary to restore plaintiffs to their rightful position. To defer to the trial judge is to all but assume the answer to the question in dispute.[26] Deference to the trial judge on the issue of scope is no more justified than would be deference to state and local officials.

Appellate courts should also consider the scope of a consent decree even when it comes to the appellate court long after it has been entered. The first time that most decrees come before an appellate court is on appeal from a decision by the trial judge on whether to enforce, modify, or terminate the decree. In such appeals, defendants are prohibited from arguing that the decree was too broad in the first place.[27] Different rules should apply when the defendants are state and local officials because no official can give away the rights of the public to an accountable government or the rights of their successors in office.[28] An explicit agreement to limit a successor's governmental authority would, in other contexts, be ultra vires—that is, void as beyond the scope of that official's authority, and it should be so considered in a consent decree as well.[29] When a trial judge does not keep the parties within appropriate limits, an appellate court is the only corrective authority available to successor officials who find that their predecessors have bargained away the powers of their office.

Managing the Decree

Judges should handle issues during the period of reform in ways that allow government to function and to preserve democracy.

DECREES SHOULD BE MODIFIED WHENEVER DEFENDANTS
HAVE A GOOD REASON TO CHANGE HOW THEY WILL
HONOR PLAINTIFFS' RIGHTS

Courts should further ease rules on the modification of decrees. Unless the decrees can be changed, governments must continue to implement failed solutions adopted long ago. Governments cannot solve new problems and experiment with different means for solving old ones. *Rufo*'s "unforeseen circumstance" test should be discarded in favor of one that allows state and local governmental defendants to gain a modification whenever they have a reasonable basis for doing so.[30] In applying this test, judges should grant elected officials the same deference they accord federal administrators seeking to change regulations, except where the circumstances suggest that the modification's purpose is to delay vindication of plaintiffs' rights.[31]

THE REMEDIAL OBLIGATIONS IN CONSENT DECREES, BUT NOT THE UNDERLYING JUDGMENT OF LIABILITY, SHOULD BE CONSTRUED TO LAST ONLY AS LONG AS THE CONSENTING CHIEF EXECUTIVE REMAINS IN OFFICE

Newly elected officials should be able to revise past choices on how to vindicate plaintiffs' rights. Unlike private people, who may divest themselves and their heirs of rights, mayors, governors, and other elected officials should not be able to give away the powers of their successors or the franchise of the voters. Successors, however, cannot be allowed to disclaim previously entered judgments of liability or the trial judge's findings on the injury done to plaintiffs. From that basis, a judge can always impose a new decree if necessary.

THE CONTROLLING GROUP SHOULD BE SUBJECT TO CHECKS AND BALANCES

The controlling group has the power of an important governmental agency yet operates like a private club. It usually works in secret and by consensus, with a closed membership restricted to lawyers and governmental officials, each likely to possess strong personal agendas and institutional concerns. The insularity of the group allows, even encourages, pursuit of idiosyncratic policy agendas and perpetration of unwarranted status marked by power, fees, and management authority over large public enterprises. Missing are independent, decision-making clients whose competence and pocketbooks must be respected, as well as the rest of society affected by the controlling group's hold on government. Outsiders are mostly kept in the dark, especially after the group switches from drafting the initial decree to the less dramatic, detailed work of managing, refining, and reviewing agency performance.

Real administrative agencies operate under formal procedures that seek to prevent secrecy and surprise and discourage arbitrariness. These administrative procedures include sunshine laws, notice of proposed actions, time for comment, articulation of the basis for the decision, and the right to appeal by those adversely affected. Similar rules and procedures should be imposed on the workings of the controlling group.

The controlling group should be required to open up its work. The judge should mandate public notice of the proposed decree and subsequent modifications; should impose sunshine rules for meetings of the controlling group, especially during the post-decree management stage; and should increase the opportunity for those affected by the decree to intervene, participate, or institute collateral challenges to the decree.

THE JUDGE SHOULD COMPEL CONTINUAL UPDATING OF
THE DECREE TO ENSURE THAT A SINGLE, CONSOLIDATED
DOCUMENT IS ALWAYS AVAILABLE

All agreements and modifications should be formally incorporated into a consolidated, up-to-date document. Consolidation should not only add new provisions, but also remove completed or discarded obligations. The court should make copies of the updated decree available to the public from an easily available source, such as a Web site, in addition to the public records rooms maintained by the clerks of the courts, a location that can be inconvenient and inaccessible. Updating should also include the plans developed pursuant to the decrees in which the key obligations are finally brought down to earth.

TO ENSURE JUDICIAL IMPARTIALITY, DECREES LASTING
LONGER THAN EIGHT YEARS SHOULD BE REASSIGNED TO
A NEW JUDGE, AND ANY TRIAL FOR CONTEMPT SHOULD
BE ASSIGNED TO A SEPARATE JUDGE

Fixed terms for elected officials are everywhere embraced to check policy makers. Elected executives, including the president, have been further restricted by term limits as an additional safeguard against the disadvantages flowing from the longevity of a single personality in a key administrative position. We suggest that a term limit of eight years on judicial supervision by any one judge would facilitate reevaluation of old orders, bring to bear additional flexibility and innovative energy, and increase the potential for earlier restoration of control to elected political officials.

This is not the case now. For example, on February 13, 1999, the *New York Times* reported that the Texas attorney general had moved to terminate a twenty-year-old federal prison condition court order. The *Times* reporter was stunned to discover that the motion was pending before Judge William Wayne Justice, the "very same [judge], 78 years old now," who had signed the original order.[32] In democracy by decree it is not unusual for the same federal judge to preside for twenty or more years. Two years later in 2001 Judge Justice denied the motion and refused to terminate the order.[33]

The judge's main role in institutional reform litigation is to keep the parties moving toward compliance. Over time, however, a judge cannot escape from forming opinions on process, policy, and personality. The risk of prejudgment and imposition of personal preferences grows to unacceptable proportions when the same judge, largely unchecked by appellate review, holds authority over a public institution for decades. Judges openly displaying outright bias can be and have been removed, but that rarely happens.[34] More likely, the judge along with the controlling group will become locked into old ideas, management options, and concerns more related to status than to obligations imposed by law.

The risk that the judge will act more like an expert than a judge is great given the extreme longevity of decrees. An appellate court in 1997 reversed an order spontaneously entered by a judge who had supervised a school district for thirty years. "[G]reat knowledge," the appellate court wrote, "is a temptation as well as a resource: a temptation to blur the separation of powers, to shift the balance between the federal courts and the state and local government too far toward the court, and to disregard procedural niceties, all in fulfillment of a confident sense of mission."[35]

Once a remedial decree has been signed, judges mainly recede into the background, reappearing only to threaten defendants with punishment and award fees to plaintiffs' attorneys. For punishment, judges have relatively few and blunt tools: fines, imprisonment, and moral outrage in the form of finger pointing and blame. When a judge feels compelled to consider contempt, it would serve the interests of justice if the judge, who had earlier endorsed the methods of reform by personally attesting to their reasonableness, did not also adjudicate the reasons for their failure.

Ending the Decree

Judges and plaintiffs do not necessarily want cases to end. They often delight in them. The hidden secret of institutional reform cases is that they are more interesting, fulfilling, and satisfying to lawyers and judges than almost any other legal work. Occasionally, the veil is lifted on this fact. An appellate court recently chastised a lower court judge for delighting in the "minutiae" of management "methodologies" and for having "lost sight of the forest for its long-time attention to the trees. We write today not only to decide the specific questions presented by these appeals, but also to clarify the district court's dual missions and, in the process, refocus the attention of all concerned on the tasks at hand: remedying the constitutional infirmities the district court found existed in 1979, and terminating this litigation as speedily as possible."[36]

"Acted to Improve Prisons" read the headline of a recent obituary in the *New York Times* for Judge Stanley Weigel.[37] Judge Weigel's prison cases began in the early 1970s and involved California's San Quentin prison, Folsom prison, Deuel Vocational Institution at Tracy, and the Correctional Training Facility at Soledad prison. The obituary lauded him but did not state that his enthusiasm was so great for his prison reform cases that the appellate court restrained him four times, the last time by ordering him to stop making personal visits to prisons looking for violations where there had been no prior allegation of illegality or wrongdoing.[38]

A DECREE SHOULD BE PROMPTLY TERMINATED WHEN THE THREAT TO PLAINTIFFS' RIGHTS CEASE

Current court doctrine calls for decrees to terminate only after they are almost fully complied with, even if plaintiffs' rights are no longer threatened.[39] This may make sense when the defendants are private people, but not when they are state and local governments or officials. We favor an automatic "term limit" for decrees.[40] Once the decree has been in effect for a certain period of time—perhaps four years—the defendant government would be allowed to have it terminated unless plaintiffs can show that it is still necessary for preventing ongoing, current violations or repairing old ones.[41] The record of the Prison Litigation Reform Act shows that by placing this burden on the proponents of keeping decrees alive, judges can, where appropriate, terminate decrees and restore public institutions to public control.

JUDGES SHOULD AT THE OUTSET ANNOUNCE AN "END GAME" FOR TERMINATING THE DECREE

An end game should be mandatory. In any institutional reform case, the decree should state up front the basis for its termination. Although decrees make concrete what government must do for plaintiffs, they often fail to make concrete the terms upon which full control can be restored to officials accountable to the voters. In *Wyatt v. Stickney,* the court in the twenty-seventh year of supervision of Alabama's mental hospitals refused to terminate its order on the basis that only the court could be trusted. The judge wrote that state officials tolerated lax management. "[A]bsent direct and continuing judicial oversight," the court wrote, "it is likely that the defendants will not remedy a serious problem, even though brought out into the open; they will often deny it without adequate inquiry."[42] There are such cases, and perhaps the facts show that the *Wyatt* case is one such case, but the logical result of this assertion as a general proposition is that court supervision should never end. A court that voluntarily gives up supervision would be guilty of abandonment and betrayal.

The self-proclaimed heroic role with its cynical view of elected officials does not stand up to close scrutiny.[43] As Professor Stephen Carter wrote in reviewing Gerald Rosenberg's book *Hollow Hope,* "Rosenberg's data confirm [that] . . . the actions of the political branches of government ultimately determine whether society changes or not. The courts, acting alone, change almost nothing."[44] More importantly, it cannot be squared with traditional principles of equitable jurisprudence that limit direct judicial supervision of elected officials. There is always a risk of failure and faithlessness, but perpetual court management is not the answer.

Planning for termination forces judges to confront the practical limitations of their own power. They must acknowledge that complete compliance with statutory and regulatory aspirations will rarely, if ever, be achieved. Between stark violations that call for judicial attention and the realistic levels of success that can actually be achieved lies a crossover point where agency violations shift from being systemic and chronic to occasional and correctable by individual remedies. It is, however, devilishly hard to pinpoint the crossover point, especially once a decree has been entered. Mistakes and violations that might have been resolved by individual lawsuits become proof that the agency has not made the necessary corrections and continues to be in need of judicial supervision.

Judges should define good faith in practical terms. Judges regularly speak of good faith but less often find it when evaluating performance under a remedial decree. Instead, they find reasons to believe government lacks good faith. We thought the same way when we represented plaintiffs. Without a court order, we felt there was no assurance that the promises would be kept. Judges, however, unlike plaintiffs, have an obligation to restore governmental institutions to the control of elected officials as soon as possible.

The term "good faith" is, in the abstract, slippery and becomes even more so when used to predict how unknown, future governmental officials will perform. For this reason, judges should define good faith in concrete rather than abstract terms at the beginning of the decree by specifying just what governmental officials must do to demonstrate it. The definition might be put in temporal terms— what must be accomplished over what period of time. This essentially is what Judge Ward did when he approved the *Marisol* settlement. During a two-year trial period, New York City's Administration for Children's Services did not have to succeed in ending its violations. Instead, it had to demonstrate that it could sustain its reform agenda in a way that satisfied a panel of outside experts. The burden was on plaintiffs to show that the city was in bad faith.[45] Once the decree ended, plaintiffs could start an entirely new lawsuit should the agency backslide. In the meantime, defendants knew what they needed to do to get out from under court supervision.[46]

Once democracy by decree begins, courts tend to devalue individual lawsuits as an appropriate remedy. Individual lawsuits look pale compared with a broad remedial decree because they can solve only a single individual's problem. Yet the availability of individual remedies should help to prompt termination of broad court supervision.[47] Individual remedies, including money damages, reflect the reality that there will always be violations. Where administrative and judicial systems adequately handle individual violations, a court will be justified in ending systemic supervision.

By stating at the outset what defendants must do to end court supervision, judges signal to the public that they understand that judicial control should be temporary. It forces the judge to appraise candidly the scope and feasibility of the tasks assigned to defendants and to come to grips with the inevitability that, in most institutional reform cases, no matter the extent to which defendants are in good faith, violations of law, misjudgment, and failures will still occur. By candidly stating at the outset what it will take to terminate the decree, the trial judge can set the stage for a later, principled decision in favor of restoring local democracy.

Summary and Conclusion

We want judges to enforce rights because government must not be above the law. Yet unless the rights that courts respect also include the right to an accountable government, we will have a government of lawyers, not of law. Judges once respected that right by adhering to sensible, self-effacing principles of equity, but some judges have deviated from these traditions. The deviations have been incremental and subtle, but their cumulative consequence is the new, self-aggrandizing conception of judges as policy makers. Legislators, seizing the opportunity, invite judges to accept an even greater policy-making role in running state and local governments. The upshot is democracy by decree.

Judges respond that they are only enforcing rights. They picture rights as coming from some source that is external to themselves, such as the Constitution or a statute. This picture is inaccurate. The rights actually enforced are often negotiated in the courthouse by the controlling group rather than found by judges in statutes or constitutions.

Judges expanded a system of remedial sanctions designed to deal with reprobates and applied them to elected officials. That made sense when officials defied the Constitution, as many did in resisting *Brown v. Board of Education* or maintaining unconscionably brutal prisons. Now, however, the values that the decrees seek to achieve are often voiced in statutes enacted by popularly elected legislators. Although society is far from perfect, judges should not suppose that they alone hold the key to improvement. Remedies designed to vindicate society's values should not put society's representatives in binds where they cannot help being outlaws.

Judges also fail to heed the lesson of experience that shows that even well-intended judicial decrees are blunt instruments with which to do the delicate work of improving governmental institutions.

Finally, judges pretend that consent by the parties means that all those with a legitimate interest have appropriately acquiesced in the decree. The plaintiffs and defendants named in the caption of the complaint are never the only interested parties, and the individuals who are before the court have conflicts of interest. Government officials have interests that differ from those of the citizens who must suffer the higher tax bills and worse service that often attend democracy by decree. Plaintiffs' attorneys often have a political or personal agenda at odds with the concrete interests of their nominal clients.

Judges have failed to appreciate these errors partly because democracy by decree crept in piecemeal, partly because attacks on decrees were associated with lawless resistance to core constitutional rights, and partly because judges do not want to see that they, of all people, oversee undertakings worthy of blame.

Courts thus succumbed to the temptation to improve constitutional government. They wanted welfare to be more readily available and conditions improved for the mentally ill, prisoners, and others identified as poor and powerless. Lawyers thought that elite judges would be smarter, higher minded, and less political than state and local officials and would do a better job of running things.

No one wants to go back to segregated schools and prisons on a par with Devil's Island. Society today lauds the bravery and determination of the judges and lawyers who helped end these terrible conditions. The wellsprings of these improvements, however, were in the main the desires of society, not the dictates of courts. Courts often played a positive role in helping society find its way when judges identified violations of rights and enforced rights against resistant officials. But the hallmark of democracy by decree is ongoing management by a controlling group operating in the name of the court for the purpose of producing better policy outcomes, not simply enforcing rights.

Judicial management has generally failed to produce the level of policy outcomes that the advocates declared to be their objectives. Time has revealed unintended downsides from judicially sanctioned management of public institutions. Courts, and the interest groups they empowered, have proved no better and often worse at running things. Their style of management is all about practical politics, not high principle, yet is too rigid and top-heavy to be efficient.

Courts and judges do not operate alone; they are part of a larger political system that collectively responds to society's desires. Providing universal education or ending the disabilities associated with poverty, as a judicially delivered right, makes sense only as an abstraction. Courts can and do work at an abstract level, which is what allows them to articulate moral judgments so forcefully in response to discrimination and oppression. But education and public health and welfare are different; they are desired results that must be delivered at a human level by human institutions such as legislatures and elected mayors and governors.

What makes people like Michael Rebell, John Gray, Marcia Lowry, and the other plaintiffs' lawyers in institutional reform cases heroes is not that they wield the power of the courts, but that they devote a lifetime of energy and skills to helping others. Public-spirited people played such a role in ordinary government long before democracy by decree became the norm, and they will be needed in ordinary government after it is reformed. Lawyers will still go to court to correct stark violations of real rights, and their advocacy and compassion for the less fortunate will still penetrate the policy-making councils of government. They will no longer, however, be able to impose their policies through judicial fiat.

Rights must still be vindicated, and judges through individual lawsuits have the power to hold officials responsible. The major difference between class actions and individual lawsuits is who is in control. Lawyers prefer class actions because they control the results, whereas clients prefer individual lawsuits because they are in control. Jose P.'s mother wanted him to be educated, whereas Jose P.'s lawyers wanted to reform special education generally. The decree that the lawyers negotiated did not mention the person Jose P. What was written into the decree and its continuation over time depended on satisfying the lawyers, not the client.

Society has conducted a long-running experiment with democracy by decree. It is time for a reevaluation, but not of the values that underlie our best intentions. What needs reevaluation is our continuing reliance on courts, judges, and lawyers to do the work that in a representative democracy should properly be done by legislatures, representatives, and the people.

The most strenuous opponents of current court practices in institutional reform cases will worry that the reforms we propose do too little because they would be incremental and would still depend on judges to enforce them. Those who, on the other hand, venerate judge-led reform of state and local governments will worry that our reforms do too much because they would make it harder for plaintiffs' attorneys to use the courts to change government.

Both are right and both are wrong. Our proposed reforms are incremental, do depend on judges to enforce them, will make it harder for plaintiffs' attorneys to use the courts to change government, and so will leave more authority to state and local officials. The result will be a major contraction of democracy by decree, and yet there will be no substantial loss of rights. What will be lost is the power that controlling groups around the country have to dictate public policy. That power and the responsibility for its use will fall on officials who are accountable the constitutional way.

Our new principles and their application, although incremental, will cumulatively close the loopholes that allow courts and their controlling groups to gain and keep unjustified control over public policy. With consent decrees, and almost all remedial decrees in institutional reform cases are by consent decree, court rules will require the trial judge to vouch that the entire decree is necessary to remedy illegal injury to plaintiffs. Appellate rules will allow scrutiny of the trial court's reasons for imposing a remedial decree. Should a newly elected governor or mayor complain that the decree is no longer needed or never was necessary to remedy any illegal injury to plaintiffs, or is broader or more intrusive than necessary to do so, the trial judge will not be able to avoid the issue by simply noting that the decree is now the law of the case.

With fixed "term limits" for remedial decrees, judges cannot automatically continue a decree unless plaintiffs, as the proponents of judicial supervision, can show that it is still needed to prevent systemic injury. Now, in contrast, governors and mayors must, to end the regime of the controlling group, show that they have complied with the detailed dictates of the original decree. This shift in burden to the plaintiffs to justify their continued control will, in itself, dramatically shrink the scope of democracy by decree, as shown by a similar provision in the Prison Litigation Reform Act.

Our proposals thus place full and ongoing responsibility on the judge whenever a court decree shifts control from the statehouse and city hall to the courthouse, not only at the outset, but later when challenged by new officials or scrutinized by appellate judges. These changes will open the trial judge to criticism from appellate courts and the court of public opinion for unwarranted judicial aggrandizement.

This responsibility on trial judges will translate into pressure on plaintiffs' attorneys. Now, plaintiffs' attorneys get a long-term lock on power by giving defendant officials temporary relief from embarrassing litigation. These transient officials ought not to be able to give away power over their constituents in perpetuity. Having to rejustify the decree would be extra work for plaintiffs' attorneys, but if illegal injury is still threatened, they will be well compensated under attorneys' fees statutes for their efforts. Not only will defendants have to pay, they will suffer the political pain that comes when a judge holds that their programs are still illegal.

Most judges, we think, would be open to persuasion that although decrees have done some good, they are not an unalloyed good and that the absence of meaningful rules to limit democracy by decree is an embarrassing hiatus in judicial good citizenship. Most judges would also want to respond to instructions from higher courts or Congress that their job is not only to remedy violations of rights, but also to bring court control to an end. Elected officials, for their part, do not want to be branded violators and will be prone to work to end violations in most cases, especially if the judge displays a realistic understanding of the difficulties that they face in governmental institutions.

The upshot of our proposed reforms will be less power for the controlling group, but not less respect for rights. It will mean for the trial court judge more responsibility for the scope of court control, but less control of public policy. Such change is not too little or too much, but just right.

Appendix
Major Federal Statutes Regulating State and Local Governments

Statutes listed through 1990 (the 101st Congress) are from the Advisory Committee on Intergovernmental Relations (ACIR), *Regulatory Federalism: Policy, Process, Impact and Reform* (Washington, D.C.: ACIR, 1984), 19–21; and ACIR, *Federal Regulation of State and Local Governments: The Mixed Record of the 1980s* (Washington, D.C.: ACIR, A-126, 1993), 8, 44–55. The ACIR's list omits some statutes imposing mandates on state and local governments such as the Adoption Assistance and Child Welfare Act of 1980 discussed in the Introduction. Statutes after 1990 have been selected by the authors.

The ACIR included statutes in its list if they had one or more of the following characteristics with respect to state and local governments:

- Crosscutting Requirements: The statute's general provisions applied across the board to many or all federal grants to advance national social and economic goals as, for example, the 1964 Civil Rights Act.
- Crossover Sanctions: The statute's grant conditions imposed fiscal sanctions on one program for failure to comply with federal requirements under another program as, for example, the Education for All Handicapped Children Act of 1975.
- Partial Preemption: The statute set minimum federal standards for certain activities, including situations in which the federal government delegated administration and enforcement to the states as, for example, the Clean Air Act of 1970.
- Direct Orders: The statute imposed legal requirements enforced by civil or criminal penalties as, for example, the Equal Employment Opportunity Act of 1972.

In adding statutes after 1990, we sought to follow the ACIR's standards, but subjectivity remains in the listing of a particular statute. In addition, some clearly important statutes are hidden among other more benign enactments. For example, the statute that reversed the Supreme Court's decision in *Suter v. Artist M.*, 503 U.S. 347 (1992), and made state adoption and foster care plans enforceable, is a single section in hundreds of pages of the 1994 federal education enactment.

Statutes Enacted Before 1960

Title   Public Law No.

Davis-Bacon Act (1931)   74–403

Assured that locally prevailing wages are paid to construction workers employed under federal contracts and financial assistance programs.

Hatch Act (1940)   76–753

Prohibited public employees from engaging in certain political activities.

Statutes Enacted in the 1960s

Civil Rights Act of 1964 (Title VI)   88–352

Prevented discrimination on the basis of race, color, or ancestry in state and local government receiving federal financial assistance.

Water Quality Act   88–668

Established federal water-quality standards for interstate waters.

Highway Beautification Act of 1965   89–285

Controlled and removed outdoor advertising signs along major highways.

National Historic Preservation Act of 1966   89–665

Protected properties of historical, architectural, archeological, and cultural significance.

Wholesome Meat Act (1967)   90–201

Established systems for the inspection of meat sold in intrastate commerce.

Architectural Barriers Act of 1968   90–480

Made federally occupied and funded buildings, facilities, and public conveyances accessible to the physically handicapped.

Civil Rights Act of 1968 (Title VIII)   90–284

Prevented discrimination on the basis of race, color, or national origin in federally assisted programs.

Wholesome Poultry Products Act (1968)   90–492

Established systems for the inspection of poultry sold in intrastate commerce.

Title   Public Law No.

National Environmental Policy Act of 1969   91–190

Assured consideration of the environmental effect of major federal agencies and procedures.

Statutes Enacted in the 1970s

Occupational Safety and Health Act (1970)   91–596

Eliminated unsafe and unhealthful working conditions.

Clean Air Act Amendments of 1970   91–604

Established national air-quality and emissions standards.

Uniform Relocation Act of 1970   91–646

Set federal policies and reimbursement procedures for property acquisition under federally assisted programs.

Equal Employment Opportunity Act of 1972   92–261

Prevented discrimination on the basis of race, color, religion, sex, or national origin in state and local government employment.

Education Amendments of 1972 (Title IX)   92–318

Prevented discrimination on the basis of sex in federally assisted education programs.

Federal Water Pollution Control Act Amendments of 1972 92–500

Established federal effluent limitations to control the discharge of pollutants.

Federal Insecticide, Fungicide, and Rodenticide Act (1972) 92–516

Controlled the use of pesticides that may be harmful to the environment.

National Health Planning and Resources Development   93–64
Act of 1974

Established state and local health planning agencies and procedures.

Rehabilitation Act of 1973   93–112

Prevented discrimination against otherwise qualified individuals on the basis of physical or mental handicap in federally assisted programs.

Endangered Species Act of 1973   93–205

Protected and conserved endangered and threatened animal species.

Flood Disaster Protection Act of 1973   93–234

Expanded coverage of the national flood insurance program.

Emergency Highway Energy Conservation Act (1974)   93–239

Established a national maximum speed limit of fifty-five miles per hour.

Age Discrimination in Employment Act (1974)   93–259

Prevented discrimination on the basis of age in state and local government employment.

Title   Public Law No.

Fair Labor Standards Act Amendments of 1974   93–259
Extended federal minimum wage and overtime pay protections to state and local government employees.

Family Educational Rights and Privacy Act of 1974   93–380
Provided student and parental access to educational records while restricting access to others.

Safe Drinking Water Act of 1975   93–523
Assured the purity of drinking water.

Age Discrimination Act of 1975   94–135
Prevented discrimination on the basis of age in federally assisted programs.

Education for All Handicapped Children Act (1975)   94–142
Provided a free, appropriate public education to all handicapped children.

Coastal Zone Management Act of 1972   94–370
Assured that federally assisted activities are consistent with federally approved state coastal zone management.

Resource Conservation and Recovery Act of 1976   94–580
Established standards for the control of hazardous waste.

Marine Protection Research and Sanctuaries Act Amend-   95–153
ments of 1977
Prohibited ocean dumping of municipal sludge.

National Energy Conservation Policy Act (1978)   95–619
Established residential energy conservation plans.

Natural Gas Policy Act of 1978   95–621
Implemented federal pricing policies for the intrastate sales of natural gas in producing states.

Public Utilities Regulatory Policies Act of 1978   95–617
Required consideration of federal standards for the pricing of electricity and natural gas.

Surface Mining Control and Reclamation Act of 1977   95–87
Established federal standards for the control of surface mining.

Statutes Enacted in the 1980s

Voting Rights Act Amendments of 1982   97–205
Extended provisions of the 1965 Voting Rights Act for twenty-five years and expanded its coverage of disabled voters and those needing language assistance; amended the Voting Rights Act to prohibit any voting practice that results in discrimination, regardless of intent, thereby overturning a Supreme Court decision.

Title   Public Law No.

Surface Transportation Assistance Act of 1982   97–424
   Enacted uniform national size and weight requirements for trucks on interstate highways.

Social Security Amendments of 1983   98–21
   Prohibited state and local governments from withdrawing from Social Security coverage; accelerated scheduled increases in payroll taxes and payment of payroll taxes by state and local governments.

Highway Safety Amendments of 1984   98–363
   Set uniform national minimum legal drinking age of twenty-one.

Voting Accessibility for the Elderly and Handicapped Act 98–435
(1984)
   Required that states and political subdivisions assure that all polling places used in federal elections are accessible and that a reasonable number of accessible registration sites be provided.

Child Abuse Amendments of 1984   98–457
   Overturned federal court ruling and authorized the promulgation of "baby doe" regulations protecting seriously ill newborns

Hazardous and Solid Waste Amendments of 1984   98–616
   Reauthorized and strengthened the scope and enforcement of the Resource Conservation and Recovery Act of 1976; established a program to regulate underground storage tanks for petroleum and hazardous substances; required annual inspections by the Environmental Protection Agency of state and locally operated hazardous waste sites.

Consolidated Omnibus Budget Reconciliation Act of 1985   99–72
   Extended Medicare hospital insurance taxes and coverage to all new state and local government employees.

Handicapped Children's Protection Act of 1986   99–372
   Reversed a Supreme Court decision to allow the recovery of attorneys' fees under the Education for All Handicapped Children Act.

Safe Drinking Water Act Amendments of 1986   99–339
   Promulgated new procedures and timetables for setting national drinking water standards; established new monitoring requirements for public drinking water systems; tightened enforcement and penalties for noncomplying water systems.

Education of the Handicapped Act Amendments of 1986   99–457
   Expanded coverage and services for preschool children aged three to five years.

Title   Public Law No.
Emergency Planning and Community Right-to-Know Act   99–499
of 1986

Promulgated new national hazardous waste cleanup standards and time-tables; established a community right-to-know program, requiring state and local notification of potential hazards and dissemination of information to the public; expanded local emergency response planning.

Asbestos Hazard Emergency Response Act of 1986   99–519

Directed school districts to inspect for asbestos hazards, develop management response plans, and take necessary actions to protect health and the environment; required state review and approval of local management response plans.

Commercial Motor Vehicle Safety Act of 1986   99–570

Established minimum national standards for licensing and testing commercial and school bus drivers; directed states to issue and administer licenses by 1992 or risk losing 5 to 10 percent of major highway grants.

Age Discrimination in Employment Act Amendments of   99–592
1986

Outlawed mandatory retirement at age seventy, with a seven-year delay in coverage for police, firefighters, and college professors.

Water Quality Act of 1987   100–4

Established new grant programs and set forth requirements for states for identifying and controlling nonpoint pollution; promulgated new requirements for testing and permitting municipal storm sewer discharges; directed the Environmental Protection Agency to develop regulations governing toxic wastes in sewage sludge; reduced and restructured funding programs for municipal waste treatment plants.

Civil Rights Restoration Act of 1987   100–259

Reversed a Supreme Court decision and expanded institutional coverage of laws prohibiting racial, gender, handicapped, and age discrimination by recipients of federal assistance.

Drug-Free Workplace Act of 1988   100–690

Required certification by all federal grantees and contractors of a drug-free workplace and creation of employee awareness, sanction, and treatment programs.

Fair Housing Act Amendments of 1988   100–430

Extended the Civil Rights Act of 1968 to cover the handicapped and families with children.

Title   Public Law No.
Lead Contamination Control Act of 1988   100–572
Amended the Safe Drinking Water Act to require that states establish programs for assisting schools with testing and remedying problems with lead contamination in water coolers.
Ocean Dumping Ban Act (1988)   100–688
Outlawed remaining ocean dumping of municipal sewage sludge.

Statutes Enacted in the 1990s

Americans with Disabilities Act (1990)   101–326
Established comprehensive national standards to prohibit discrimination in public services and accommodations and to promote handicapped access to public buildings and transportation.
Cash Management Improvement Act of 1990   101–453
Created new management procedures for the disbursement of federal aid funds to states, resulting in an overall reduction of interest earned on federal funds by states.
Clean Air Act Amendments of 1990   101–459
Imposed strict new deadlines and requirements dealing with urban smog, municipal incinerators, and toxic emissions; enacted a new program for controlling acid rain.
Education of the Handicapped Act Amendments of 1990   101–476
Prevented states from claiming sovereign immunity under the Eleventh Amendment from lawsuits by parents seeking tuition reimbursement under the Handicapped Education Act, thereby reversing a Supreme Court decision.
Older Workers Benefit Protection Act of 1990   101–433
Overturned a Supreme Court decision and broadened the Age Discrimination in Employment Act's prohibitions against discrimination in employee benefit plans.
Social Security: Fiscal 1991 Budget Reconciliation Act   101–508
Extended Social Security coverage to all state and local government employees not otherwise covered by a public employee retirement system.
Individuals with Disabilities Education Act Amendments   102–119
of 1991
Extended the federal program first passed in 1975.
Intermodel Surface Transportation Efficiency Act of 1991   102–240
Imposed extensive statewide planning requirements of transportation facilities.

Title   Public Law No.
Juvenile Justice and Delinquency Prevention Amend-   102–586
ments of 1992
   Required states to adopt plans for incarcerated juveniles and prohibited use
of common prison staff for juveniles and adults.
Rehabilitation Act Amendments of 1992   102–569
   Added additional mandatory requirements to state plans.
Family and Medical Leave Act of 1993   103–3
   Required family and medical leave benefits to be given to state and local
government employees.
National Voter Registration Act of 1993   103–31
   Required states to include a voter registration application with a drivers
license application and set other standards for voter registration in federal
elections. Included a citizen suit provision for enforcing the statute in federal
court.
Brady Handgun Violence Prevention Act of 1993   103–159
   Regulated the purchase and sale of handguns. Was partially declared un-
constitutional insofar as the statute imposed an obligation on state officials to
execute federal laws. *Printz v. United States,* 521 U.S. 898 (1997).
Religious Freedom Restoration Act of 1993   103–141
   Prohibited state and local governments from placing "substantial" burdens
on religious institutions. Was declared unconstitutional in *City of Boerne v.
Flores,* 521 U.S. 507 (1997).
Improving America's Schools Act of 1994   103–382
   Reversed the Supreme Court decision in *Suter v. Antist M.*, 503 U.S. 347
(1992), by making obligations in state plans under the Social Security Act en-
forceable against state and local governments. Title V, §555.
Safe Drinking Water Act Amendments of 1996   104–182
   Extensively revised the federal requirements for public water supplies.
Personal Responsibility and Work Opportunity Recon-   104-193
ciliation Act of 1996
   Reformed the national welfare program.
Adoption and Safe Families Act, 1997   105–89
   Added additional requirements for state plans to compel states to move
children from foster care to adoption and to act within fifteen months to end
parental rights where required.
Individuals with Disabilities Education Act Amendments   105–17
of 1997
   Expanded the federal mandates under the act.

Title	Public Law No.
Foster Care Independence Act of 1999	106–169

Added requirements for children remaining in foster care and for Medicaid eligibility to age twenty-one.

Ticket to Work and Work Incentives Improvement Act of 1999	106–170

Expanded the availability of health-care coverage for working individuals with disabilities.

Notes

Introduction

1. The facts concerning Shirley Wilder's life and the history of *Wilder v. Bernstein* are taken from Nina Bernstein, *The Lost Children of Wilder* (New York: Pantheon Books, 2001).

2. *Wilder v. Sugarman*, 385 F. Supp. 1013 (S.D.N.Y. 1974).

3. *Wilder v. Bernstein*, 645 F. Supp. 1292 (S.D.N.Y. 1986), *aff'd*, 848 F. 2d 1338 (2d Cir. 1988).

4. Nina Bernstein, "Despite 20-Year Effort, City Can't Fix System," *Newsday*, July 13, 1993, p. 77.

5. Ibid.

6. Malcolm M. Feeley and Edward L. Rubin, *Judicial Policy Making and the Modern State: How the Courts Reformed America's Prisons* (Cambridge: Cambridge University Press, 1998), 13.

7. Wendy Parker, "The Future of School Desegregation," 94 *Northwestern University Law Review* 1157, 1159 (2000).

8. Dirk Johnson, "From Guiding Planes to Guiding Long-Troubled Schools," *New York Times*, May 5, 2000, p. A7. On spending and educational results, compare the dueling characterizations of the data in Judge Ross's concurring opinion of *Jenkins v. Missouri*, 216 F. 3d 720, 730–31 (8th Cir. 2000) (en banc) (Heaney, J., concurring), and 216 F. 3d 733–35 (Beam, J., dissenting). The data tell a sorry story, however characterized.

9. *LaShawn A. v. Kelly*, 887 F. Supp. 297 (D.D.C. 1995), *aff'd*, 107 F. 3d 923 (1996), *cert. denied*, 520 U.S. 1264 (1997).

10. Sari Horwitz and Scott Higham, "D.C. Regains Control of Foster Care; Child Welfare Goes to a New Agency," *Washington Post*, October 24, 2000, p. AO1.

11. See, for example, Abram Chayes, "The Role of the Judge in Public Law Litigation," 89 *Harvard Law Review* 1281, 1309 (1976) ("varying degrees of

success" with some that "may turn out to be pretty thorough going failures"); Richard A. Posner, *The Federal Courts: Challenge and Reform*, (Cambridge, Mass.: Harvard University Press, 1996), 340–42; Susan P. Sturm, "The Legacy and Future of Corrections Litigation," 142 *University of Pennsylvania Law Review* 639, 659 (1993) (acknowledging "concerns about courts' unilateral capacities to reform institutions" and "the potential for unintended negative consequences from judicial intervention and the limitations of the adversary process as a means of achieving reform"); Donald L. Horowitz, *The Courts and Social Policy* (Washington, D.C.: Brookings Institution, 1977); Peter H. Schuck, *Suing Government: Citizen Remedies for Official Wrongs* (New Haven, Conn.: Yale University Press, 1983); John J. DiIulio, Jr., *Governing Prisons: A Comparative Study of Correctional Management* (New York: Free Press, 1987).

12. Feeley and Rubin, *Judicial Policy Making*, at 26, 362.

13. Statement by Muzzy Rosenblatt, an attorney in the Boston, Massachusetts, homeless litigation, Panel Presentation on Homelessness sponsored by New York University's Robert F. Wagner Graduate School of Public Service, New York City (May 23, 2001). His point was that attorneys for the homeless have quite different agendas from those of their clients and that homeless litigation has kept government from meeting the real needs of homeless people.

14. See discussion concerning *Rhem v. Malcolm*, Chapter 5 below.

15. See discussion of the *Ho* case, Chapter 5 below.

16. See discussion of combined sewage systems, Chapter 6 below.

17. See, for example, Linda Greenhouse, "Justices Curb Federal Power to Subject States to Lawsuits," *New York Times*, March 28, 1996, sec. A1; Nina Bernstein, "An Accountability Issue," *New York Times*, April 1, 1996, sec. A1 ("Many federal laws on the environment, business, health and safety now have provisions that allow people hurt by violations of those laws to sue in Federal court. But the new decision . . . says states are immune from such suits and holds that Congress is powerless to authorize them."); Linda Greenhouse, "States Are Given New Legal Shield by Supreme Court," *New York Times*, June 24, 1999, sec. A1; Linda Greenhouse, "Justices Give the States Immunity From Suits by Disabled Workers," *New York Times*, February 22, 2001, sec. A1.

18. See, for example, *Seminole Tribe of Florida v. Florida*, 517 U.S. 44 (1996); *Alden v. Maine*, 527 U.S. 706 (1999); *College Savings Bank v. Fla. Prepaid Postsecondary Educ. Expense Bd.*, 527 U.S. 666 (1999).

19. *The Adoption Assistance and Child Welfare Act of 1980*, Pub. L. No. 96–272, 94 Stat. 500.

20. National Center for Youth Law, *Foster Care Reform Litigation Docket, 2000* (Oakland, Calif.); Robert Pear, "Many States Fail to Fulfill Child Welfare," *New York Times*, March 17, 1996, sec. A1 (reporting twenty-one states and the District of Columbia under court order).

21. Of the rich literature on the topic, we have learned from many authors, but particularly from the following: Abram Chayes, "The Role of the Judge in

Public Law Litigation," 89 *Harvard Law Review* 1281 (1976); Donald L. Horowitz, *The Courts and Social Policy* (Washington, D.C.: Brookings Institution, 1977); Owen M. Fiss, *The Civil Rights Injunction* (Bloomington: Indiana University Press, 1978). These authors were writing when democracy by decree was young and hopes were high. We have the advantage of seeing how these early decrees have turned out and the proliferation of decrees that enforce statutory rights. Other authors have studied this phenomenon more recently but either emphasized other aspects of democracy by decree, did not pinpoint the importance of the controlling group, or offered different kinds of corrective recommendations: Phillip J. Cooper, *Hard Judicial Choices: Federal District Court Judges and State and Local Officials* (New York: Oxford University Press, 1988); DiIulio, Jr., *Governing Prisons*; Gerald N. Rosenberg, *The Hollow Hope: Can Courts Bring About Social Change?* (Chicago: University of Chicago Press, 1991); Schuck, *Suing Government*; R. Shep Melnick, *Between the Lines: Interpreting Welfare Rights* (Washington, D.C.: Brookings Institution, 1994). Finally, a recent book candidly admits that federal judges set out from the beginning to assume the policy-making powers of state and local government rather than stick to enforcing rights; it nonetheless argues that this is a good thing: Feeley and Rubin, *Judicial Policy Making*. Other authors take the opposite position. Some of the most thoughtful works include the following: Jeremy Rabkin, *Judicial Compulsions: How Public Law Distorts Public Policy* (New York: Basic Books, 1989); Lino A. Graglia, *Disaster by Decree: The Supreme Court Decisions on Race and the Schools* (Ithaca, N.Y.: Cornell University Press, 1976); Raoul Berger, *Government by Judiciary: The Transformation of the Fourteenth Amendment*, 2d ed. (Indianapolis, Ind.: Liberty Fund, 1997).

Chapter 1. How Courts Came to Govern

    1. *Brown v. Bd. of Educ.*, 347 U.S. 483 (1954).

    2. Alexander M. Bickel, *The Least Dangerous Branch: The Supreme Court at the Bar of Politics*, 2d ed. (New Haven, Conn.: Yale University Press, 1986), 267–68.

    3. Gerald N. Rosenberg, *The Hollow Hope: Can Courts Bring About Social Change?* (Chicago: University of Chicago Press, 1991).

    4. Daniel P. Moynihan, *Maximum Feasible Misunderstanding: Community Action in the War on Poverty* (New York: Free Press, 1969).

    5. At least since the 1950s, issues surrounding strings tied to federal aid programs had been of political concern. In 1965, there were 125 separate federal aid programs to the states. *Five-Year Record of the Advisory Commission on Intergovernmental Relations and Its Future Role: Joint Hearings Before the Subcomm. on Intergovernmental Relations of the Senate and House Committees on Government Operations*, 89th Cong., 1st Sess., 5 (1965) (remarks of Sen. Edmund S. Muskie, chairman of the Senate Subcommittee on Intergovernmental

Relations). The Advisory Commission on Intergovernmental Relations (ACIR) began reporting on the implications of federal mandates and federally induced costs to the states in its 1978 report *Categorical Grants, Their Role and Design* (Washington, D.C.: ACIR) and continued reporting on the problem under different nomenclature ("regulatory federalism," "federal preemption," and "unfunded mandates") right up to the final draft report issued by the commission in 1996.

6. *Calvert Cliffs' Coord. Comm. v. AEC*, 449 F. 2d 1109, 1111 (D.C. Cir. 1971). The defendant in the case was a federal commission, but the judicial attitude toward state and local governments was no less aggressive.

7. There was one narrow exception for auto manufacturers who had to meet air-quality standards set by Congress for newly manufactured cars. *Clean Air Amendments of 1970*, Pub. L. No. 91–604, §202, 84 Stat. 1676, 1690–93.

8. R. Shep Melnick, *Regulation and the Courts: The Case of the Clean Air Act* (Washington, D.C.: Brookings Institution, 1983).

9. David Schoenbrod, *Power Without Responsibility: How Congress Abuses the People Through Delegation* (New Haven, Conn.: Yale University Press, 1993), 136–37.

10. *Train v. NRDC*, 421 U.S. 60, 64 (1975).

11. Irvin Molotsky, "Koch Tells Fellow Mayors Reasons to Beware of Mandated Programs," *New York Times*, January 25, 1980, p. B3.

12. Advisory Commission on Intergovernmental Relations, *Federal Statutory Preemption of State and Local Authority: History, Inventory, and Issues* (Washington, D.C.: ACIR, 1992).

13. Advisory Commission on Intergovernmental Relations, *The Role of Federal Mandates in Intergovernmental Relations: A Preliminary ACIR Report for Public Review and Comment* (Washington, D.C.: ACIR, 1996), 1.

14. Advisory Commission on Intergovernmental Relations, *Federal Court Rulings Involving State, Local, and Tribal Governments, Calendar Year 1994: A Report Prepared Under Section 304, Unfunded Mandates Reform Act of 1995* (Washington, D.C.: ACIR, 1995).

15. Perry A. Zirkel, "The 'Explosion' in Education Litigation: An Update," 114 *West's Education Law Reporter* 341 (1997). Both the Zirkel and ACIR study cited above relied entirely on decisions included in the West Reporter system, a protocol that substantially understated actual court litigation activity and ignored entirely the related administrative proceedings, most of which do not get to court.

16. Paul L. Posner, *The Politics of Unfunded Mandates: Whither Federalism?* (Washington, D.C.: Georgetown University Press, 1998).

17. The Council for Public Interest Law in 1976 defined the term *public interest law* broadly and without using either the term *civil rights* or *constitution*: "Public interest law is the name that has been given to efforts to provide legal representation to interests that historically have been unrepresented and under-

represented in the legal process. These include not only the poor and the disadvantaged but ordinary citizens who, because they cannot afford lawyers to represent them, have lacked access to courts, administrative agencies, and other legal forums in which basic policy decisions affecting their interests are made. Public interest lawyers have tried to provide systematic representation to these excluded individuals and groups in order to assure that their interests are understood and acknowledged by decision-makers." Council for Public Interest Law, *Balancing the Scales of Justice: Financing Public Interest Law in America: A Report* (Washington, D.C.: Council for Public Interest Law, 1976), 3; see also, Ford Foundation Report, *The Public Interest Law Firm: New Voices for New Constituencies* (New York: Ford Foundation, 1973).

18. Earl Johnson, Jr., *Justice and Reform: The Formative Years of the OEO Legal Services Program* (New York: Russell Sage Foundation, 1974), 71, 181.

19. Revenue Procedure 71–39 (1971–2 Cum. Bull. 575). The IRS decision is discussed in the Council for Public Interest Law, *Balancing the Scales of Justice,* at 65–66.

20. *Abrams v. N.Y.C. Transit Auth.,* 39 N.Y. 2d 990 (1976).

21. *Friends of the Earth v. Carey,* 535 F. 2d 165, 172 (2d Cir. 1976).

22. Donald L. Horowitz, "Decreeing Organizational Change: Judicial Supervision of Public Institutions," 1983 *Duke Law Journal* 1265, 1295–96.

23. Robert F. Wagner, Jr., Richard A. Chudd, David Schoenbrod, and Ross Sandler, *A New Direction in Transit: A Report to Mayor Edward I. Koch* (New York: Dept. of City Planning, No. 78–28, 1978).

24. Leo Tolstoy, *War and Peace,* trans. Louise and Aylmer Maude, vol. 2 (New York: Heritage Press, 1938), 8.

25. Ibid., at 5–6.

26. See Edward L. Rubin, "Puppy Federalism and the Blessings of America," 574 *Annals of the American Academy of Political & Social Science* 37 (2001).

Chapter 2. How Congress Creates Rights

1. The curb ramp saga was first described in Adam D. Lancer, "Two City Efforts: Curb Ramps and Preferred Sources," 3 *City Law* 125 (1997).

2. Poor drainage at a curb ramp can be costly. A Manhattan jury in 1999 awarded $709,222 to a woman who slipped on ice that accumulated at a curb ramp. *Brownell v. City of New York,* 715 N.Y.S. 2d 405 (App. Div. 1st Dep't 2000).

3. *Rehabilitation Act of 1973,* Pub. L. No. 93–112, §504, 87 Stat. 355, 394.

4. *Americans with Disabilities Act of 1990,* Pub. L. No. 101–336, 104 Stat. 327.

5. "Final Rule: Nondiscrimination on the Basis of Disability in State and Local Government Services," 56 *Federal Register* 35,694 (July 26, 1991) (codified at 28 C.F.R. Part 35).

6. *Uttilla v. City of Memphis,* 40 F. Supp. 2d 968 (W.D. Tenn. 1999), *aff'd,*

Uttilla v. Tenn. Highway Dep't, 208 F. 3d 216 (6th Cir. 2000); *Simpson v. City of Charleston*, 22 F. Supp. 2d 550 (S.D. W. Va. 1998); *Deck v. City of Toledo*, 29 F. Supp. 2d 431 (N.D. Ohio 1998), *class certified*, 1999 U.S. Dist. LEXIS 17853 (N.D. Ohio 1999); *Tyler v. City of Manhattan*, 857 F. Supp. 800 (D. Kan. 1994); *Kinney v. Yerusalim*, 812 F. Supp. 547 (E.D. Pa. 1993), *aff'd*, 9 F. 3d 1067 (3d Cir. 1993), *cert. denied, Hoskins v. Kinney*, 511 U.S. 1033 (1994). Portland, Oregon, defeated a claim involving an arena, *Independent Living Resources v. Oregon Arena Corp.*, 1 F. Supp. 2d 1124 (D. Or. 1998); as did Carlsbad, California, *Schonfeld v. City of Carlsbad*, 978 F. Supp. 1329 (S.D. Cal. 1997). A complaint remains pending against the City of New York, *Eastern Paralyzed Veterans Ass'n v. City of New York*, No. 94 Civ. 0435 (S.D.N.Y. filed Jan. 26, 1994).

7. Letter in files of the authors.

8. 60 *Federal Register* 58,462 (Nov. 27, 1995).

9. *Unfunded Mandates Reform Act of 1995*, Pub. L. No. 104–4, 109 Stat. 48.

10. "Remarks on Signing the Unfunded Mandates Reform Act of 1995," *Public Papers of the Presidents of the United States: William J. Clinton, 1995*, Book I (Washington, D.C.: GPO, 1996), 382.

11. Advisory Commission on Intergovernmental Relations, *The Role of Federal Mandates in Intergovernmental Relations: A Preliminary ACIR Report for Public Review and Comment* (Washington, D.C.: ACIR, 1996), 11–12, A-27. The fourteen statutes were the following. *For repeal with respect to state and local governments:* the Fair Labor Standards Act, Family and Medical Leave Act, Occupational Safety and Health Act, Drug and Alcohol Testing of Commercial Drivers, Metric Conversion for Plans and Specifications, Medicaid's Boren Amendment, and the required use of recycled crumb rubber. *For modification of deadlines and greater federal funding:* the Clean Water Act, Individuals with Disabilities Education Act, and the Americans with Disabilities Act. *For revisions to provide greater flexibility:* the Safe Drinking Water Act, Endangered Species Act, the Clean Air Act, and laws related to the Davis-Bacon Act.

12. Spencer Rich, "Exemptions From 7 Federal Mandates Sought for Local, State Governments," *Washington Post*, January 25, 1996, sec. A, p. 23. The lawsuit to which he referred was *Kinney v. Yerusalim*.

13. Letter to the Hon. William F. Winter, chairman, ACIR, from Marcia Hale, assistant to the president (March 1, 1996); letter to the Hon. William F. Winter, chairman, ACIR, from Janet Reno, attorney general (February 8, 1996); letter to the Hon. William F. Winter, chairman, ACIR, from Robert B. Reich, secretary of labor (March 1, 1996); letter to the Hon. William F. Winter, chairman, ACIR, from Carol M. Browner, administrator, EPA (March 5, 1996); letter to the Hon. William Winter, chairman, ACIR, from Richard W. Riley, secretary of education (March 6, 1996); letter to the Hon. William Winter, chairman, ACIR, from Gilbert F. Casellas, chairman, U.S. Equal Opportunity Commission (March 29, 1996); letter to the Hon. William F. Winter, chairman, ACIR, from Frank E. Kruesi, assistant secretary of transportation (March 1, 1996); and letter

to the Hon. William F. Winter, chairman, ACIR, from George T. Frampton, Jr., assistant secretary of the interior (March 1, 1996). Copies of the letters, obtained from ACIR's files, are in the files of the authors.

14. Amy D. Burke, "Shoot the Messenger," *The American Prospect,* January–February 1998, p. 56.

Chapter 3. How Courts Enforce Rights

1. *Education for All Handicapped Children Act of 1975,* Pub. L. No. 94-142, 89 Stat. 773. The history of advocacy and congressional alliances that led to the passage of this act is told in R. Shep Melnick, *Between the Lines: Interpreting Welfare Rights,* Chap. 7 (Washington, D.C.: Brookings Institution, 1994).

2. New Mexico at first refused to comply, but its resistance wilted when a federal court in 1982 ruled that because it accepted other federal education money, the state would have to meet federal special education standards anyway. *N.M. Ass'n for Retarded Citizens v. New Mexico,* 678 F. 2d 847 (10th Cir. 1982).

3. *Jose P. v. Ambach,* No. 79 Civ. 270 (E.D.N.Y. Feb. 1979).

4. S. Rep. No. 94–168, at 20–21 (1975), *reprinted in 1975 U.S.C.C.A.N.* 1425, 1444–45.

5. *Education for All Handicapped Children Act of 1975,* §611(a)(1)(B)(i–v), 89 Stat. 773, 776–77.

6. S. Rep. No. 94–168, 8 (1975), *reprinted in 1975 U.S.C.C.A.N.* 1425, 1432.

7. *Pa. Ass'n for Retarded Children v. Pennsylvania,* 343 F. Supp. 279 (E.D. Pa. 1972).

8. Mayor's Task Force on Special Education, "Reforming Special Education in New York City: An Action Plan," June 9, 1998; *Reid v. Bd. of Educ.,* 453 F. 2d 238, 243 (2d Cir. 1971).

9. The story of these wars has been told in many places, but perhaps best in Diane Ravitch, *The Great School Wars, New York City, 1805–1973: A History of the Public Schools as Battlefield of Social Change* (New York: Basic Books, 1974).

10. "The City in Transition: Prospects and Policies for New York: The Final Report of the Temporary Commission on City Finances" (Ray Horton, staff director), June 1977, 132.

11. Edward I. Koch, *Mayor* (New York: Simon and Schuster, 1984), 64–65.

12. Much of this history is well told in Joseph P. Viteritti's lively and authoritative *Across the River: Politics and Education in the City,* Chaps. 2 and 4 (New York: Holmes & Meier, 1983).

13. Mark Hamblett, "Law Journal Profile: Judge Experienced With Jury Race Issues," *New York Law Journal,* April 13, 1999, p. 1.

14. *Jose P. v. Ambach,* 3 *Education for the Handicapped Law Reporter* 551:245 (E.D.N.Y. May 16, 1979).

15. *Reid v. Bd. of Educ.,* 453 F. 2d at 238.

16. *United Cerebral Palsy of New York City v. Bd. of Educ.*, No. 79 Civ. 560 (E.D.N.Y.).

17. *Jose P. v. Ambach*, 551:245 at 247.

18. Ibid. The case quoted by Judge Nickerson is *Hart v. Cmty. Sch. Bd.*, 383 F. Supp. 699, 766 (E.D.N.Y. 1974).

19. *Dyrcia S. v. Bd. of Educ.*, No. 79 Civ. 2562 (E.D.N.Y.).

20. Michael A. Rebell, "*Jose P. v. Ambach:* Special Education Reform in New York City," in *Justice and School Systems: The Role of the Courts in Education Litigation,* ed. Barbara Flicker (Philadelphia: Temple University Press, 1990), 58 n. 41.

21. *Jose P. v. Ambach*, 3 *Education for the Handicapped Law Reporter* 551:245 (E.D.N.Y. May 16, 1979).

22. Interview with Marvin E. Frankel in New York City (March 8, 1999).

23. *Education for All Handicapped Children Act: Hearings on S. 6 Before the S. Subcomm. on the Handicapped of the Comm. on Labor and Public Welfare,* 93d Cong., 1st Sess., 1245 (1973) (statement of Dr. Jerry C. Gross, assistant director for program services, Special Education Division, Minneapolis Public Schools).

24. Interview with Frank J. Macchiarola in Brooklyn, N.Y. (March 25, 1999).

25. Kay Hymowitz, "Special Ed: Kids Go In, But They Don't Come Out," 6(3) *City Journal* 27, 32 (summer 1996).

26. Interview with Marvin E. Frankel in New York City (March 8, 1999).

27. Rebell, "*Jose P. v. Ambach*," at 35.

28. Ibid., at 36.

29. Interview with Joseph P. Viteritti in New York City (January 21, 2000).

30. *Jose P. v. Ambach*, No. 79 Civ. 270 (E.D.N.Y.), Special Master Rep. No. 3, at 2 (Nov. 10, 1980).

31. William L. Riordan, *Plunkett of Tammany Hall* (New York: E. P. Dutton & Co., 1973), 3.

32. Viteritti, *Across the River,* at 183–84.

33. *Jose P. v. Ambach*, No. 79 Civ. 270 (E.D.N.Y.), Special Master. Rep. No. 3 (Nov. 10, 1980).

34. *Jose P. v. Ambach*, No. 79 Civ. 270 (E.D.N.Y. filed Jan. 9, 1981), at 3.

35. Dorothy J. Gaiter, "Chief of Section on the Disabled Leaves Schools," *New York Times,* March 11, 1981, sec. B2.

36. *Jose P. v. Ambach*, No. 79 Civ. 270 (E.D.N.Y.), Special Master Rep. No. 8 (Dec. 14, 1981); Special Master Rep. No. 9, 3 *Education for the Handicapped Law Reporter* 555:304.

37. *Jose P. v. Ambach*, 3 *Education for the Handicapped Law Reporter* 553:298 (1982).

38. Affidavit of Frank J. Macchiarola, *Jose P. v. Ambach*, No. 79 Civ. 270 (E.D.N.Y. March 3, 1982).

39. Dena Kleiman, "Disabled Pupils Termed Victims of Legal Action," *New York Times*, March 4, 1982, sec. B3.

40. Ibid.

41. *Jose P. v. Ambach*, No. 79 Civ. 270 (E.D.N.Y.), Special Master Rep. No. 12, at 5–6 (Sept. 7, 1982).

42. *Jose P. v. Ambach*, 557 F. Supp. 1230, 1243 (E.D.N.Y. 1983).

43. Hymowitz, "Special Ed," at 32.

44. Jay Gottlieb, "Report to the Mayor's Commission on Special Education on COH Practices in New York City," (February 11, 1985), p. 11, Appendix B in Commission on Special Education (Richard I. Beattie, chairman), "Special Education: A Call for Quality" (April 1985) (herein after "Beattie Commission Report").

45. Beattie Commission Report, at 12, 20.

46. Ibid., at 24.

47. Ibid., at 34.

48. Ibid., at 40–41.

49. Ibid., at 58.

50. *Jose P. v. Ambach*, No. 79 Civ. 270 (E.D.N.Y.), Memorandum and Order (July 17, 1986).

51. *Jose P. v. Ambach*, 1987 WL 6232 (E.D.N.Y. Jan. 15, 1987).

52. Ibid., at 8.

53. *Jose P. v. Ambach*, 1987 WL 9684 (E.D.N.Y. Apr. 13, 1987).

54. *Jose P. v. Ambach*, No. 79 Civ. 270 (E.D.N.Y.), Stipulation (July 28, 1988).

55. Emily Sachar, "Not So Special Education; Nation's Largest Program Widely Viewed as Failure," *Newsday*, April 10, 1988, p. 4.

56. *Jose P. v. Ambach*, No. 79 Civ. 270 (E.D.N.Y.), Memorandum and Order (June 26, 1990), at 7, 9, 10.

57. *Jose P. v. Sobol*, No. 79 Civ. 270 (E.D.N.Y.), Report and Recommendation (Aug. 14, 1995), at 8.

58. *Jose P. v. Ambach*, No. 79 Civ. 270 (E.D.N.Y.), Memorandum and Order (Sept. 20, 1995).

59. Sam Dillon, "A Class Apart: Special Education in New York City," *New York Times*, April 7, 1994, sec. A1, col. 2.

60. Norm Fruchter, et al., NYU Institute for Education and Social Policy, "Focus on Learning: A Report on Reorganizing General and Special Education in New York City" (October 1995).

61. Fee data supplied by the New York City Law Department.

62. Michael Rebell, attorney for the United Cerebral Palsy plaintiffs, did not participate in the negotiations. The reference to plaintiffs and their attorneys in this section refers to the *Jose P.* and *Dyrcia S.* plaintiffs, and the amicus, Advocates for Children.

63. *Jose P. v. Mills*, No. 96 Civ. 1834 (E.D.N.Y.), Stipulation (Nov. 29, 2000).

The new case number for *Jose P.* was assigned when the Brooklyn federal court computerized its dockets.

64. Ibid., at 12.

65. Ibid., at 11.

66. Fee data supplied by the New York City Law Department.

67. Nick Chiles, "Legacy of Jose P. Still Haunts City: City on the Brink: Education: Sixth in a Series," *Newsday*, December 15, 1989, p. 32

68. New York City, *The Mayor's Management Report*, vol. 2 (New York: The Mayor, September 21, 2000), 153, 158; New York Bd. of Educ., *School Based Expenditure Reports—School Year 1999–2000*.

69. New York City, *The Mayor's Management Report*, at 153.

70. Ibid., at 158.

71. Hymowitz, "Special Ed," at 41.

72. Rebell, "*Jose P. v. Ambach*," at 27.

73. Interview with John Gray in New York City (February 19, 1999). Michael Rebell reaches somewhat similar conclusions about the efficacy of courts as implementers of remedies in social change litigation. Michael A. Rebell and Arthur R. Block, *Educational Policy Making and the Courts: An Empirical Study of Judicial Activism* (Chicago: University of Chicago Press, 1982), 215.

74. Hymowitz, "Special Ed," at 41.

75. Joseph Berger, "Costly Special Classes Serving Many With Minimal Needs," *New York Times*, April 30, 1991, sec. A1, col. 1.

76. Mary-Beth Fafard, Robert E. Hanlon, and Elizabeth A. Bryson, "*Jose P. v. Ambach:* Progress towards Compliance," 52 *Exceptional Children* 313 (January 1986).

77. Interview with Frank J. Macchiarola in Brooklyn, N.Y. (March 25, 1999). See also Frank J. Macchiarola, "The Courts in the Political Process: Judicial Activism or Timid Local Government?" 9 *St. John's Journal of Legal Commentary* 703 (1994).

78. U.S. Dept. of Education, *Twenty-second Annual Report to Congress on the Implementation of the Individuals with Disabilities Education Act (IDEA)* (Washington, D.C.: U.S. Dept. of Education, 2000), II-20 to II-21, *available at* http://www.ed.gov/offices/OSERS/OSEP/PRODUCTS/OSEP2000AnlRpt/ (last modified Oct. 25, 2001).

79. New York City Bd. of Educ., PD-1 Report (December 2001).

80. Kate Zernike, "Special Education Debate Shifts From Money to New Ideas," *New York Times*, May 13, 2001, sec. 1., p. 27.

81. Michael Winerip, "A Disabilities Program that 'Got Out of Hand,' " *New York Times*, April 8, 1994, sec. A1, col. 1. See also Wade F. Horn and Douglas Tynan, "Revamping Special Education," *The Public Interest* 36, 40 (summer 2001), reporting that "while children from families with more than $100,000 in annual income account for just 13 percent of the SAT test-taking population,

they make up 27 percent of those who receive special accommodations when taking the SAT."

82. *Hart v. Cmty. Sch. Bd., aff'd,* 512 F. 2d 37 (2d Cir. 1975). The idea of a "polycentric" problem was a central feature of an important article by Professor Lon Fuller, "Adjudication and the Rule of Law," 54 *Proceedings of the American Society of International Law* 1 (1960).

83. Colin S. Diver, "The Judge as Political Powerbroker: Superintending Structural Change in Public Institutions," 65 *Virginia Law Review* 43 (1979).

84. Anemona Hartocollis, "U.S. Questions The Placement of City Pupils," *New York Times,* November 21, 1998, sec. B1, col. 5. Memorandum of Understanding, entered into by the U.S. Dept. of Education, Office for Civil Rights, the Board of Education of the City of New York, and the New York State Education Dept. in Conjunction with the U.S. Dept. of Education, Office of Special Education Programs, May 30, 1997 (Case Nos. 02–96–5004).

85. Frederick J. Weintraub and Bruce A. Ramirez, *Progress in the Education of the Handicapped and Analysis of P.L. 98–199, the Education of the Handicapped Act Amendments of 1983* (Reston, Va.: Council for Exceptional Children, 1985), 17.

86. U.S. Dept. of Education, *Nineteenth Annual Report to Congress on the Implementation of the Individuals with Disabilities Education Act (IDEA)* (Washington, D.C.: Dept. of Education, 1997), I-28, I-29, I-32, *available at* http://www.ed.gov/offices/OSERS/OSEP/Research/OSEP97AnlRpt/(last modified Oct. 15, 2001). The Department of Education's estimates of the federal share were based on a 1993–94 survey of twenty-four states that did *not* include New York, New Jersey, Illinois, Texas, Ohio, or the District of Columbia, among others. While this study is the only one that has been published in recent years, it presents a better face on the size of the federal share of special education expenses than is likely the case because the study omitted so many high-cost states.

87. *New York City Bd. of Educ. FY '00 Ex. Rep.,* No. 1 (February 2000), p. 3.

88. In 1988 the parties developed a partial exit strategy by defining "substantial compliance." The definition, couched with many provisos and sounding a lot like full compliance, called for a 90 percent success rate for one year in meeting the sixty-day deadline on evaluating, placing, and arranging for transportation for children needing special education, and a 99 percent success rate within eighty days. Certain adjustments were allowed when parents failed to consent. Substantial compliance also called for a 97 percent success rate in performing triennial evaluations within the month due, and a 99 percent success rate within the following month. The agreement further conditioned termination on meeting other targets for students with limited English proficiency and for hiring bilingual professionals. Not defined, however, was the meaning of substantial compliance on providing related services. The parties noted the

disagreement and agreed to keep trying. *Jose P. v. Sobol*, No. 79 Civ. 270 (E.D.N.Y.), Stipulation (July 28, 1988), par. 49–60. The termination provision has been a dead letter since it was agreed to.

Chapter 4. Something New Is Going On In Court

1. Charles A. Reich, "The New Property," 73 *Yale Law Journal* 733 (1964). For a cogent argument that the rights-benefit distinction generally did not bar the recipients of most forms of new property from being heard in court, see R. Shep Melnick, *Between the Lines: Interpreting Welfare Rights* (Washington, D.C.: Brookings Institution, 1994), 44.

2. Reich, "The New Property," at 733.

3. *Goldberg v. Kelly*, 397 U.S. 254 (1970). Reich's views were very much on the minds of all the key participants in the *Goldberg* litigation, including Justice William J. Brennan, who wrote the Court's majority opinion. The story of the decision and Reich's effect on it is told by Martha F. Davis in *Brutal Need: Lawyers and the Welfare Rights Movement, 1960–1973* (New Haven, Conn.: Yale University Press, 1993), 104–18.

4. The contrast between traditional remedies as simple and quick and those in institutional reform cases as complicated and ongoing was first prominently pointed out by Professor Abram Chayes. We discuss his work at length in Chapter 5. Although Chayes lauded the new litigation, others of its supporters worried that the very newness of it would make it seem unprecedented and therefore illegitimate. In particular, Theodore Eisenberg and Stephen C. Yeazell, in "The Ordinary and the Extraordinary in Institutional Reform Litigation," 93 *Harvard Law Review* 465 (1980), argued that the new was not as new as Chayes made it out to be. There is something to their point. Chayes's descriptions were in generalities that admitted exceptions. Nonetheless, we think Eisenberg and Yeazell strain too hard to make the new look like the old. They point out that traditional courts were willing to undertake ongoing management of complex institutions, such as in probate and bankruptcy (ibid., at 481–86). The cases they cite deal, however, with *private* trusts and *private* bankrupts (ibid.). Such cases do not provide precedent for ongoing judicial control of *governmental* institutions, at least those that are not bankrupt. To the extent that government involves trusts, the trustees are, in a republican form of government, electorally accountable officials, not appointed judges with life tenures. To bridge this gap from private to public defendants, Eisenberg and Yeazell point out that British courts routinely issued writs of mandamus. They must acknowledge, however, that "it is only in comparatively recent centuries that such 'extraordinary' writs have been transformed from the stuff of everyday political life into exotics of the legal firmament" (ibid., at 490). And for good reason—democratic accountability. Early in our republic, mandamus was recognized as a writ reserved for

compelling performance of ministerial duties, not to control the kind of discretionary duties that in a republic are left to politically accountable officials. *Marbury v. Madison,* 5 U.S. (1 Cranch) 137, 170–71 (1803). Eisenberg and Yeazell try to justify the modern institutional reforms by pointing out they are "a response to problems of intransigence and complexity that the law has dealt with in 'extraordinary' ways for centuries" (ibid., at 491). Yet they cite no instances of complicated, ongoing remedies against government defendants in old American case law. Besides, the lack of full compliance in democracy by decree often stems more from the aspirational nature of the rights and the decrees than from the resistance of defendants, as we show in Chapters 4 and 5. Finally, Eisenberg and Yeazell argue that many modern institutional reform cases "are little more than judicial opinions blessing settlements negotiated by the parties" (ibid., at 493). We disagree and show why in Chapters 5 through 7.

5. James A. Henderson, Jr., and Richard N. Pearson, "Implementing Federal Environmental Policies: The Limits of Aspirational Commands," 78 *Columbia Law Review* 1429 (1978).

6. *Swann v. Charlotte-Mecklenberg Bd. of Educ.,* 402 U.S. 1, 15 (1971).

7. *Milliken v. Bradley,* 433 U.S. 267 (1977).

8. See *Swann v. Charlotte-Mecklenberg Bd. of Educ.,* 402 U.S. at 26.

9. Douglas Laycock, *Modern American Remedies: Cases and Materials* (Boston: Little, Brown, 1985), 259.

10. Examples include *Missouri v. Jenkins,* 11 F. 3d 755, 759, 764–66 (8th Cir. 1993), *rev'd, Missouri v. Jenkins,* 515 U.S. 70 (1995); *Missouri v. Jenkins,* 959 F. Supp. 1151, 1157–65, 1179 (W.D. Mo.), *aff'd,* 122 F. 3d 588 (8th Cir. 1997); *San Francisco NAACP v. San Francisco Unified Sch. Dist.,* 576 F. Supp. 34 (N.D. Cal. 1983).

11. See Malcolm M. Feeley and Edward L. Rubin, *Judicial Policy Making and the Modern State: How the Courts Reformed America's Prisons* (Cambridge: Cambridge University Press, 1998), 13–17.

12. This is most clearly stated in cases not dealing with prisons. *Rizzo v. Goode,* 423 U.S. 362, 371–72 (1976); *Gen. Bldg. Contractors Ass'n v. Pennsylvania,* 458 U.S. 375, 400–01 (1982).

13. See *Swann v. Charlotte-Mecklenberg Bd. of Educ.,* 402 U.S. at 16; *Rizzo v. Goode,* 423 U.S. at 377.

14. Henderson and Pearson, "Implementing Federal Environmental Policies," at 1429.

15. Michael A. Rebell, "*Jose P. v. Ambach:* Special Education Reform in New York City," in *Justice and School Systems: The Role of the Courts in Education Litigation,* ed. Barbara Flicker (Philadelphia: Temple University Press, 1990), 26–27.

16. See, for example, *Swann v. Charlotte-Mecklenberg Bd. of Educ.,* 402 U.S. at 1.

17. Dan B. Dobbs, *Law of Remedies: Damages, Equity, Restitution*, vol. 1, 2d ed. (St. Paul, Minn.: West Pub. Co., 1993), 224–25.

18. See, for example, *Virginia v. West Virginia*, 246 U.S. 565 (1918).

19. Feeley and Rubin, *Judicial Policy Making*, at 5, 9–14, 208, 337–40.

20. *Sobky v. Smoley*, 855 F. Supp. 1123 (E.D. Cal. 1994).

21. *Esteban v. Cook*, 77 F. Supp. 2d 1256 (S.D. Fla. 1999).

22. *Frew v. Gilbert*, 109 F. Supp. 2d 579 (E.D. Tex. 2000).

23. *Westside Mothers v. Haveman*, No. 99–73442 (E.D. Mich. filed July 12, 1999); *Dajour B. v. City of New York*, No. 00 Civ. 2044 (S.D.N.Y. Mar. 17, 2000); *Advocates for Special Kids v. Or. State Bd. of Educ.*, No. CV 99-26 KI (D. Or. filed Feb. 22, 1999); *John v. Menke*, No. 3–98–0168 (M.D. Tenn. Feb. 25, 1998).

24. 20 U.S.C. §1401 et seq.

25. *Smith v. Wheaton*, No. H-87–190 (D. Conn. Apr. 26, 2000); *Blackman v. District of Columbia*, 185 F.R.D. 4 (D.C.C. 1999); *LIH v. New York City Bd. of Educ.*, 103 F. Supp. 2d 658 (E.D.N.Y. 2000).

26. 42 U.S.C. §12101 et seq.

27. 23 *Mental & Physical Disability Law Reporter* 9 (1999), and subsequent annual counts.

28. *Olmstead v. L.C. by Zimring*, 527 U.S. 581 (1999).

29. Data come from the National Association of Protection and Advocacy Web site, *available at* http://www.protectionandadvocacy.com (last visited Feb. 27, 2002).

30. *Barthelemy v. Louisiana Dep't of Health & Hosps.*, No. 00–1083 (E.D. La. filed July 14, 2000); *Olesky v. Haveman*, No. 5:99 cv-105 (W.D. Mich. May 2, 2000).

31. Donald L. Horowitz, "Decreeing Organizational Change: Judicial Supervision of Public Institutions," 1983 *Duke Law Journal* 1265, 1288.

32. Colin S. Diver, "The Judge as Political Powerbroker: Superintending Structural Change in Public Institutions," 65 *Virginia Law Review* 43 (1979).

Chapter 5. How Court Management Works

1. Abram Chayes, "The Role of the Judge in Public Law Litigation," 89 *Harvard Law Review* 1281 (1976).

2. Ibid., at 1282–83.

3. Ibid., at 1283.

4. See, for example, *Adams v. Richardson*, 480 F. 2d. 1159 (D.C. Cir. 1973); *Sierra Club v. Ruckelshaus*, 344 F. Supp. 253 (D.C. 1972), *aff'd*, 412 U.S. 541 (1973).

5. Chayes, "The Role of the Judge," at 1282.

6. Donald L. Horowitz, *The Courts and Social Policy* (Washington, D.C.: Brookings Institution, 1977), 45–56.

7. See also Margo Schlanger, "Beyond the Hero Judge: Institutional Reform Litigation as Litigation," 97 *Michigan Law Review* 1994, 1999–2000 (1999)

(pointing out that Malcolm M. Feeley and Edward L. Rubin also mistake the judge as the central actor in *Judicial Policy Making and the Modern State: How the Courts Reformed America's Prisons* (New York: Cambridge University Press, 1998).

8. *Missouri v. Jenkins*, 495 U.S. 33 (1990) (considering how to finance implementation of a consent decree in the face of limits on local taxation in the state constitution); *Spallone v. United States*, 493 U.S. 265 (1990) (considering how to force city council members to enact a measure needed to implement consent decrees).

9. See, for example, David I. Levine, "The Chinese American Challenge to Court-Mandated Quotas in San Francisco's Public Schools: Notes from a (Partisan) Participant-Observer," 16 *Harvard BlackLetter Law Journal* 39 (spring 2000).

10. *R.C. v. Petelos*, No. 88-D-1170-N (M.D. Ala. 1988).

11. *G.L. v. Stangler*, No. 77-242-CV-W-3-JWO (W.D. Mo. 1977). Of the many litigation events of this lawsuit, only two resulted in published opinions: *G.L. v. Zumwalt*, 564 F. Supp. 1030 (W.D. Mo. 1983) (approving the initial consent decree), and *G.L. v. Zumwalt*, 731 F. Supp. 365 (W.D. Mo. 1990) (threatening the defendants in contempt sanctions).

12. Ellen Borgersen and Stephen Shapiro, "*G.L. v. Stangler:* A Case Study in Court-Ordered Child Welfare Reform," 1997 *Journal of Dispute Resolution* 189, 211.

13. National Center for Youth Law, "Foster Care Reform Litigation Docket: 2000." The report is helpful because key events for each of the cases listed are described, a valuable service since most of the decisions and orders in the cases are unreported. Available at http://www.youthlaw.org/Fcdocket.htm (last updated Sept. 20, 2000).

14. Edward V. Sparer, "The Role of the Welfare Client's Lawyer," 12 *UCLA Law Review* 361, 375 (1965).

15. Borgersen and Shapiro, "*G.L. v. Stangler:* A Case Study," at 209.

16. Murray Levine, "The Role of Special Master in Institutional Reform Litigation: A Case Study," 8 *Law and Policy* 275 (1986).

17. Michele Herman, "Rhem v. Malcolm: A Case Study of Public Interest Litigation" (master's thesis, Harvard Law School, 1977), p. 41.

18. See, for example, Derrick A. Bell, Jr., *Race, Racism and American Law* (Boston: Little, Brown, 3d ed., 1992), 613–23 (on the clash between the NAACP and parents who wanted the emphasis to be on better schools, not racial balance).

19. *Rufo v. Inmates of Suffolk County Jail*, 502 U.S. 367, 377 (1992).

20. For example, in *Benjamin v. Jacobson*, 1995 WL 681297 (S.D.N.Y. Oct. 2, 1995), plaintiffs' attorneys opposed a change in who provides meals to prisoners. The litigation on this matter took several months.

21. See generally, Robert A. Kagan, "Adversarial Legalism: Tamed or Still

Wild," 2 *New York University Journal of Legislation & Public Policy* 217, 238 (1999).

22. 924 F. Supp. 1323 (S.D.N.Y. 1996).

23. *N.Y. Real Prop. Acts.* §711 (5) and §715 (Consol. 1981).

24. Valerie D. White, "Modifying the *Escalera* Consent Decree: A Case Study of the Application of the *Rufo* Test," 23 *Fordham Urban Law Journal* 377 (1996); see also Kierna Mayo Dawsey, "Strike Out," *City Limits,* May 1996, p. 8, reporting that tenants were split over fast-track evictions of criminals.

25. *Board of Education v. Dowell,* 498 U.S. 237, 249–50 (1991). ("The District Court should address itself" to whether the board had complied in good faith with the desegregation decree since it was entered, and whether the vestiges of past discrimination had been eliminated to the extent practicable.) *Freeman v. Pitts,* 503 U.S. 467, 492 (1992). The leading modification case holds that it is the decree rather than the underlying law that sets the floor. *Rufo v. Inmates of Suffolk County Jail,* 502 U.S. 367, 391 (1992).

26. *Wilder v. Bernstein,* 645 F. Supp. 1292 (S.D.N.Y. 1986). Fee data provided by the New York City Administration for Children's Services.

27. *Marisol A. v. Giuliani,* 111 F. Supp. 2d 381 (S.D.N.Y. 2000).

28. *United States v. City of Yonkers,* 181 F. 3d 301, 310 (2d Cir.), *vacated on reh'g,* 197 F. 3d 41 (2d Cir. 1999). See also, *Jenkins v. Missouri,* 515 U.S. 70, 99 (1995); *Ho v. San Francisco Unified Sch. Dist.,* 147 F. 3d. 854 (9th Cir. 1998); Levine, "The Chinese American Challenge," at 39, 72–73, 124–25 (discussing *Ho* and other examples).

29. *McLaughlin v. Boston Sch. Comm.,* 938 F. Supp. 1001 (D. Mass. 1996).

30. Deborah L. Rhode, "Class Conflicts in Class Actions," 34 *Stanford Law Review* 1183, 1217 (1982) (quoting David Kirp, "The Bounded Politics of School Desegregation Litigation," 51 *Harvard Education Review* 395, 402 [1981]).

31. If a decree is not terminated yet is also not under active supervision, it may still be enforced. *Bd. of Educ. v. Dowell,* 498 U.S. 237 (1991).

32. 451 U.S. 1 (1981).

33. *Halderman v. Pennhurst State Sch. & Hosp.,* 9 F. Supp. 2d 544 (E.D. Pa. 1998).

34. Rhode, "Class Conflicts," at 1183.

35. Despite the lack of consent from interveners, the court may still be able to enter the decree. *Local No. 93, Int'l Ass'n of Firefighters v. City of Cleveland,* 478 U.S. 501, 528 (1986). Nonetheless, the threat of appeal makes the interveners a force to be reckoned with in settlement talks.

36. This account is a brief summary of the much fuller account in Levine, "The Chinese American Challenge."

37. *Ho v. San Francisco Unified Sch. Dist.,* 147 F. 3d 85 (1998) (dismissing appeal of the denial of summary judgment, yet going on to provide an advisory opinion on the standard to be applied at trial); Order, *Ho v. United States Dist. Ct.,* No. 98–71415 (filed Dec. 14, 1998) (granting writ of mandamus against the

trial judge appointing a special master to take up the burden of proof that defendants should shoulder).

38. Charles J. Cooper, "The Collateral Attack Doctrine and the Rules of Intervention: A Judicial Pincer Movement on Due Process," 1987 *University of Chicago Legal Forum* 155, 156 n. 4; *Harris v. Reeves,* 946 F. 2d 214 (3d Cir. 1991).

39. Rhode, "Class Conflicts," at 1187.

40. The states are Connecticut (two cases), Kansas, Kentucky (two cases), Louisiana, Missouri, New Mexico, New York (three cases), and Pennsylvania, as well as Washington, D.C. National Center for Youth Law, "Foster Care Reform Litigation Docket: 1998."

41. "Public interest law," the Council for Public Interest Law wrote in 1976, "has been a response to the problem that policy formulation in our society is too often a one-sided affair—a process in which only the voices of the economically or politically powerful are heard." Council for Public Interest Law, *Balancing the Scales of Justice: Financing Public Interest Law in America: A Report* (Washington, D.C.: Council for Public Interest Law, 1976), 8.

42. Chayes, "The Role of the Judge," at 1313.

Chapter 6. A Good Thing Gone Wrong

1. *TVA v. Hill,* 437 U.S. 153 (1978).

2. David S. Schoenbrod, "The Measure of an Injunction: A Principle to Replace Balancing the Equities and Tailoring the Remedy," 72 *Minnesota Law Review* 627, 636–70 (1988).

3. Colin S. Diver, "The Judge as Powerbroker: Superintending Structural Change in Public Institutions," 65 *University of Virginia Law Review* 43, 45 (1979).

4. Douglas Martin, "Water Projects' Bill Worries Even Environmentalists," *New York Times,* June 15, 1998, sec. B1 (emphasis added). Another environmental attorney with the Natural Resources Defense Council echoed the thought: "There is a need for some sensible priority setting and triage" (ibid.).

5. New York City, "Mayor's Management Report" (preliminary FY 2000), vol. II, p. 131.

6. In July 1996, Judge Robert J. Ward issued an opinion favorable to plaintiffs' attorneys on many issues of law. *Marisol A. v. Giuliani,* 185 F.R.D. 152 (S.D.N.Y. 1999). They began aggressive pretrial discovery.

7. The road to improvement has been every bit as rocky as Scoppetta expected. See Nina Bernstein, "Pattern Cited in Missed Signs of Child Abuse," *New York Times,* July 22, 1999, sec. A1.

8. James Q. Wilson, *Bureaucracy: What Government Agencies Do and Why They Do It,* Chap. 1 (New York: Basic Books, 1989).

9. *Marisol A. v. Giuliani,* 185 F.R.D. 152 (S.D.N.Y.), *aff'd sub nom. at Joel A. v. Giuliani,* 218 F. 3d 132 (2d Cir. 2000); Report of Special Child Welfare Advisory Panel, December 7, 2000.

10. As Donald L. Horowitz put it, "The assumptions carried by the traditional model into institutional reform litigation are easily stated. A decree, when rendered, demands compliance. If the requirements of a decree were not fulfilled, there must be noncompliance, typically because of 'bureaucratic intransigence.' To achieve compliance, some combination of coercion (or threat of coercion), persistence, and expertise—the latter of the two often embodied in the person of a special master—is necessary." "Decreeing Organizational Change: Judicial Supervision of Public Institutions," 1983 *Duke Law Journal* 1265, 1295.

11. Robert Pear, "Many States Fail to Fulfill Child Welfare," *New York Times*, March 17, 1996, sec. 1, p. 1, col. 6. Utah's attempts to extricate itself from the decree can be found in *David C. v. Leavitt*, 13 F. Supp. 2d 1206 (D. Utah 1998), *aff'd*, 242 F. 3d 1206 (10th Cir. 2001), *cert. denied*, 122 S. Ct. 56 (2001).

12. Peter H. Schuck, *Suing Government: Citizen Remedies for Official Wrongs* (New Haven, Conn.: Yale University Press, 1983), 155, citing many of the commentaries on the efficacy of decrees. See also, case studies in Phillip J. Cooper, *Hard Judicial Choices: Federal District Court Judges and State and Local Officials* (New York: Oxford University Press, 1988).

13. Gerald N. Rosenberg, *The Hollow Hope: Can Courts Bring About Social Change?* (Chicago: University of Chicago Press, 1991). Rosenberg examined in detail the litigation campaigns on school desegregation, abortion, prison conditions, and other famous examples of judicial "success" in constitutional cases. He concluded that the decrees were effective in achieving their objectives only when they had the support of the politically accountable branches of government. Where they lacked such support, there was little or no progress. Rosenberg also examined the hypothesis that court decisions led public opinion and thereby created the conditions for the eventual, successful enforcement of rights. But he found the evidence to be to the contrary; judicial opinions did not so much lead public opinion as follow it. The judges "cut the ribbon" for social change that was in the works anyway.

14. Neal Devins, "Review Essay: Judicial Matters," 80 *California Law Review* 1027, 1068 (1992). Devins finds that Rosenberg overstates his case. Devins argues, however, that Rosenberg's evidence sustains a milder thesis in which courts can sometimes help to sway the rest of government, if not unilaterally then by engaging in a dialogue with it. We agree with this milder thesis. See also, R. Shep Melnick, *Between the Lines: Interpreting Welfare Rights* (Washington, D.C.: Brookings Institution, 1994), 236–37.

15. "What Judges Can Do to Improve Prisons and Jails," Chap. 11 in *Courts, Corrections, and the Constitution*, ed. John J. DiIulio, Jr. (New York: Oxford University Press, 1990). A similar point was made by Ellen Borgersen and Stephen Shapiro in their study of the Kansas City child welfare case. They emphasize the role of experts, both in the substance of the mission and in governmen-

tal processes, collaboration rather than litigation between the plaintiffs and the defendants, and efforts to build "grass-roots political support for sustained reform." *"G.L. v. Stangler:* A Case Study in Court-Ordered Child Welfare Reform," 1997 *Journal of Dispute Resolution* 189, 211–12. See also, James B. Jacobs, *New Perspectives on Prisons and Imprisonment,* Chap. 2 (Ithaca, N.Y.: Cornell University Press, 1983).

16. E-mail from American Civil Liberties Union President Nadine Strossen to authors, August 26, 2001 (noting shift in resources at her organization and in the allocation of resources by leading foundations). We have noted a parallel shift in strategy by environmental organizations, including the Natural Resources Defense Council.

17. Michael A. Rebell and Robert L. Hughes, "Special Educational Inclusion and the Courts: A Proposal for a New Remedial Approach," 25 *Journal of Law & Education* 523 (1996). The proposal was made in the context of individual cases, not class actions, but its logic applies to all actions, and Rebell himself has begun implementation of his model in a class action dealing with school funding.

18. Ibid., at 566.

19. Ibid., at 567.

20. *City of Boerne v. Flores,* 521 U.S. 507 (1997) (discussing Congress's power under section 5 of the Fourteenth Amendment).

21. Donald L. Horowitz, *The Courts and Social Policy* (Washington, D.C.: Brookings Institution, 1977), 298.

22. *Printz v. United States,* 521 U.S. 898, 930 (1997).

23. Horowitz, *The Courts and Social Policy,* at 52.

24. *The Federalist,* No. 10 (James Madison), ed. Jacob E. Cooke (Middletown, Conn.: Wesleyan University Press, 1961), 58–59.

25. Ibid., at 64–65; *The Federalist,* No. 51 (James Madison), 351.

26. Robert E. Buckholz, Jr., et al., Special Project, "The Remedial Process in Institutional Reform Litigation," 78 *Columbia Law Review* 784, 904 n.199.

27. Jeremy A. Rabkin, *Judicial Compulsions: How Public Law Distorts Public Policy* (New York: Basic Books, 1989), 248, 270.

28. Peter H. Schuck, "Benched: The Pros and Cons of Having Judges Make the Law," *Washington Monthly,* December 1, 2000, pp. 35, 41.

29. Robert H. Jackson, *The Struggle for Judicial Supremacy: A Study of a Crisis in American Power Politics* (New York: A. A. Knopf, 1941), 321.

Chapter 7. Why the Wrong Thing Continues

1. *Mt. Healthy City Sch. Dist. v. Doyle,* 429 U.S. 274 (1977); *Rizzo v. Goode,* 423 U.S. 362 (1976); *Lewis v. Casey,* 518 U.S. 343 (1996).

2. For prison condition cases, see Malcolm M. Feeley and Edward L.

Rubin, *Judicial Policy Making and the Modern State: How the Courts Reformed America's Prisons* (Cambridge: Cambridge University Press, 1998), 8–15, 24, 146, 162, 209, 265. For school desegregation cases, see Douglas Laycock, *Modern American Remedies: Cases and Materials* (Boston: Little, Brown, 1985), 260–61.

3. The Constitution limits the power of courts to deciding "cases and controversies." U.S. Constitution, art. 3, sec. 2, cl. 1. That limitation serves to keep courts from wandering from judicial to political business. *Seminole Tribe v. Florida,* 517 U.S. 44, 73 (1996); *Pennsylvania v. Union Gas Co.,* 491 U.S. 1 (1989); *Warth v. Seldin,* 422 U.S. 490, 499 (1975) ("The Art. III judicial power exists only to redress or otherwise protect against injury to the complaining party, even though the court's judgment may benefit others collaterally."). See also, *Lujan v. Nat'l Wildlife Fed'n,* 497 U.S. 871, 891 (1990); *City of Los Angeles v. Lyons,* 461 U.S. 95, 101 (1983); George Rutherglen, "Notice, Scope, and Preclusion in Title VII Class Actions," 69 *Virginia Law Review* 11 (1983). For protecting everybody, see, for example, *Casey v. Lewis,* 834 F. Supp. 1553 (D. Ariz. 1992), *aff'd in part, vacated in part,* 43 F. 3d 1261 (9th Cir. 1994), *rev'd,* 518 U.S. 343 (1996); *San Francisco NAACP v. San Francisco Unified Sch. Dist.,* 576 F. Supp. 34 (N.D. Cal. 1983).

4. Feeley and Rubin, *Judicial Policy Making,* at 81, 100.

5. *City of Los Angeles v. Lyons,* 461 U.S. at 102–3; *Hecht Co. v. Bowles,* 321 U.S. 321 (1944).

6. *Lewis v. Casey.*

7. Lacey Mudge, "Whether Lower Courts Follow the Holding of *Lewis v. Casey,*" May 15, 1999, 19 (student paper on file with authors).

8. See, for example, *Milliken v. Bradley,* 433 U.S. 267, 280–81 (1977); *Missouri v. Jenkins,* 515 U.S. 70, 102 (1995); *Rufo v. Inmates of Suffolk County Jail,* 502 U.S. 392 n. 14 (1992).

9. *Milliken v. Bradley,* 433 U.S. at 280–88.

10. See, for example, Laycock, *Modern American Remedies,* at 291.

11. Feely and Rubin's account of prison condition litigation describes how judges set out to reform entire institutions rather than correct specific violations of law asserted by individual plaintiffs. Some judges even asked lawyers to bring lawsuits on behalf of all the inmates. See Feeley and Rubin, *Judicial Policy Making,* at 175.

12. *Turner v. Safley,* 482 U.S. 78 (1987); *Pennhurst State Sch. & Hosp. v. Halderman,* 465 U.S. 89, 106 (1984) (stating that "it is difficult to think of a greater intrusion on state sovereignty than when a federal court instructs state officials on how to conform their conduct to state law"); *Rufo v. Inmates of Suffolk County Jail,* 502 U.S. at 367.

13. *Lewis v. Casey,* 518 U.S. at 349.

14. See Feeley and Rubin, *Judicial Policy Making,* at 303–7, 329.

15. *Gilligan v. Morgan,* 413 U.S. 1, 8–9 (1973). A concurring opinion by Justice Blackmun went on to state: "This case relates to prospective relief in the

form of judicial surveillance of highly subjective and technical matters involving military training and command. As such, it presents an '(inappropriate) . . . subject matter for judicial considerations,' for respondents are asking the District Court, in fashioning that prospective relief, 'to enter upon policy determinations for which judicially manageable standards are lacking.' *Baker v. Carr,* 369 U.S. 186, 198, 226 (1962)." 413 U.S. at 13. While *Gilligan* involved the National Guard, whose control the Constitution vested in Congress, as the Court noted at 413 U.S. at 6, the decrees discussed in this book would have involved institutions whose control the Constitution vested in state government.

16. Ralph Winter, "The Activist Judicial Mind" in *Views from the Bench: The Judiciary and Constitutional Politics* 291 (Mark W. Cannon and David M. O'Brien, eds.) (Chatham House, N.J., 1985).

17. *Newman v. Alabama,* 559 F. 2d 283 (5th Cir. 1977) (a decree may require a prison to provide recreation, even through not a right, to repair harm done to prisoners by unconstitutionally deficient prison conditions).

18. See *Hutto v. Finney,* 437 U.S. 678, 687 (1978).

19. Ibid., at 688; *Missouri v. Jenkins,* 515 U.S. at 100.

20. Circuit Judge Sonia Sotomayor of the Second Circuit Court of Appeals speaking at the New York Law School Law Review banquet on April 7, 1999.

21. *Federal Rules of Appellate Procedure* 4.

22. *Rufo v. Inmates of Suffolk County Jail,* 502 U.S. at 367 (refusing to allow reopening of the consent decree except upon special showing); *Missouri v. Jenkins,* 495 U.S. 33, 53 (1990) (refusing to consider the scope of a decree in an enforcement proceeding on the basis that certiorari was not granted in that issue); *Walker v. City of Birmingham,* 388 U.S. 307 (1967) (invoking the collateral bar rule).

23. "Both parties to the litigation . . . may want a judicial decree that ties the hands of the successor." Frank H. Easterbrook, "Justice and Contract in Consent Judgments," 1987 *University of Chicago Legal Forum* 19, 34.

24. See, for example, *LaShawn A. v. Dixon,* 887 F. Supp. 297 (D. D.C. 1995), *aff'd,* 107 F. 3d 923 (D.C. Cir. 1996), *cert. denied,* 520 U.S. 1264 (1997).

25. The dialogue between Burt Neuborne and Frederick A. O. Schwarz, Jr., on the settlement of *Wilder v. Bernstein,* 645 F. Supp. 1292 (S.D.N.Y. 1986), explores many of these issues, including the importance to the defendant of becoming a problem solver rather than a defender of past programs. Neuborne and Schwarz, "A Prelude to the Settlement of *Wilder,*" 1987 *University of Chicago Legal Forum* 177, 205.

26. *Education for All Handicapped Children: Hearing on S. 6 Before the Senate Subcommittee on the Handicapped of the Committee on Labor and Public Welfare,* 93rd Cong., 2d Sess., 1441 (March 18, 1974) (statement of John C. Pittenger, secretary of education, Commonwealth of Pennsylvania).

27. Margo Schlanger, "Beyond the Hero Judge: Institutional Reform Litigation as Litigation," 97 *Michigan Law Review* 1994, 2012 (1999).

28. Robert Pear, "Many States Fail to Fulfill Child Welfare," *New York Times,* March 17, 1996, sec. A1, col. 6. See also, for example, *Missouri v. Jenkins,* 495 U.S. 33 (1990) (school board defendant gets state help to fund the cost of implementing a decree).

29. *Lewis v. Casey,* 518 U.S. at 362.

30. *Pa. Ass'n for Retarded Children v. Pennsylvania,* 343 F. Supp. 279, 300 (E.D. Pa. 1972).

31. See, for example, discussion of the New York State constitutional provisions restricting the state's ability to issue general obligation bonds. *Schulz v. State,* 84 N.Y. 2d 231 (1994).

32. *Local No. 93, Int'l Ass'n of Firefighters v. City of Cleveland,* 478 U.S. 501, 525 (1986). In addition, the court may not enter a decree that conflicts with positive statutory requirements. *Firefighters Local Union No. 1784 v. Stotts,* 467 U.S. 561 (1984). See generally, Judith Resnik, "Judging Consent," 1987 *University of Chicago Legal Forum* 43.

33. Owen Fiss, "Justice Chicago Style," 1987 *University of Chicago Legal Forum* 1, 12.

34. Michael W. McConnell, "Why Hold Elections? Using Consent Decrees to Insulate Policies from Political Change," 1987 *University of Chicago Legal Forum* 295, 301–4; Easterbrook, "Justice and Contract," at 35–36.

35. Easterbrook, "Justice and Contract," at 35–37; McConnell, "Why Hold Elections?," at 299.

36. For examples, see McConnell, "Why Hold Elections?," at 311–17. For other examples, see Chapter 6.

37. Eugene McQuillin, *The Law of Municipal Corporations,* 3rd ed., vol. 2A (Eagan, Minn.: The West Group: 1996), §10.39. ("Unless authorized by statute or charter, a municipal corporation, in its public character as an agent of the state, cannot surrender, by contract or otherwise, any of its legislative and governmental functions or powers, including a partial surrender of such powers. The principle is fundamental and rests upon policies the soundness of which has never been seriously questioned.") McQuillin, *Municipal Corporations,* vol. 6A, §24.41 (1997). ("[W]hen authority to exercise the police power within a defined sphere is delegated by the state to a municipal or other public corporation, the authority is inalienable in the corporation, and it cannot in any manner be contracted away or otherwise granted, delegated, diminished, divided, or limited by the corporation. The authority, until withdrawn by the legislature or by the people through a constitutional change, continues to exist in the corporation unfettered and unrestricted by anything done by it, by its legislative body, or by any other part of it. The power when delegated to a city must at all times be available to it to meet any public need that may arise.")

38. Easterbrook, "Justice and Contract," at 36; McConnell, "Why Hold Elections?," at 299.

39. Ibid., at 308–9.

40. See ibid., at 309 (arguing that the contract clause of the Constitution offers no justification for ongoing enforcement of overbroad institutional reform consent decrees).

41. 521 U.S. 567 (1997).

42. Ibid.

43. *United States v. Swift & Co.*, 286 U.S. 106, 119 (1932). It may well have been that the "grievous wrong" requirement was meant to be applicable only when the grounds for changing the decree were that undue hardship had arisen in trying to implement a decree entered on the assumption that the circumstances of the case would remain the same. David I. Levine, "The Latter Stages of Enforcement of Equitable Decrees: The Course of Institutional Reform Cases After Dowell, Rufo, and Freeman," 20 *Hastings Constitutional Law Quarterly*, 579, 638–39 (1993).

44. *Inmates of Suffolk County Jail v. Kearney*, 734 F. Supp. 561 (D. Mass. 1990), *aff'd*, 915 F. 2d. 1557 (1st Cir. 1990).

45. *Rufo v. Inmates of Suffolk County Jail*, 502 U.S. at 367, 383–93.

46. *Benjamin v. Jacobson*, 124 F. 3d 162 (2d Cir. 1997), *vacated en banc*, 172 F. 3d 144 (2d Cir.) (en banc), *cert. denied*, Benjamin v. Kerik, 528 U.S. 824 (1999) carried this thought to its logical conclusion, ruling that even if a consent decree is vacated by a federal court, the decree could still be enforced as a contract in state court.

47. *Benjamin v. Jacobson*, 172 F. 3d 144, 157 (2d Cir. 1999) (en banc).

48. *King v. Greenblatt*, 52 F. 3d 1, 4 (1st Cir. 1995).

49. *King v. Greenblatt*, 127 F. 3d 190 (1st Cir. 1997).

50. *King v. Greenblatt*, 149 F. 3d 9, 12 (1st Cir. 1998).

51. Ibid., at 19. The twenty-seven-year saga of this case ended a year later when, on motion by the state, the district court finally terminated the decree. *King v. Greenblatt*, 53 F. Supp. 2d 117 (D. Mass. 1999).

52. Other cases have had to run similar courses. See, for example, *Escalera v. New York Hous. Auth.*, 924 F. Supp. 1323 (S.D.N.Y. 1996), discussed in Chapter 5; *Gilmore v. Hous. Auth. of Baltimore City*, 170 F. 3d 428 (4th Cir. 1999) (litigation over whether a change in the applicable federal law was sufficient for modifying an old consent decree).

53. Abram Chayes, "The Role of the Judge in Public Law Litigation," 89 *Harvard Law Review* 1281, 1284 (1976).

54. *Freeman v. Pitts*, 503 U.S. 467 (1992).

55. See *Milliken v. Bradley, Turner v. Safley*. See also, Eugene V. Rostow, "The Democratic Character of Judicial Review," 66 *Harvard Law Review* 193, 210 (1952).

56. As Justice Holmes wrote, "[g]reat constitutional provisions must be administered with caution. Some play must be allowed for the joints of the machine, and it must be remembered that legislatures are ultimate guardians of the liberties and welfare of the people in quite as great a degree as the courts."

Missouri, Kansas & Texas R. Co. v. May, 194 U.S. 267, 270 (1904). See also *Bivens v. Six Unknown Named Agents of the Federal Bureau of Narcotics*, 403 U.S. 388 (1971) (Harlan, J., concurring).

57. See Neuborne and Schwarz, "A Prelude," at 195.

58. *Scheuer v. Rhodes*, 416 U.S. 232, 242 (1974).

59. *Waters v. Churchill*, 511 U.S. 661, 675 (1994).

60. *Larson v. Domestic & Foreign Commerce Corp.*, 337 U.S. 682, 704 (1949).

Chapter 8. Road to Reform

1. Pub. L. No. 104–134, 110 Stat. 1321, 1321–66 to 1321–70 (codified at 18 U.S.C. §3626). Our discussion of the act is limited to those provisions concerning decrees controlling prison conditions.

2. *Harris v. Pernsley*, 113 F.R.D. 615 (E.D. Pa. 1986).

3. *Harris v. Pernsley*, 820 F. 2d 592 (3d Cir. 1987) (affirming the denial of standing).

4. 18 Pa. Cons. Stat. Ann. §1108 (West 1998), adopted March 25, 1988. *Harris v. Reeves*, 946 F. 2d 214 (3d Cir. 1991), *cert. denied sub nom., Abraham v. Harris*, 503 U.S. 952 (1992).

5. Sarah B. Vandenbraak, "Bail, Humbug! Why Criminals Would Rather Be in Philadelphia," *Policy Review* 73, 75 (summer 1995). The data come from documents prepared at Sarah Vandenbraak Hart's request by the Pretrial Services Division of the Philadelphia Court of Common Pleas.

6. John J. DiIulio, Jr., ed., *Courts, Corrections, and the Constitution: The Impact of Judicial Intervention on Prisons and Jails* (New York: Oxford University Press, 1990).

7. *Harris v. Levine*, 1993 WL 209582 (E.D. Pa. June 14, 1993) and 1993 WL 441728 (E.D. Pa. Oct. 28, 1993), *aff'd, Harris v. City of Phila.*, 47 F. 3d 1311 (3d Cir. 1994) and 47 F. 3d 1333 (3d Cir. 1995).

8. *Harris v. City of Phila.*, 1995 WL 527383 (E.D. Pa. Aug. 17, 1995).

9. Senate Committee of the Judiciary, *Prison Reform: Enhancing the Effectiveness of Incarceration: Hearing before the Committee on the Judiciary*, 104th Cong., 1st Sess., July 27, 1995.

10. 18 U.S.C. §3626(a)(1).

11. 18 U.S.C. §3626(a)(3)(F).

12. 18 U.S.C. §3626(b).

13. 18 U.S.C. §3626(f).

14. See for example, *Ruiz v. Johnson*, 178 F. 3d 385 (5th Cir. 1999).

15. *Benjamin v. Jacobson*, 124 F. 3d 162 (2d Cir. 1997), *rev'd en banc*, 172 F. 3d 144 (2d Cir.), *cert. denied sub nom., Benjamin v. Kerik*, 528 U.S. 824 (1999).

16. *Miller v. French*, 530 U.S. 327, 347 (2000). The Court wrote that "[p]rospective relief under a continuing, executory decree remains subject to alteration due to changes in the underlying law." 530 U.S. at 344. This principle

supports the constitutionality of the act's basic requirement that the decree terminate unless the plaintiffs can demonstrate that it is still needed to protect the prisoners' federal rights. The issue before the Court in *Miller* was not, however, the constitutionality of this basic requirement, but rather the constitutionality of another provision in aid of it. That auxiliary provision automatically stays the operation of a prison decree ninety days after the defendant moves to terminate it unless the district court finds in the meantime that the decree is needed to protect the prisoners' rights. All of the justices raised concerns that the ninety-day period may not be sufficient for plaintiffs to shoulder the burden of showing that the decree is still needed. The five-justice majority held that the ninety-day automatic stay provision did not offend separation of powers, but might, in some complex cases, offend due process. It decided, however, that the due process issue had not been presented in this case. 530 U.S. at 350. Justice Souter joined by Justice Ginsburg, concurring in part and dissenting in part, argued that the case should be remanded for factual development of the issues of due process and separation of powers. 530 U.S. at 350–53. Justice Souter's opinion did not throw into question the constitutionality of the act's basic requirement. To the contrary, he wrote that "Congress has the authority to change rules of this sort by imposing new conditions precedent for the continuing enforcement of existing, prospective remedial orders and requiring courts to apply the new rules to those orders." 530 U.S. at 351. Justice Breyer, joined by Stevens, dissenting, argued that the automatic stay provision should be interpreted to allow district courts to extend the ninety-day period. Nothing in Justice Breyer's opinion suggests that he believed the act's basic requirement to be unconstitutional.

17. Scholars have already begun to call for expansion of the Prison Litigation Reform Act. David I. Levine, "The Chinese American Challenge to Court-Mandated Quotas in San Francisco's Public Schools: Notes from a (Partisan) Participant-Observer," 16 *Harvard BlackLetter Law Journal* 39, 126 (spring 2000).

Chapter 9. New Principles

1. *Marisol A. v. Giuliani*, 185 F.R.D. 152 (S.D.N.Y. 1999), *aff'd sub nom., Joel A. v. Giuliani*, 218 F. 3d 132 (2d Cir. 2000).
2. The Annie E. Casey Foundation Panel, *Advisory Report on Family Permanency Issues in the New York City Child Welfare System* (initial report, February 11, 1999), 3.
3. *Hecht Co. v. Bowles*, 321 U.S. 321 (1944).
4. *Hecht Co. v. Bowles*, 321 U.S. 321, at 325–26. *Hecht's* holding that plaintiffs who have been the victims of violations are not automatically entitled to an injunction is still the law. Plaintiffs must show that the injunction will help to ward off significant future harm to plaintiffs by the defendant. *City of Los Angeles v. Lyons*, 461 U.S. 95 (1983), and *O'Shea v. Littleton*, 414 U.S. 488 (1974).

The Court's application of this law to the facts of *Los Angeles* and *O'Shea* is controversial, but the holding of *Hecht* was the governing principle.

5. The Supreme Court has not prevented Congress from delegating legislative powers to federal agencies, *Whitman v. American Trucking Ass'ns*, 531 U.S. (2001), and has taken only modest measures to prevent Congress from regulating state and local governments. *Printz v. United States*, 521 U.S. 898 (1997); *City of Boerne v. Flores*, 521 U.S. 507 (1997); *United States v. Lopez*, 514 U.S. 549 (1995); *New York v. United States*, 505 U.S. 144 (1992). For an analysis, see Marci A. Hamilton, "Reflections on *City of Boerne v. Flores*: A Landmark for Structural Analysis," 39 *William & Mary Law Review* 699 (1998).

6. Harry T. Edwards, "The Growing Disjunction Between Legal Education and the Legal Profession," 91 *Michigan Law Review* 34, 45 (1992).

7. Many liberal scholars would agree. See, for example, Donald H. Zeigler, "Federal Court Reform of State Criminal Justice Systems: A Reassessment of the *Younger* Doctrine from a Modern Perspective," 19 *UC Davis* 31 (1985) (limit remedies to redress of violations of the federal Constitution); Wendy Parker, "The Supreme Court and Public Law Remedies: A Tale of Two Kansas Cities," 50 *Hastings Law Journal* 475, 479–80 (1999).

8. David I. Levine, in "The Chinese American Challenge to Court-Mandated Quotas in San Francisco's Public Schools: Notes from a (Partisan) Participant-Observer," 16 *Harvard BlackLetter Law Journal* 39 (spring 2000), describes how, after a decree was adopted in the name of desegregating San Francisco's schools, a court-appointed advisory committee found that the school district had "largely achieved the Decree's desegregation goals," but went on to find that the court supervision should continue to serve other purposes. See also, for example, *Wilder v. Bernstein*, 153 F.R.D. 524 (S.D.N.Y. 1994), *appeal dismissed*, 49 F. 3d 69 (2d Cir. 1995) (district judge interpreted the consent decree to extend to an area unmentioned in the decree and not alleged as a violation in the underlying complaint).

9. It is sometimes said that defendants would not agree to findings of wrongdoing because of concerns about liability to others. But Rule 36 of the *Federal Rules of Civil Procedure*, dealing with requests for admissions, provides a way to fill the bill without locking the defendants into open-ended liability.

10. Peter H. Schuck similarly called for a reexamination of how judges bifurcate litigation into separate liability and remedy stages in *Suing Government: Citizen Remedies for Official Wrongs* (New Haven, Conn.: Yale University Press, 1983), 186–87.

11. *Weinberger v. Romero-Barcelo*, 456 U.S. 305, 310 (1982).

12. *Hecht Co. v. Bowles*, 321 U.S. at 321.

13. *In re Birmingham Reverse Discrimination Employment Litig.*, 20 F. 3d 1525, 1543 (11th Cir. 1994), *cert. denied sub nom., Arrington v. Wilks*, 514 U.S. 1065 (1995).

14. Samuel Issacharoff, "Program: AALS Section on Civil Procedures: Class Action Conflicts," 30 *UC Davis* 805, 822–23, 830 (1997).

15. In evaluating whether decrees are necessary to repair or prevent illegal injury to plaintiffs, courts should rely on expert testimony only if experts stick to what experts have proved by accepted scientific methods. "[T]he guidelines for the admissibility of expert testimony that the Supreme Court laid down in *Daubert v. Merrell Dow Pharmaceuticals, Inc.* . . . apply to the testimony of social scientists as well as to that of natural scientists. . . . And not only to their testimony at the liability stage of a lawsuit, but also to testimony offered at the remedy stage." *People Who Care v. Rockford Bd. of Educ.,* 111 F. 3d 528, 534 (7th Cir. 1997). See also, *Davis v. New York City Hous. Auth.,* 166 F. 3d 432 (2d Cir. 1999) (reversing the decree because the trial judge relied on vague speculations of an expert witness).

16. For a cogent argument that such discretion is strongly rooted in established doctrine, see David L. Shapiro, "Jurisdiction and Discretion," 60 *New York University Law Review* 543 (1985). Professors Anthony M. Bertelli and Laurence C. Lynn, Jr., "A Precept of Managerial Responsibility: Securing Collective Justice in Institutional Reform Litigation," 29 *Fordham Urban Law Journal* 317 (2001), argue that federal courts should defer to state and local governments on such questions of policy under the doctrine of *Burford v. Sun Oil Co.,* 319 U.S. 315, 317–18 (1943). In that opinion Justice Black wrote, "Although a federal equity court does have jurisdiction of a particular proceeding, it may, in its sound discretion, whether its jurisdiction is invoked on the ground of diversity of citizenship or otherwise, 'refuse to enforce or protect legal rights, the exercise of which may be prejudicial to the public interest'; for it 'is in the public interest that federal courts of equity should exercise their discretionary power with proper regard for the rightful independence of state governments in carrying out their domestic policy.'"

17. *City of New York v. United States EPA,* 543 F. Supp. 1084 (S.D.N.Y. 1981). See also, *Baker v. State,* 744 A. 2d 864, 889 (Vt. 1999), where the Vermont Supreme Court remanded to the state legislature the job of coming up with a constitutionally acceptable remedy to ensure that same-sex couples receive the same benefits and protections afforded married couples.

18. See, for example, *Lewis v. Casey,* 518 U.S. 343 (1996); *Hecht v. Bowles,* 321 U.S. at 321.

19. *King v. Walters,* 190 F. 3d 784 (7th Cir. 1999); see also, *United States v. North Carolina,* 180 F. 3d 574 (4th Cir. 1999), where the attorneys representing the state consented to a decree, but before the judge approved it, the state legislature enacted a statute requiring legislative approval before the state agreed to certain settlements. The district court decided not to enter the decree, but the court of appeals reversed.

20. Professor Peter H. Schuck examines such a hierarchy of remedies in his book *Suing Government: Citizen Remedies for Official Wrongs* and suggests that a more logical and effective remedy system depends on an expansion of remedies other than mandatory injunctions.

21. *Illinois v. Costle*, 12 Env't Rep. Cas. (B.N.A.) 1597 (D.D.C. 1979). The controlling section of the Administrative Procedure Act permits the court to "set aside" agency action. 5 U.S.C. §706 (2000). Courts normally respond to illegality by remanding to the agency. *SEC v. Chenery Corp.*, 332 U.S. 194 (1947). The wording of this particular provision of the United States Code is no accident, but rather is part of a broader pattern of conduct that results in federal courts being less prone to take over federal than state and local policy making. One source of the difference is that Congress, in writing procedural rules for suits in federal court, has predictably shown more concern for federal than state and local policy makers. It has not seen fit to include a comparable provision in the United States Code limiting remedies against state and local agencies.

22. *Illinois v. Costle*, 12 Env't Rep. Cas. 1599.

23. *Kaspar v. Bd. of Election Comm'rs*, 814 F. 2d 332 (7th Cir. 1987).

24. Ibid., at 340.

25. Once it is determined that the scope of the decree is appropriate, issues about its specific design inevitably require more deference. *People Who Care v. Rockford Bd. of Educ.*, 171 F. 3d 1083, 1087 (7th Cir. 1999). ("We can decide which provisions of the remedial decree are valid and which invalid, but when it comes to the design of specific programs for achieving the objectives of the valid provisions, and to the funding for those programs, we have no practical alternative to deferring broadly to the judgment of the district court.")

26. See discussion of Judge Henry Friendly's version of a deferential test of modification in David I. Levine, "The Modification of Equitable Decrees in Institutional Reform Litigation: A Commentary on the Supreme Court's Adoption of the Second Circuit's Flexible Test," 58 *Brooklyn Law Review* 1239 (1993).

27. The "collateral bar rule" generally forbids someone charged with contempt to challenge the scope of the decree. *Walker v. City of Birmingham*, 388 U.S. 307 (1967). In motions for modifications, courts treat the parties as stuck with the bargain they originally made, absent special circumstances justifying a change. *Rufo v. Inmates of Suffolk County Jail*, 502 U.S. 367 (1992).

28. The approach we suggest is implicit in *Rufo's* observation that defendants cannot consent to something illegal.

29. The ultra vires doctrine is a particularly powerful doctrine. See, for example, *Chemical Bank v. Washington Public Power Supply System*, 99 Wash. 2d 772, 666 P. 2d 329 (1983), where the Washington Supreme Court voided $7.2 *billion* of existing local government debt as beyond the authority of the officials who had agreed to the obligation.

30. Levine, "The Modification of Equitable Decrees," at 1269-70.

31. *Motor Vehicle Mfrs. Ass'n v. State Farm Mutual Auto. Ins. Co.*, 463 U.S. 29 (1983).

32. Rick Lyman, "Texas Acts to Free Its Prisons of Long Court Oversight," *New York Times*, February 13, 1999, sec. A15.

33. *Ruiz v. Johnson*, 154 F. Supp. 2d 975 (S.D. Tex. 2001).

34. See, for example, *Reserve Mining Co. v. Lord,* 529 F. 2d 181 (8th Cir. 1976) (long-running public law environmental case).

35. *United States v. Bd. of Sch. Comm'rs,* 128 F. 3d 507, 512 (7th Cir. 1997).

36. *Glover v. Johnson,* 138 F. 3d 229, 233 (6th Cir. 1998).

37. The full headline of the article, by Wolfgang Saxon, reads "Judge Stanley Weigel, 93, Dies; Acted to Improve Prisons," *New York Times,* September 4, 1999, sec. A11, col. 1.

38. The Ninth Circuit in 1981 reversed one of Judge Weigel's orders, which covered everything from the condition of each prisoner's bedding to access to educational TV. The appellate court wrote that Judge Weigel had ventured too "far into the realm of prison reform. Prison reform, beyond the standards required by the Eighth Amendment, is the function of state government officials." *Wright v. Rushen,* 642 F. 2d 1129, 1133 (9th Cir. 1981). On another occasion, the Ninth Circuit vacated an order issued by Judge Weigel concerning prison food service because there was no supporting factual basis for the order. *Toussaint v. Yockey,* 722 F. 2d 1490 (9th Cir. 1984). In 1985, the Ninth Circuit reversed and modified portions of another decree by Judge Weigel, ruling that the judge, in general, "assumed too much control over the day to day affairs of the prisons." *Toussaint v. McCarthy,* 801 F. 2d 1080, 1085 (9th Cir. 1986), *cert. denied,* 481 U.S. 1069 (1987). In 1988, the Ninth Circuit ruled that Judge Weigel had strayed so far from his legitimate jurisdiction that it issued a rare writ of mandamus prohibiting him from inspecting prisons where there had not been any allegations of illegality or unconstitutional conduct. *Rowland v. United States Dist. Court,* 849 F. 2d 380 (9th Cir. 1988).

39. *Freeman v. Pitts,* 503 U.S. 467, 491 (1992); *Bd. of Educ. v. Dowell,* 498 U.S. 237, 249–50 (1991).

40. Ross Sandler and David Schoenbrod, "Government by Decree: The High Cost of Letting Judges Make Policy," 4(3) *City Journal* 54 (summer 1994).

41. For an early version of this idea, see Michael Greve, "Terminating School Desegregation Lawsuits," 7 *Harvard Journal of Law & Public Policy* 303, 312–15 (1984).

42. *Wyatt v. Rogers,* 985 F. Supp. 1356, 1375 (M.D. Ala. 1997).

43. Gerald N. Rosenberg, *The Hollow Hope: Can Courts Bring About Social Change?* (Chicago: University of Chicago Press, 1991).

44. Stephen L. Carter, "Do Courts Matter?," 90 *Michigan Law Review* 1216, 1221–22 (1992).

45. One of the Supreme Court's leading cases on termination of decrees, *Freeman v. Pitts,* is a step in the right direction because it speaks of the absence of "bad faith." 503 U.S. 467, 499 (1992). The effect is to put the burden on plaintiffs to show that defendants still cannot be trusted without ongoing judicial oversight.

46. The panel in the *Marisol* case assessed the good faith efforts of the New York City Administration for Children's Services (ACS) by focusing on efforts

rather than outcomes. They asked: "To what extent has ACS identified, both on its own initiative and with the Panel's assistance, the key changes needed to reform this system? How quickly and how thoroughly has it responded to each of these needs? How relevant have its responses been? To what extent has it secured the resources needed to make change possible? How thoroughly has it communicated its vision of change and worked to influence other key stakeholders whose actions are also essential to the reform effort?"

They answered these questions positively but quickly noted that a positive assessment of the agency's good faith did not mean that the work was complete: "It would be a very serious misreading of our Final Report if these [positive] conclusions regarding good faith were read as a judgment that this system has been fixed. In our view, ACS has made remarkable progress in many areas that must be changed if children and families are to have a better experience. The reforms already implemented were necessary, but they are not yet sufficient, to produce that better experience. Throughout this report, we identify critical areas in which we cannot yet observe sufficient change in the front line and supervisory practice that really determines what happens to the citizens who come into contact with New York's child welfare system." Special Child Welfare Advisory Panel, Letter accompanying its Final Report, December 7, 2000.

47. See generally, Schuck, *Suing Government*.

Acknowledgments

Our first efforts on what eventually became this book began with a suggestion from Edward N. Costikyan, then a partner at Paul, Weiss, Rifkin, Wharton & Garrison and a long-time participant in the reform politics of New York City. He and Lawrence Mone, the president of the Manhattan Institute, questioned the limitations that court decrees placed on elected officials and suggested that we prepare an article on court orders for *City Journal*. Two articles resulted: "Government by Decree" in 1994 and "How to Put Lawmakers, Not Courts, Back in Charge" in 1996. The articles were ably edited by Myron Magnet, the iconoclastic editor in chief of *City Journal*, along with James Taranto and Gary Rosen. Peter Salins made helpful suggestions from his position on the *City Journal* editorial board. Recognizing that much was at stake in how the courts reacted to the Prison Litigation Reform Act, Melanie Kirkpatrick, deputy editor of the *Wall Street Journal* editorial page, gave us the opportunity to express our point of view in two columns, "By What Right Do Judges Run Prisons?" and "In New York City, the Jails Still Belong to the Judges."

Robert Rosenkranz, a board member of the Manhattan Institute and a leader in the investment industry, first suggested that we undertake a longer, book-length examination of the issues presented by court decrees and encouraged us to begin. Over the years his friendship has been demonstrated through many discussions about court decrees as well as many other topics. His advice as the manuscript developed helped to clarify our ideas and enabled us to make it more comprehensible for the general reader.

We would like to acknowledge two others who indirectly helped us to understand court decrees. John Adams, our friend and longtime executive director of the Natural Resources Defense Council (NRDC) where we both worked in the 1970s, never let NRDC's lawyers forget the political side of their court cases. He always emphasized results, and his insights about the limits of litigation taught us important lessons. Edward I. Koch, mayor of New York City from 1978 through 1989, faced repeated lawsuits on homelessness, welfare, foster care, prisons, AIDS, special education, and more. We are both privileged to enjoy his friendship and to have worked with him and his administration. Despite Mayor Koch's personal compassion, leadership, and effectiveness, his administration was never able to produce the results that lawyers and judges demanded. His example in grappling with these issues, and his own lucid accounts of his administration in his several books, taught us much about these matters.

New York Law School has been enormously supportive, both materially and intellectually. Deans Harry Wellington and Richard A. Matasar, and the law school's large, diverse faculty encouraged us to pursue the topic of institutional reform litigation despite the fact that many colleagues had questions or doubts about our views. We presented a chapter at one of the law school's regular, well-attended Tuesday faculty seminars and received much significant feedback. Among our New York Law School faculty colleagues who gave special help were Steven J. Ellmann, Jethro Lieberman, Denise C. Morgan, Edward Purcell, Nadine Strossen, and Donald Ziegler. New York Law School's Center for New York City Law offered us the opportunity to more easily follow cases affecting New York City, while its publication, *City Law,* gave significant space to our articles and comments on particular cases. We also learned a great deal from the students at New York Law School who participated in our seminar "Reforming Government by Court Order." Their varied reactions to an early version of the book helped to deepen our understanding of court remedies.

Other law teachers, academics, and observers generously offered significant help by reading and commenting on our drafts. Among them were Lynn Chu of Writers' Representatives, Inc.; James B. Jacobs of NYU Law School; Michael Greve of the American Enterprise Institute; Marci Hamilton of Cardozo Law School; Walter Olsen of the Manhattan Institute; Neal D. Peterson, formerly chief of Vice President Hubert H. Humphrey's office of liaison with state and local governments; Peter Salins of the City University of New York; Margo Schlanger of Harvard Law School; and Peter H. Schuck of Yale Law School. Mark Reibling, an independent editor, helped immeasurably in pointing the way toward a more effective outline and in providing a keen editorial review.

For particular parts of the story, the help of many people benefited us. For the history of the Advisory Commission on Intergovernmental Relations (ACIR) during its final years we acknowledge the help of Richard Nathan, a member of the ACIR board, who made his files available to us; Charles Griffin, the last executive director of ACIR, who described ACIR's final days for us; and Theresa A. Gullo, chief of the state and local government unit at the congressional budget office, who saved the files of the ACIR from the garbage bin and allowed us to review them.

We could not even have attempted to understand the *Jose P.* litigation without the help of John C. Gray and Michael A. Rebell, plaintiffs' attorneys, who opened their court document files for our review, allowed themselves to be interviewed, and were always courteous and available to answer our questions about the twists and turns of the litigation. They are among the very best the public interest bar has to offer. We learned much from Joseph P. Viteritti, who was special assistant to the chancellor during the first three years of the *Jose P.* litigation. His book, *Across the River: Politics and Education in the City,* provides an indispensable analysis of the motivations and actions taken by the chancellor and the board of education in response to the *Jose P.* complaint. We also acknowledge the help provided by Marvin Frankel, the first special master, who allowed himself to be interviewed concerning his role as special master; Frank Macchiarola, chancellor during the first years of the court order, who shared his thoughts with us; David Goldin and Dan McCray of the New York City Law Department, who took over the case in its later years and continued to struggle with the order; Anthony Shorris, Kate Goldmark, Mary McKenna Rodriguez, and Linda Wernikoff of the New York City Board of Education, who explained the board's budgeting and special education data to us, and who, with their colleagues, have the obligation to deliver special education services in a school system with 1.1 million children, and Nancy Oskow-Schoenbrod of the New York State Department of Education, who provided us with insights into the current debate on federal special education legislation. We also thank Richard I. Beattie, Norm Fruchter, and Peter J. Powers for making their respective reports on special education in New York City available to us.

For the *Marisol* litigation we thank Commissioner Nicholas Scoppetta of the Administration for Children's Services (ACS), who was always available to talk about the case and who made a presentation on *Marisol* to our seminar at New York Law School. Other ACS and New York City law department staff members who provided documents and explanations were Gerald Harris, ACS general counsel; Linda Gibbs, ACS deputy commissioner; Valerie Russo, special assistant to the commissioner; Don Shacknai, associate general counsel; and Gail Rubin, senior litigator at the law department.

For the background of the Prison Litigation Reform Act and its adoption by Congress, we acknowledge the help of Sarah B. Vandenbraak Hart, who made the problem of court-ordered prison population caps a national issue. Lorna Bade Goodman of the New York City law department helped us to understand the New York City prison cases, a prime example of an early, long-lived prison case. Other New York City attorneys who helped us with the prison cases, as well as other court decrees, included Leonard Koener, chief assistant corporation counsel, and Lawrence S. Kahn, chief litigating assistant corporation counsel. Jeff Schanback, general counsel of the New York City Housing Authority, helped us with the *Escalera* case. We also thank U.S. district court judge Harold Baer, Jr., the judge currently supervising the New York City prison cases, for sharing his thoughts with us on the role of the judiciary and prison court orders and for meeting with our seminar. Finally, we thank Judge Guido Calabresi for sharing his thoughts on the Prison Litigation Reform Act. Like the kind teacher he remains, he reacted to our disagreements by trying to educate us and, in the process, helped us to sharpen our presentation.

The staff at New York Law School's Mendik Library labored hard to identify and track down sources. We acknowledge the generous and professional assistance of Marta Kiszely, Joseph F. Molinari, and William R. Mills. Endless versions of the manuscript were prepared by Joan Argento and Gemma Jacobs of the law school's administrative staff. Student research help was provided by Mark Atlee, Lori Quinn, Adam Pinto, and Sena Kim-Reuter. We feel especially grateful to Deborah K. Paulus of the Brooklyn Law School, who gave the manuscript the style of a book (along the way saving us from many errors) and prepared the index.

Generous grants allowed us to devote uninterrupted time to the research and preparation of the book. We are indebted to the Manhattan Institute, New York Law School, the John M. Olin Foundation, and the Smith Richardson Foundation as well as Dr. James Piereson, executive director of the John M. Olin Foundation, and Mark Steinmeyer, senior program officer of the Smith Richardson Foundation.

We are especially grateful to Yale University Press for its decision to publish this book and for the enthusiastic support provided by senior editor Jean E. Thomson Black. We also thank Jessie Dolch for her helpful editing of the manuscript, and Nancy Moore Brochin for her care in seeing the book through the production process.

Over the years we have learned much from the many lawyers and judges with whom we have had the privilege of working and, in some cases, litigating against. In drawing on these experiences, we have tried to provide a fully rounded picture: why judges issue the orders they do; how Congress takes advantage of the judicial forum; how lawyers control the process; and how court decrees affect government and governmental officials. We offer these stories and analyses in hopes that readers will come to a greater understanding of the court's role in protecting rights, including the right for a democratically elected government.

Index